PSYCHIC WHOLENESS AND HEALING

PSYCHIC WHOLENESS AND HEALING

Using ALL the Powers of the Human Psyche

—*Second Edition*—

ANNA A. TERRUWE, M.D.
and CONRAD W. BAARS, M.D.

Foreword by Alexis E. McCarthy

Edited and Revised by
SUZANNE M. BAARS, M.A.
and BONNIE N. SHAYNE, M.A.

WIPF & STOCK · Eugene, Oregon

Wipf & Stock
An Imprint of Wipf and Stock Publishers
199 W. 8th Ave., Suite 3
Eugene, OR 97401

www.wipfandstock.com

PAPERBACK ISBN 13: 978-1-4982-8812-5
HARDCOVER ISBN 13: 978-1-4982-8814-9

Manufactured in the U.S.A.   03/29/2016

CONTENTS

FOREWORD

AFTER CITING THE GENESIS story of creation, in a presidential address to the American Psychiatric Association, Abraham Maslow remarked that the role of the psychiatrist was to restore man to God's image.

Two essential areas of such a restoration are the psychological and the spiritual. Man's psyche or soul cannot be separated from his spirit. For too long a time, there seemed to exist a conflict between theology and applied psychology (of whatever school). Fortunately, and especially since Vatican II, the clergy are turning to the resources of psychology, though sometimes at the expense of theology.

On the other hand, man's relationship to a Power outside himself—God in the Judaeo-Christian tradition; Jesus Christ in the Christian tradition—a relationship expressed and developed through the various theologies, is fairly commonly accepted as a psychological necessity. With more and more of the clergy being involved in the field of counseling, the present status might be better described as synergy than as symbiosis. The clergy and the psychiatrists can quite simply acknowledge a need for what they have to offer each other.

In the U.S., we have had priest-psychiatrists (e.g. Dom T.V. Moore, O.S.B., James Gill, S.J., et al) and many articulate priest-psychologists. In Drs. Baars and Terruwe, we have psychiatrists who are at ease with theological concepts, and who find no difficulty in applying them to theory and therapy. This, to me, is a major contribution of the present work.

It should be obvious that years of experience with therapy afford a great support for all who are offering or receiving counseling services. The total human person is too precious to be made raw material for a learning process. In other scientific fields, experiments can be scrapped if they fail. Who would dare say the same of a human person?

Making use of the insights and methodology offered in this work will help many to avoid long-lasting mistakes. Some years ago, writing to Dr. Baars about the positive response of women religious to his presentation of the need for affirmation in communities, I asked the question: "Where do we go from here?" I am deeply grateful that Dr. Baars has continued to bring out new works to lead so many along the way to psychic wholeness.

Dr. Terruwe's insights on emotional maturity in marriage were extremely helpful for me during the early years of Cana and Pre-Cana work in Chicago, and also in the preparation of marriage courses for high school seniors and college students.

Since Vatican II, the concept of wholeness has been crucial both for counseling individual religious and for guiding religious community development. In some dioceses, the program for the restoration of the catechumenate is under way. In time, we hope, it will spread through the entire Church in America. If "psychic wholeness" becomes recognizable as a mark of Christian life, this present work and others like it will have contributed to the growth of the Body of Christ on earth.

May all who read this work become part of that future.

Alexis E. McCarthy, O. Carm.

PREFACE

IN HIS FOREWORD TO the first American edition of Dr. Anna Terruwe's doctoral thesis—*The Neurosis in the Light of Rational Psychology*—Francis Braceland, M.D., 85th president of the American Psychiatric Association, wrote: "It is said that the love of God is an adventure of the spirit and the sad thing in our day is that there are few adventurers who, like Dr. Terruwe, are willing to soar intellectually. It is a delight to welcome her ideas . . . and evidences of original thinking as are exemplified in this book. . . . Any psychiatric theory which takes into account the spiritual nature of man will be particularly welcome in many areas."

One might well wonder whether at that time in 1960 Dr. Braceland already foresaw "Psychiatry's depression" (*Time*, 4/2/79) of the late seventies with "Psychiatrists battling for survival" (*American Medical News*, 5/26/78) as the profession of "Psychiatry (was) running into an identity crisis" (*U.S. News & World Report*, 4/78), and, if so, did he consider the profession's reluctance to include man's spiritual dimension in its research of man and his mental disorders as one of the main contributing factors? I, for one, see an incontrovertible cause and effect relationship between psychiatry's secular humanistic, scientific study of man and modern man's ever deepening sense of frustration in searching for effective psychiatric treatment of his "Emotional turmoil, increasingly blamed on the stress of American life" (*WSJ*, 4/79).

I could not help but detect an unspoken rebuke of psychiatry and the modern human sciences when I read the words of John Paul II, spoken at Puebla, Mexico, in January 1979: "The truth that we owe to man is, first and foremost, a truth about man. Perhaps one of the most obvious weaknesses of present-day civilization lies in an inadequate view of man. Without doubt, our age is the one in which man has been most written and spoken of, the age of the forms of humanism and the age of anthropocentrism.

Nevertheless it is paradoxically also the age of man's deepest anxiety about his identity and his destiny, the age of man's abasement to previously unsuspected levels, the age of human values trampled on as never before.

"How is this paradox explained? It is the inexorable paradox of atheistic humanism. It is the drama of man being deprived of an essential dimension of his being, namely his search for the infinite, and thus faced with having his being reduced in the worst way."

It is reasonable to assume that psychiatrists and others who like to call themselves "mental health professionals," when in a reflective mood, must be painfully aware of the irony that there exists no truly satisfactory definition of "mental health." How many of them realize that there cannot be such a definition unless the spiritual dimension were included? Yet, if serious consideration were given to the existence and role of the spiritual powers of man, the profession would possess a clearer diagnostic criterion and therapeutic goal to aid it in promoting what then would better be called "psychic wholeness."[1]

There are many who are unconvinced that it is the psychology of man that needs a radical reassessment, because they prefer to see social, cultural, political or other factors as the chief causes of "man's deepest anxiety about his identity and destiny." I invite them to ponder the words of an eminent philosopher, author and survivor of too many years of profound suffering in Russian gulags, Alexander Solzhenitsyn, written in 1975: "I insist that the problems of the West are not political. They are psychological and moral. When dissatisfaction with government is expressed, it should be understood not in terms of political failure, but of weakened religious and ethical foundations of modern society. A problem like inflation in the midst of plenty is a psychological and moral problem. I am convinced that the only salvation for the West—and the East—lies in a moral and psychological rebirth." Obviously, Solzhenitsyn perceives in man an indestructible, not to be ignored, link between his psychological and spiritual powers, which affect each other positively or negatively depending on the extent to which they are recognized and cultivated, or misunderstood and ignored.

1. Editors' note: Dr. Terruwe and Dr. Baars used the term *psychic wholeness* as referring to the emotional, intellectual, and spiritual aspects of the human person as well as the life of the will. It is unfortunate that this term has sometimes been confused with occult terminology. Therefore, throughout this revised edition of *Psychic Wholeness and Healing* the terms "psychic" and "psychological" will be used interchangeably and should be understood in the context of psychological wholeness and *not* as referring to anything mystical, magical or telepathic.

PREFACE

The basis of Dr. Terruwe's doctoral thesis—the psyche of man in the light of philosophical anthropology—is presented in the first chapter of this book, though in a newly revised and modernized version, with new terminology replacing the outdated one of medieval times. I am most grateful for the suggestions received from Robert E. Joyce, Ph.D., Professor of Philosophy at St. John's University, Collegeville, Minnesota, and his wife Mary, a gifted and intuitive philosopher in her own right. Their teachings and writings fully support our clinical-philosophical insights and discoveries. Additional contributions to this first chapter have been received with my sincere appreciation from Cornelis van Paassen, SCJ, Ph.D., Professor of Philosophy at the Institute for Philosophy and Theology, Yogyakarta, Indonesia. Further testimony to the considerable labor involved in readying this very same chapter is the valuable help received from a Professor of Philosophy at Our Lady of the Lake University, San Antonio, Texas. Both the editor and I consider ourselves gratefully beholden to Sister Mary Christine Morkovsky, CDP, Ph.D.

The remainder of this book contains a detailed description of the various types of neuroses, discovered by Freud to be caused by repression, in the light of philosophical anthropology, as well as their specific therapies illustrated with numerous clinical case histories. However, in this, the fourth revised edition in English of Dr. Terruwe's thesis—the second edition was contained in *Loving and Curing the Neurotic*[2]—a special section has been added. This special sub-chapter offers a detailed presentation of our psychotherapy of obsessive-compulsive neurotics who have repressed their sexual feelings. We have always refrained from committing this subject with its delicate moral aspects to paper because it lends itself, especially when read out of context, to serious misinterpretations and possible harmful applications. Not that these unfortunate occurrences could not happen without a formal written presentation. They have happened. But because it was precisely some of the best educated and most influential persons in the Church who failed to grasp the truth and potential benefits of Dr. Terruwe's thesis—which failure led to condemnation of ideas and persons, yet ultimately also to public apologies and even the acknowledgement of my colleague's work as "a gift to the Church" by the late Pontiff Paul VI—that we did not want to invite similar painful occurrences on an even larger scale. However, we cannot close our eyes to the fact that we will not live forever,

2. by A.A. Terruwe, M.D. and C.W. Baars, M.D., Arlington House Publ., New Rochelle, N.Y., 1972

and therefore owe it to all obsessive-compulsive neurotics, the members of our profession and orthodox moral theologians, to share in written form what has proven beneficial to countless repressive neurotics.

I am most grateful to Rev. William B. Smith, STD, and Rev. Daniel V. Flynn, JCD, both of the Office of the Censor of Books, Archdiocese of New York, St. Joseph's Seminary, Dunwoodie, Yonkers, N.Y., for their critical evaluation of this special sub-chapter, "Moral aspects of our therapy of obsessive-compulsive neurotics who have repressed their sexual feelings." Their determination, *"Nothing against faith and morals"* should prove a most valuable help to those patients who need to obtain absolute certainty that they can fully trust their therapist in this most important area by consulting a moralist. In our respective practices we have always encouraged our patients to consult the most competent moralist they can find, since we know that without this moral certainty they cannot follow our advice one hundred percent. Yet this is absolutely necessary if they are to be freed of the tyranny of their obsessions and compulsions, and become capable of performing truly human, i.e. freely willed acts. However, the paucity of moralists possessing the required knowledge of sound psychological concepts sometimes kept some patients from attaining this moral certainty, or caused them to experience considerable delay in their therapeutic progress while searching for such a qualified moral theologian.

In conclusion, I want to acknowledge my indebtedness to Father Anthony Chenevey, SSP, editor of ALBA HOUSE, for his continued interest in our work. When *Loving and Curing the Neurotic* was out of print it was he who offered to make its contents available in two smaller volumes. This has now become a reality with *Psychic Wholeness and Healing* joining its companion volume, *Healing the Unaffirmed*, first published in 1976 [edited and revised in 2002] and presently in its fourth printing. The two volumes comprise the sum total of everything—the psychology of normal man, particularly his emotional life; a new interpretation of the basic mechanism of repression; the newly discovered syndromes of energy neurosis [now being called *energy-based repression*] and deprivation neurosis [now called *Emotional Deprivation Disorder*] (not caused by repression); our therapies of these neuroses; the matter of freedom of the will in neurotics; and numerous clinical case histories—of everything that has evolved from the original and brilliant introductory lecture given in the Netherlands before the Society for Thomistic Philosophy in 1935 by the late Professor W.J.A.J.

Duynstee, C.SS.R., LL.D., entitled, "The Theory of Repression Judged from the Thomistic Viewpoint."

Lastly, a brief reflection on the "Adventurous Soaring of the Intellect" by the main author, Dr. Anna Terruwe (for the sake of bibliographic reference in English-speaking countries not listed as such by the publisher for the English language edition only). There is a valuable lesson to be learned in what I consider the fundamental reasons for her unique contribution to psychiatry: her being a woman and her liberal arts education.

The proper balance between her intuitive and reasoning intellects, or better, between her heart and her mind, developed harmoniously in the affirming atmosphere of her parental home. A sound liberal arts education gave her a profound grasp of the multi-dimensional aspects of the human person, and enhanced her sensitivity and compassionate openness to human suffering so firmly that they could never be diminished by the secular scientific training in psychiatry.

Dr. Terruwe's academic and clinical achievements offer abundant proof of the claim by William Marra, Ph.D., that the liberal arts can and must humanize the professions. By this he means that specialists must see their subjects, whether medicine, law, business, or whatever, "in terms of the total picture of man on earth in the midst of death and life, man with problems of good and evil, man with problems of beauty." Real progress in the human sciences, particularly psychiatry, demands mandatory study by all students of the classics, philosophy, theology, literature, history and languages. The humanizing effects of a liberal arts education should be fully appreciated by all professional schools, in particular by those of psychology, which, Marra states, "has nothing to say about humanizing life because it itself is a mixture of all kinds of second rate philosophical theories which are served up as if they were scientific."

What Marra has to say about the special benefits a liberal arts education offers to women in terms of humanizing the home, as well as the professional and business world, should be required reading for every woman today.[3] Suffice it to say here, that my colleague, Dr. Terruwe, single, physician, psychiatrist, author and lecturer, personifies the truth of Marra's words. Speaking for myself, as a man, married, father, physician, psychiatrist, author and lecturer, I owe much to her. Without her revolutionary ideas and the benefit of her personal teachings I would have abandoned

3. "A Humanist's View of Engineering," William A. Marra, Ph.D., *Engineering Education*, Vol. 63, No. 8, May, 1973.

my specialty long ago, disenchanted as I was with its secular humanistic, scientific view of man, a view that in its failure to understand and integrate the spiritual dimension of man, is clinically sterile in terms of healing emotionally ill people.

Conrad W. Baars, M.D.
San Antonio, Texas
Fall, 1980

INTRODUCTION TO
INTEGRACJA PSYCHICZNA[1]

Is ALCOHOLISM A SICKNESS or a sin? Are persistent returning obsessive thoughts the subject matter of conversation with a psychiatrist or with a confessor? Why do we object to people who have a sick ambition? If their ambition is sick, then maybe it is sinless, and so it does not merit our indignation? We are not outraged by people who are suffering from a catarrh. Are resentments and festering signs of enmity emerging from a wounded heart always sinful for which we bear full moral culpability? How is it that some people are capable of love, they are friendly, cordial and open, and others, even though they want to love, have a heart of stone? Religion makes these others aware of the need of loving, but they do not know how – they are closed, cold, in the company of others they feel awkward, and they cannot experience fascination in anything. They experience their religious life only as an ethical obligation, fulfilled pragmatically, in a cold way. They cannot recognize in religion the immersion in divine mercy, and the joyful transmission of the mercy that they have received. And how can we help a scrupulous person, who understands that he or she has not done anything wrong, and yet the judgment of reason is paralyzed by fear? Such people know that they have not sinned, but they feel guilty, because they are struck with fear, being afraid of self, of their own emotions, of their sexuality? They are afraid of distant, unpredicted and doubtful consequences of their acts, because in a sick way, they are afraid of God.

The way one handles the emotions and their internal liberty, or conversely, their neurotic blocking has an impact on the moral and spiritual

1. Anna. A Terruwe, Conrad W. Baars, *Integracja Psychiczna* (Poznań: W drodze, 1989), the Polish Edition of: Anna. A Terruwe, Conrad W. Baars, *Psychic Wholeness and Healing Using All the Powers of the Human Psyche* (New York: Alba House, 1981)

life. The affirmation of the fundamental goodness of the emotions enables fully humane reactions. A person that is at ease with the emotions can both receive and give human warmth. Not only is such a person happy, but also awakens happiness in others. Whereas if educators have conveyed distrust towards the emotional sphere, or if, what is even worse, somebody has never experienced cordial contact with significant others, the emotional life of such a person is then injured. The wounding of the emotional sphere is very painful, sometimes even more painful than mental sickness, because it is conscious. Simplest human relationships then become a torture. With-out the healing of the psychic foundation, the establishment of mature hu-man relationships becomes difficult, and this is echoed in the religious and spiritual life. Grace builds upon nature, and its growth presumes a natural capacity for free and creative response to the divine gift.

Emotional inhibitions are not rare. In some sense they concern all. Even though distrust of the emotions, in particular of the sexual emotions, was never so severe in Poland as in Protestant countries, we are not com-pletely free from the repression of sexuality. Of course, we all know that sexuality is inherently good, but are our emotional reactions in accord with what our reason perceives? Do we not transmit to children, who by nature are more sensitive to the emotional atmosphere than to arguments, a cer-tain distrust and embarrassment when out of curiosity they raise questions about "tender issues"?

In our country maybe an even greater spiritual devastation is caused by the repression of the assertive emotions. The exclusion of independent initiatives dictated by the social system and the accompanying feelings of frustration and fear cause the underdevelopment of the emotions of cour-age and anger. This generates in individuals apathy, the incapacity to act, to be angry at true evil, with the cultivation, sometimes for years, of past resentments and humiliations. It is normal for men to find satisfaction in their work. But if the conditions in our work places are so enslaved by bu-reaucratic rules, that no one is allowed to manifest any initiative, the net result is that men return home frustrated – and they often drown their dissatisfaction with alcohol. And how many middle-aged priests are bit-ter, complaining, talking constantly about the neurotic atmosphere that was dominant in the seminaries twenty or thirty years ago? Mother Te-resa of Calcutta wrote into the Constitutions of the Congregation of the Missionaries of Charity an admonition that in the convents the complete freedom to respond to the inspirations of the Holy Spirit who invites with force and gentleness is to be respected and cultivated. Cardinal Ratzinger in his famous *Report on Faith* writes about the strange incapacity of many bishops, who fail to use the emotion of anger. It was forgotten that charity requires sometimes courage and endurance. Christians have been taught to be pleasant, compliant, and without expression. Such a formation generates people who are soft, wounded, without personal initiatives, incapable of defending basic values.

Emotional disturbances are not only a field of observation of professional medicine, but also of ethics, pedagogy and moral theology. Neuroses often come about due to an inappropriate reception of the correct moral law and from a faulty approach towards religious obligations. That is why this book that explains the mechanism of the integration of the personality is addressed not only to the limited circle of psychiatrists, but also to the wider public, to educators, parents, pastors and confessors. The priest in the confessional does not fulfill the task of a psychiatrist. He transmits divine mercy. But by his attitude, by presenting the forgiving God, he can greatly help in the liberation from neurosis. He can also, unfortunately, intensify an existing neurosis.

Where the boundary between sin and sickness is thin, one needs to know how to differentiate, both theoretically and practically whether one is dealing with a sinner or with a sick person. For this one needs a language that is useful both for medicine and for moral discourse. Such a moral reflection is needed that perceives sicknesses and is capable of describing them comprehensively to the medical professions, and such a psychiatry is needed that is open towards ethics, towards common sense, happiness, and even more, towards the world of grace. Medicine and theology will communicate with one another, when both sciences will base themselves on common philosophical presuppositions.

A true science of man, and so also psychology and psychiatry needs to proceed beginning with an understanding of the healthy person – sinful or virtuous, but healthy, and with a common sense vision of human nature. Without such a base, which by nature is philosophical, psychology and psychiatry are incapable of even giving a definition of "psychic health." The transposition on healthy people of conclusions worked out through the observation of the sick or even worse of animals always ends in the mutilation of man.

The authors of this book undertook a courageous effort. Not fearing the critique of their medical colleagues they introduced into their clinical practice philosophical principles taken from the rational psychology of St. Thomas Aquinas. Furthermore, they discovered that the genial intuitions of S. Freud about the genesis of repressive neuroses can be interpreted best through the application of a terminology that has been worked out in the Middle Ages. They abandoned therefore Freudian concepts – *id, ego, superego*, which unnecessarily complicate the picture. The terms of rational psychology are more comprehensible for patients and they allow for the making of appropriate distinctions, so that the liberation from neurotic repression is not identified with a permissive liberation from the moral law. The application of Thomism in the medical consulting room has allowed for the reaching out beyond a phenomenological description of the symptoms of neurosis towards the understanding of their causes. It is possible therefore to lead the neurotic along the narrow path that unblocks the repression at the same time maintaining the objective moral order.

Kraków, 1989
Wojciech Giertych OP

The years that have passed since the writing of this introduction invite a further comment. The prophetic words "Do not be afraid!" of John Paul II have greatly contributed to the liberation from the repression of the assertive emotions in many countries of central Europe. The almost global however contemporary explosion of sexual hedonism has generated new and not easy psychic and moral problems, distinct from that of sexual repression. The careful putting together of the emotions with the spiritual faculties of the reason and the will as they point towards the true good in such a way that the emotions will continue to supply their natural dynamism requires a precise understanding of the virtues and their cultivation. The art of forming these moral virtues will always be needed, whatever psychic and moral distortions happen to be dominant in society. The wise understanding of anthropology, built not only upon the intuitions of Aristotle, but also being the fruit of gazing upon that unique and perfect man, that is the Incarnate God, Jesus Christ, have allowed Aquinas to develop a comprehensive synthesis that will always be worth studying as a necessary point of reference for psychic integration.

It may also be worth noting that the repression of the emotional sphere is not the only source of moral and psychic difficulties. Also the nature and functioning of the spiritual faculty of appetition, that is, the will, may be misunderstood or even mistaken for the emotions of the irascible appetite, thereby leading to the will's paralysis. Furthermore, the cognitive faculties also at times suffer from an intellectual repression, when ideologies, restrictive philosophical assumptions or even mere fads disenable the reason from reaching out towards the plenitude of truth. And last but not least, the spiritual life of grace, infused in the depths of the soul at the moment of baptism, may suffer from a spiritual repression. The opening up and the flowering of the spiritual life of grace that enables a truly maintained and lived out encounter with the living God as a side effect liberates the mind, the will and the emotions from any repressions from which they may suffer. It is therefore true to say, that the best cure for all these levels of psychic repression is the true living out of the theological virtues of faith, hope and charity, that centered upon God open up to life giving grace.

This of course is apart from the simpler but also valid natural cure for neurosis that is a sense of humor, applied to oneself. Blessed are those, who know how to laugh at themselves, because they will have good fun all their lives!

The Vatican, 2009

Wojciech Giertych OP
Theologian of the Papal Household

Using ALL the Powers of the Human Psyche

CHAPTER I

THE HUMAN PSYCHE

The truth that we owe to man is, first and foremost, a truth about man.

(John Paul II, Puebla, Mexico, January, 1979)

TO UNDERSTAND THE NOTION of *psychic*[1] or *psychological wholeness*, as well as the kind of emotional afflictions whose healing we describe in this book, it is necessary to be familiar with the powers and functions of the human psyche and their relationship with innate drives. Like everything created, human beings are by their very nature directed to a certain good. It follows, therefore, that the person also possesses a drive to obtain this good. This drive is not dependent on any conscious knowledge in human beings themselves, but presupposes the knowledge of Him who has created and directed human nature to this goal.[2] It exists in humans as a blind drive which functions independently of knowledge or consciousness; it drives one on continuously and can never be made to disappear, nor is it depen-

---

1. Editors' note: Dr. Terruwe and Dr. Baars used the term *psychic wholeness* as referring to the emotional, intellectual, and spiritual aspects of the human person as well as the life of the will. It is unfortunate that this term has sometimes been confused with occult terminology. Therefore, throughout this revised edition of *Psychic Wholeness and Healing*, the terms "psychic" and "psychological" will be used interchangeably and should be understood in the context of psychological wholeness and *not* as referring to anything mystical, magical or telepathic.

2. Cf. *Summa Theol.*, Ia IIae, q. 26, a.1, q.g., a.1.

dent on reason for its existence. This natural drive is directed to that which is an essential and necessary good for the human person.

This drive is, therefore, directed first of all to life itself, for it is human nature to be a composite of soul and body; without this union a human being is no longer a human being. Second, there is a drive directed to pro-creation because a human being, by virtue of his or her nature, is a specific being who does not exhaust that nature, existing as it does in numerous subjects; and is, therefore, directed at this multiplication. It is a drive of the human being as social, not as individual.

Both of these *innate drives*, that of *self-preservation* and that of *procreation*, are therefore the most fundamental drives in the human being; they are present from the moment a person begins to exist. The drive of procreation, of course, will make itself fully felt only when a person is physically capable of the procreative act; however, potentially it is always present and may also manifest itself in an elementary form before the age of puberty. On the other hand, the drive for self-preservation is completely developed from the very beginning; in fact, in the baby it plays the predominant role. (Eating and drinking are biological necessities, unlike sexual gratifications.)

These innate natural drives are directed to the most elementary human goods: life and procreation. Human nature, however, extends beyond this basic level by reason of the sensory and intellectual knowledge which it acquires. Similarly, human drives do not remain restricted to these elementary drives of human nature but develop into a wealth of sensory and intellectual inclinations by which persons are able to perfect all the potentialities of their being. These are the so-called *acquired inclinations* and are all the result of a personal cognitive act: the sensory inclinations, of a sensory cognitive act; the spiritual inclinations, of an intellectual cognitive act. Their objects are goods which in some way or other can satisfy a human need.

The sum total of these acquired inclinations has been constructed, so to speak, on the foundation of the two natural innate drives. The latter have to do only with the most essential goods; they *push* the human person, so to speak, toward these necessary, essential goods. The acquired inclinations, on the other hand, have to do with everything that encompasses these essential goods and elevates life and procreation to their fullest human value. We might say that these inclinations *pull* the human person toward the perfection of his or her being. The natural or innate drives are independent of any knowledge in the subject while the acquired inclinations are activated by sensory knowledge.

To understand how human persons attain their good and how neurotic disorders due to repression impede attainment, it is important to understand the sub-sensory, sensory, and intellectual dimensions of the human person. The *sub-sensory powers*—nutrition, growth, reproduction—comprise life's most elementary processes, which are directly concerned with the preservation and reproduction of the living being. These processes are found in every living being; therefore, animals and plants have them in common with humans. The more highly developed the being, the greater and more complex will be the differentiation in the organization of these functions. The sub-sensory physiological dimension has no direct bearing on this study. It has meaning only to the extent that the consequences of repression make themselves felt in human biological functions other than the senses.

In addition to the physiological dimension, we find the *sensory dimension* in human beings similar to, but different by nature from, that in animals. This sense life is characterized by the fact that it enables the living being, human as well as animal, to step outside itself through the ability to know, desire, and pursue concrete, external material things. Thus, an entirely new life comes into existence—the life of sense cognition, sense appetite, and motion—through which the living being passes beyond the limitations of its own being and extends itself through sense knowledge, emotional arousal, and motion. This is the proper and distinctive feature of all sense life. The higher the type of animal, the more varied its sensory life. According to the principle of philosophical anthropology that emotions are always aroused by given perceptions and interpretations, and since the cognitive powers are more perfectly developed in higher forms of sensory life, the corresponding emotions will likewise be more refined until they reach their higher perfection in humans. Although human beings are animal-like in these emotions, they are not in essence (brute) animals.

The *intellectual dimension* of the human being transcends or goes beyond the sense life. The objects of sense perception and emotions are limited to concrete, sensory, material things. The human, not the animal, also grasps the nonsensory and immaterial meaning of things through universal ideas which abstract from the concrete and individual features of singular concrete objects.

It is self-evident that the universal and immaterial can never be known or desired by the sensory powers. There is a necessary and essential relationship between a power and its object because a power is directed to a specific object and necessarily belongs to the same order. If the intended object is concrete and material, then the intending power which is directed to it will also have to be concrete and material. If the intended object is not material, however, it can never be grasped by a sensory and material power.

Consequently, faced with the fact that human beings know the immaterial meaning of things through universal ideas, it is necessary to postulate the existence of an immaterial power through which they are able to know the immaterial meaning of things and ideas.

The same is true for the accompanying appetite. Human beings desire what they know. If they know immaterial things, their appetite will also direct itself to immaterial things. Therefore, because of the necessary and essential relation between a power and its object, human beings must possess an *immaterial power of desiring*.[3] This power is called the will.

These two dimensions, the sensory and the intellectual, constitute the human person's psychic or psychological life. By nature they are meant to function in unison, and when one's development is natural and normal, there will be perfect harmony and integration between the sensory and intellectual powers of knowing and desiring, between sense knowledge and intellectual knowledge, between desire and will. Because this development

---

3. Modern empirical psychology does not admit such powers. It is true that the existence of these powers cannot be demonstrated empirically. One observes the act and the function. The organ too can be observed, but the postulation of the existence of a power always requires an inference, however simple and obvious it may be. One makes the observation that a certain function occurs which is peculiar to a particular being, and one infers from this that the being must possess a certain disposition from which that function originates. This disposition is the power which, in a further logical step, is ascribed to certain organs, but again, this is not an observation of empirical psychology; it is an inference from philosophical anthropology, which, however, does not prevent it from being a valid conclusion.

If empirical psychology rejects the immaterial powers, it oversteps its own boundaries, because this is not a question for purely empirical investigation. On the other hand, some scientific investigators, who no longer recognize the distinction between empirical psychology and philosophical anthropology, have accepted the immaterial powers as empirically determined facts. This opinion must be rejected, although it can never weaken the proof of philosophical anthropology, which is the proper place for the investigation of the immaterial powers.

For further study of this subject *see* Robert E. Brennan, O.P., Ph.D., *Thomistic Psychology—A Philosophic Analysis of the Nature of Man* (New York: Macmillan, 1941), pp. 35–38, and *General Psychology* (New York: Macmillan, 1937), pp. 428–443.

is not always normal, deviations occur, of which neurotic disorders are some of the most serious. Before analyzing their mutual relationship, we shall take a closer look at both the sensory life and the intellectual life.

The Senses

In the human person's sense life, we must distinguish, first of all, between sense knowledge and desire. Sense knowledge is obtained by means of the sensory cognitive powers. These are partly external (the senses of sight, hearing, smell, taste, and touch) and partly internal. Although all senses are somehow rooted in the brain, the internal senses are associated more fully with the brain, but as yet we cannot specify their precise locations.

First of all, there is the *central unifying sense*.[4] It is necessary to postulate the existence of such a sense, because we are able to discriminate between the several kinds of sensations that arrive from the external senses and at the same time unite them into a perceptual whole. Thus, by means of this unifying or centralizing sense, all the sensations individually received are blended into a unit of psychological experience. The importance of this sense for the formation of percepts cannot be overestimated. Experimental psychology has shown that sensory perception of an object always utilizes a variety of sensations from different senses.

A second internal sense is the *imaginative sense* or *imagination*, which enables us to re-present to mind sense objects which are not actually present. The imagination works with material received from the external senses; it stores away the impressions received from the outside world and reproduces them whenever necessary. It also provides a vast reservoir for fictive representation, as in daydreaming or night dreaming.

Besides the central unifying sense and imagination, philosophical anthropology delineates two other internal sensory cognitive powers: that of *usefulness judgment*[5] and the *power of memory*. These cognitive powers are entirely different from the central unifying sense and the imagination, because the proper object of the imagination and the central unifying sense, as well as of the external senses, is the concrete thing itself as perceived by the senses. The usefulness judgment attains in the known object a certain

---

4. In philosophical anthropology, *sensus communis or common sense*.

5. Our term for instinct penetrated by the intellect. At birth it is, for all practical purposes, strictly sensory, but from then on it is increasingly penetrated, first by the intellect of the child's educators, and then more and more by its own.

aspect which is not its goodness or badness,[6] but a relation between the object and the knowing subject, that, in its pragmatic aspect, is the object's usefulness or harmfulness for the subject. Since neither the external senses nor the central unifying sense nor the imagination are able to judge these qualities, one is forced to postulate the existence of another power for the perception of the aspects of usefulness and harmfulness.

Animals, who have a similar power, know these aspects without a shadow of a doubt. Every bird knows at once, without previous experience, how it must build its nest and what it needs for this purpose. Likewise, all animals recognize their natural enemies as dangerous and react accordingly. It is a well-known fact that the usefulness and harmfulness of certain things are known at once and *instinctively*[7] by animals, whereas these same qualities in other things are learned only by experience or training.

A bird that has once built its nest in a certain spot will often return there the following year. As it is not necessitated to this spot by nature, it cannot be nature alone that makes it return. Something has been added, namely, the recollection of its experience that *this spot* was useful. Consequently, in addition to the innate knowledge which causes it to recognize objects which are useful or harmful, the bird must possess a power by which it recalls its own experience of these qualities. This is called *sense memory* or the *power of experience*. Its significance is emphasized by the fact that in the final analysis all animal training is based on this power.[8]

Again, the number of these powers possessed by an animal depends on the degree of perfection of the species. In the lowest species one may

6. Whenever we use the terms "good" and "evil" ("bad") in this book, we refer to a sensory good or to something that is bad or evil for our sensory nature. If it is necessary to speak of moral good or evil, we shall do so explicitly.

7. This usefulness judgment, or "the faculty of estimation" in rational psychology (i.e., philosophical anthropology), "which is shared by man and brute alike, represents the cognitive part of what the modern psychologist calls *instinct*, the other parts being supplied by the sensitive appetites and the faculty of locomotion." Brennan, *Thomistic Psychology*, p. 134.

8. "According to Aquinas, the principle of memory in animals is the experience of biological values, that is of the usefulness or harmfulness of certain things. Just as imagination is complementary to common sense, whose objects it is able to conserve when they are absent, so memory is complementary to estimative sense, whose objects it is able to recall when they are past. The point about the matter is this: that although memorial power can exercise itself with any sensible event that has previously occurred, it is particularly designed, in its pragmatic aspect, to enable the animal, and ourselves as animals, to remember the objects that have special biological implications." Brennan, *Thomistic Psychology*, p. 130.

find only one sense, that of touch, with possibly a rudimentary instinct for survival, but in the higher species, the number of sensory powers is greater, and they are more perfect.

This brief résumé of the sensory cognitive powers of the human person has dealt only with the powers as such. We must now consider them *in their close integration with the higher cognitive power, the intellect.*

The human intellect not only utilizes the sensory knowing powers, but it also intensifies them by its greater penetrating power and by giving them a broader horizon. The range of the sensory knowing powers is limited to the boundaries of place and time; the intellect goes beyond those boundaries and grasps the universal meaning of things, free from the limitations of place and time. When the intellect penetrates and overflows into the sensory cognitive powers, the singular object in its concreteness is seen in the light of the universal and thus loses something of its forceful impact upon the appetite.

The imaginative power, for example, evidently retains the impressions received from the senses and is able to reproduce them; and, presumably, this is the extent of its function in the animal. In the human, however, the imagination, under the influence of the intellect, is able to separate and combine them at will, and to rearrange them into fantasies, which is the function of the so-called *creative imagination.* Although the creative imagination functions under the influence of the intellect, its operation is strongly, and even primarily, influenced by the emotions. Since the imagination is a *sensory* knowing power, its most immediate and direct stimulation will come from the sense appetites. Hence, it is not the intellect alone that makes the artist, but a deeply sensitive emotional life.

The activity of the imagination is also of considerable importance for the appreciation and understanding of human *dream life.* Dreams are products of the imagination, products free from the rational control of the intellect. It follows that the human being's emotional life is manifested directly in dreams. In these dreams, the person gives expression to his or her desires, fears, anger, frustrations, and so forth—many of which he or she is not conscious of while awake—and to resistances that are deeply rooted in the emotional life. These may be expressed in their manifest form or—because the imagination is not only reproductive but also creative—in a disguised form. When the sense appetite provokes a certain image and this image, in turn, arouses sensory resistances, the imagination will then reflect these reactions by producing an image that is a compromise between the sense appetite and the resistance. This phenomenon, discovered by Freud, is called *symbolism*.

A human being's usefulness judgment is also subject to the influence of the intellect. In fact, people possess this power in its strictly sensory character only to a limited extent. This is evident in the baby instinctively searching for its mother's breast and in the boy and girl in whom the sexual urge awakens who are instinctively drawn to each other. Therefore, it would be more correct to say that this power operates *predominantly* under the influence of the intellect. As a rational being, the human person discovers with the intellect what is useful and harmful about natural instinctive urges. By the power to see, for example, a person sees a particular sex object, but by the intellectual power the person knows sexuality. Here, too, we see an elevation of the lower powers and a transformation of the need and urgency of their drives, and as a result, a wider scope of activity in relation to their objects. In this way, there is the possibility of choice even in the sensory life. The human person no longer acts blindly and impulsively but is guided by reasoned comparisons and judgments.

The utility or usefulness judgment is closely associated with the power of reproducing previous experiences of what is useful or harmful. In this reproduction we must distinguish the element of pastness and only secondarily the content of the experiences themselves. In regard to the element of pastness, this power, which is then called *memory*, is influenced by the intellect in the sense that the need for the reproduction of the useful or harmful aspects is lessened. Here, too, as in the case of the imagination, the human person experiences a certain freedom to reproduce previous experiences according to his or her own desire; this is called the *power to reminisce*.

The content of the experiences themselves is also influenced by the intellect. The usefulness judgment, which in general functions under the influence of the intellect, judges the value of past experiences for subsequent particular actions. Thus, the *usefulness judgment in human beings becomes a power which is of the utmost importance*. The aspect of usefulness plays a role to some degree in all of one's acts, except those which are purely pleasurable. For all practical purposes, one may say that human persons employ this power almost continually.[9]

9. For this reason this power is given a name of its own: the cogitative power or *particular reason*. In experimental psychology, this function is included in the word "intelligence."

This conception of usefulness judgment has a profound bearing on the subject of our book because certain disorders of the emotional life can be traced to this power. The transition from instinct to usefulness judgment, or the penetration of the purely sensory "instinctive" power by intellect, constitutes a most important developmental process of the human psyche. *A retarded or impaired penetration of this power by the intellect will result in a psychopathic personality;*[10] *a precocious or excessive penetration will result in a repressive disorder.*[11]

The Sense Appetites

We now proceed to the most important part of the present discussion: the theory of the sense appetites. As we have already stated, for every type of cognition there is a corresponding appetite. When we know a thing as good, as something that suits or pleases our nature and thus perfects that nature, we are moved to like it; when we know something as evil, as something unsuitable or displeasing to our nature, we are moved to dislike it. *These movements are emotions.*

Proceeding from this principle and applying it to our sense life, we must distinguish *two kinds of sense appetite* related to the two kinds of cognitive powers in the sense life. One group (the external senses, the central unifying sense and the imagination) knows the quality of goodness

10. Editors' Note: "Psychopathic personality" was used in the original text, but is an outdated term. It is defined as an emotional disorder with a somatic basis in which "the normal subordination of the emotions to the intellect is not present." It is characterized by extreme egocentricity, instability of the emotional life, and unpredictability. Individuals with this disorder are "incapable of understanding" when their actions are objectively wrong, and they feel no remorse for their actions later on. We consider this to be an innately or congenitally based disorder, unlike a neurotic disorder, which is essentially a developmentally based disorder. A neurotic disorder is "acquired, the result of a certain mental attitude which caused the emotional life to develop in a distorted manner." The persons that the authors referred to as psychopathic personalities would now generally be diagnosed with one of the different personality disorders listed in the American Psychiatric Association's *Diagnostic and Statistical Manual of Mental Disorders* (*DSM; DSM-IV-TR*, Washington, DC, American Psychiatric Association, 2000). Because the term does not have an exact equivalent in the current DSM, we have left it throughout the book where changing it would have changed the authors' meaning. These topics are described fully in *Psychopathic Personality and Neurosis* by Anna A. Terruwe, M.D., translated and edited by Conrad W. Baars, M.D., New York: P.J. Kenedy, 1958.

11. For further details on the nature and function of the internal senses, *see* Brennan, *Thomistic Psychology*, pp. 121–146, especially the clarifications at the end of Chap. 5.

PSYCHIC WHOLENESS AND HEALING

or badness of an object, of being good for me or not; the other group (the usefulness judgment and the power of experience) knows the quality and degree of the usefulness or harmfulness of whatever prevents us from possessing the desired object. For example, the external senses and the central unifying sense tell me that the apple in my hand is good for me because of its healthy natural appearance and aroma, or bad for me because it is rotten. When the luscious apple is hanging high in a tree, however, it is the usefulness judgment which informs me about the difficulty involved in climbing that tree, or, when the rotten apple is held threateningly in the hands of an enemy, my harmfulness judgment tells me of the gravity of this particular threat.

Since we distinguish two entirely different kinds of qualities in objects—the goodness and the usefulness—we must also distinguish two distinct kinds of emotional response and two distinct kinds of appetite. The first kind will move us to be attracted to or repelled by the known object insofar as it is good or bad, pleasing or displeasing; the second will move us to deal with the obstacle or the threat in a positive or negative manner. The first kind of appetite we call the pleasure appetite; the second, the *utility appetite* or *assertive drive*.[12]

Although we have inferred the need for the existence of both these appetites from the nature of cognition, it may also be deduced from the nature of the appetites themselves. In our emotional life we observe emotions which cause us to be moved by a known object because it arouses pleasure and offers a promise of joy when possessed.

It is likewise evident that sensory beings also seek things which of themselves do not give pleasure but are nevertheless sought because through them we can obtain something that does give pleasure. For example, a dog will exert considerable effort to obtain a piece of meat which has been placed out of its reach; or it will attack an intruder in its territory. Although in either case the effort itself is not pleasurable, the dog exerts it in order to obtain that which it desires, the meat or its liberty. Similarly, a medical student will study night after night in order to pass his exams while his friends go out on the town or he will grapple with the mugger who attacks him at night on the street. Again, the effort is not particularly

12. In philosophical anthropology the pleasure appetite is called the concupiscible appetite; the utility appetite or assertive drive is called the irascible appetite. Because of the confusion associated with the word concupiscible, we prefer to call the concupiscible appetite the *pleasure appetite*. It describes the arousal of the emotional life in response to something which is good or bad, pleasing or displeasing.

pleasurable, but he exerts it in order to obtain what he desires: his medical degree in the one instance; his safety in the other.

It is not the pleasure appetite that causes the animal and the student to exert the effort, because that which is difficult cannot constitute an object of the pleasure appetite, which is activated only by a pleasurable good. Consequently, we are forced to postulate the existence of another emotive power which moves one to seek things that are not desired in themselves but only as useful for obtaining some other pleasurable object. This we call the *utility appetite* or *assertive drive*.[13]

The foregoing can be put in the following diagram:

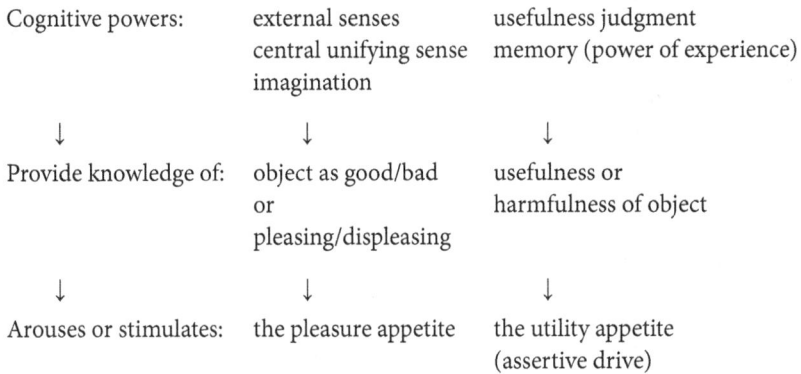

Cognitive powers:	external senses central unifying sense imagination	usefulness judgment memory (power of experience)
↓	↓	↓
Provide knowledge of:	object as good/bad or pleasing/displeasing	usefulness or harmfulness of object
↓	↓	↓
Arouses or stimulates:	the pleasure appetite	the utility appetite (assertive drive)

The Pleasure Appetite

There are *several emotions* or *psychological motors* to be recognized in the pleasure appetite, but there is only one appetitive power because, although its objects differ materially, they are always desired for one thing: for being good.[14] In philosophy, this is expressed by saying that formally the object is always the same.

---

13. The term "utility appetite" is ours. In philosophical anthropology it is called the irascible appetite, which has as its object the *bonum arduum* ("the difficult good"). *Arduum* refers to a good that is not desired in itself; it is not a *bonum delectabile* (pleasing good) and as such is not an object of the pleasure appetite. One strives for the difficult only because it is necessary as a means for obtaining some other pleasurable good. Because the striving for the difficult represents a *useful* means to obtain the desired good, we prefer to call the irascible appetite the utility appetite (also known as the *assertive drive*). Cf. *Summa Theol.*, Ia, q.81, a.2, ad 2 um.

14. There is only one pleasure appetite, in spite of the fact that its objects are many

Pleasure is the first emotion to manifest itself when an object is recognized as good.[15] To know the goodness of an object can only please, but because one knows the object as good and pleasing, one also wants to possess it. This creates *desire*, which is the second emotion. When one has taken possession of the desired object, and the desire has attained its end, the last emotion in this series is experienced: *joy*. These emotions are described by various names, depending on the object. Thus, pleasure is called *love*, liking, complacence, affection, sympathy; desire is called longing, concupiscence, craving, or striving; joy is called satisfaction, delight or happiness. These words indicate subtle variations or nuances, but no essential difference.

In regard to what is known as bad, one must distinguish the opposite emotions: *displeasure*, dislike, or *hate; aversion* from the evil; and if it is possessed, nevertheless, sorrow or *sadness*. Not to obtain what is desired as good is bad, and therefore causes sorrow; escape from what is evil is good, and thus creates joy.[16]

---

and varied. We make a comparison here with Freud's idea of the *libido*, which represents the sum total of pleasure instincts, but we cannot follow Freud in reducing the libido to the sex urge. The sexual experience is one of the objects of the pleasure appetite, but certainly not the only one, nor the most important one. Any of the countless sense goods constitutes the proper object of the pleasure appetite. When human beings recognize an object as a sense good, they naturally experience a movement of the pleasure appetite toward that object. We may distinguish many different kinds of sense goods from the most materialistic to the most immaterial; but all, without exception, can be included under the object of the sensory pleasure appetite.

Since it is the nature of all sensory objects to stimulate the pleasure appetite directly, we cannot say that one of them is the original and that all others are merely derived from it. Naturally, one of these objects presented to a given individual may exert a greater attraction than another object; this depends on the individual's particular psychological disposition. Fundamentally, however, all objects exert their influence on the same level, without being subordinate to each other. It is possible, however, that when the pleasure appetite is inhibited in its emotional response to one object, it intensifies its emotional response to another. In that case, the person's natural energy will be oriented in another direction.

15. The word "pleasure," as the first of the concupiscible or pleasure emotions, is not to be understood as the delight which proceeds from the possession of a good, but simply as the feeling of complacency or contentment which is caused by an object which pleases. Aquinas uses the word "love" to designate this passion, but he defines love in this sense as complacence in the object. Cf. *Summa Theol.*, Ia IIae, q.26, a.2: q.31. Proportionately speaking, the same distinctions apply to the use of the words "hate" and "displeasure."

16. Nowadays the first emotions of this appetite, love and hate, and sometimes also the last ones, joy and sorrow, are often attributed to a separate power: feeling. Feeling then is the opposite of desire. Yet there is no reason to adhere to this idea, which was introduced into psychology by Wundt. According to this theory the object, in experiencing

Finally, we must call attention to the fact that the reactions of this appetite differ in each individual. This is the result of differences in somatic constitution. For the sensory powers are rooted in the body and consequently their functions likewise depend on the condition of the body. One person will love, desire, or enjoy sooner or more intensely than another; one individual will be moved more by certain objects, another by others. Since there are no two people entirely alike as far as their bodies are concerned, so there are no two people whose emotional reactions are entirely the same. Constitutional and developmental factors together bring about an individuality—emotionally, intellectually and spiritually—which is peculiar to each person.

The Utility Appetite/The Assertive Drive

The second sensory appetite—the utility appetite or assertive drive—has an entirely different character. It is not directly responsive to what is pleasurable or displeasing, but provides the emotional responses by which they may be obtained or avoided. Consequently, the assertive drive serves the emotion of desire, for as soon as this has been aroused, it begins to operate in order to prepare the way for the desire to attain its object, to provide that which is wanting, and to remove any obstacle in its path. This drive is characterized by assertiveness and optimism, or their opposites.[17] The emphasis here is on the manner in which a person reacts emotionally to the many possible ways and means of attaining what he or she desires. The variety of reactions then determines the different emotions belonging to this appetite.

If it is a matter of overcoming an obstacle to a desired good and the person reacts with an attitude of "I can do it," he or she gets a feeling of

---

pleasure and joy, is exactly the same as in the case of desire, namely a sense good. The only difference is that feeling constitutes the beginning and the end, while desire constitutes the middle part of the appetite. This is not sufficient reason for dividing this appetite into two different appetites, however. It is necessary to invoke a different power or faculty when desire proceeds to utilize means for attaining its goal. In that case, as we have already explained, another aspect of the object must be considered, and as a result, the utility appetite is brought into play. This utility appetite was probably identified by Wundt with desire. Understandable as this mistake may be—for it is desire which sets this utility appetite in motion in order to achieve its goal—it is nevertheless erroneous and obscures our insight into the emotional life.

17. We do not consider it unlikely that Freud's aggressive drives must be regarded as emotions belonging to this appetitive power. For an explanation of our use of the terms "assertive" and "aggressive," *see* Chapter VII.

hope, energy, confidence, complacency, or whatever one wishes to call it. If the person reacts with an attitude of "I can't do it," however, he or she experiences a feeling of *despair*, dejection and weakness. If a man senses himself capable of overcoming possible harm, and is optimistic that he can successfully defend himself against a threatening evil, he gets a feeling of *courage*, boldness, assertiveness; but if he senses the threatening harm to be inescapable, he will experience *fear*, the emotion which is of such tremendous psychological significance in the human person's psychological life.

Thus, there are four basic emotions of the utility appetite or assertive drive; on the one hand, hope and courage when one feels the obstacle to be surmountable (and thus the desired good obtainable) or the threatening harm avoidable; on the other hand, despair and fear when the opposite is true. In order to simplify matters we combine the assertive emotional responses of hope and courage under the term "*energy*," the nonassertive emotional responses under "*fear*."

These emotions change constantly in one and the same person. It is peculiar to the emotional life that it is completely determined by the concrete object; as soon as that changes, the emotion changes also. This may often be seen in children, since in the young the emotional life has not yet been influenced noticeably by the intellect: Johnny laughs and Johnny cries. This is true not only for the pleasure appetite but for the assertive drive as well. At one moment a desired object is considered obtainable; the next moment, unobtainable: from having great hope one yields to despair. One moment one is fearful, a moment later one dares again. All these emotions are potentially present in each individual. No matter how strongly one emotion prevails, its opposite may manifest itself any time.

Not every effort, obstacle, or threat will always call forth the same emotions in a person. A person may be very energetic at certain times but fearful at others; he or she may be energetic and fearful at the same time, but in regard to different objects. This depends to a large extent on the person's upbringing and development. Although constitutional factors undoubtedly ought to be taken into account, they are modified by environmental influences.

We have not yet mentioned another emotion of the assertive drive, namely *anger*. When someone resists but still has to suffer a threatening harm, he or she experiences anger. The person also feels anger when all efforts to overcome the obstacles separating him from a desired object prove to be in vain, and the object escapes him. This reaction must be distinguished from the emotion of courage. Courage is aroused by the mere threat of harm, but anger presupposes its presence.[18] The emotion of anger is of great importance in every person's life. Unfortunately, its function as a natural and necessary psychological motor has been largely misunderstood, and consequently many people have been emotionally crippled. As we have written extensively on the function, control and repression of anger elsewhere, this brief mention must suffice here.[19]

Diagram of Emotions of the Sensory Appetites

Pleasure Appetite (Humane Emotions)		Utility Appetite (Assertive Emotions)	
love	hate	hope	courage
desire	aversion	despair	fear
joy	sadness	anger	

18. Although we have presented the commonly accepted doctrine, it is not clear to us why *ira* or anger has to be differentiated as a separate emotion. Our objections are twofold. First, according to the prevailing theory, *ira* always presupposes a present or past evil (cf. *Summa Theol.*, Ia IIae, q.23, a.2). Yet, the way we understand it, it is also possible for a threatening danger to bring about all the symptoms of anger and rage, and when the manifestations are the same, one might well assume that the emotions are one and the same.

The second objection is of a different nature. St. Thomas defines *ira* as a reaction to injustice with a view to revenge (cf. *ibid.*, qq. 46–47). For St. Thomas, therefore, *ira* is also an emotion, but obviously one which is accompanied by an act of reason. When animals experience *ira*, it is because they have a natural instinct given to them by the divine reason, in virtue of which they are gifted with movements, both internal and external, similar to rational movements (cf. *ibid.*, q.46, a.4, ad 2 um). It seems strange to us that an emotion which in essence is purely sensory would derive its distinguishing characteristics from the *ratio*, while it would occur in the animal more or less by accident, having some resemblance to that of human beings. Moreover, we would like to know how rage in an animal could ever have anything to do with revenge. Rather, it appears to us, an animal's rage constitutes a defense against further threatening evil.

If one were to drop *ira* as a separate emotion, it would be necessary to reduce its manifestations to expressions of *audacia*, often modified by expression of hatred.

19. *See* Chapter VII of this book; *Feeling and Healing Your Emotions* by Conrad W. Baars, M.D. (rev. ed., Suzanne M. Baars & Bonnie N. Shayne, eds., Bridge-Logos, Gainesville, FL, 1979, 2003); and also *Born Only Once* by Conrad W. Baars, M.D. (Rev. ed., Suzanne M. Baars and Bonnie N. Shayne, eds., Eugene, OR: Wipf & Stock, 2016.)

The Relation between the Two Appetites

We must see how these two appetites are related to each other. Because the proper guidance of the emotional life must be based on the natural relationship between these two appetites, this question is of great importance.

When comparing the pleasure appetite with the assertive drive, we realize that the latter is subordinated to the former. The *assertive drive operates to enable the pleasure appetite to reach its goal*; therefore, it is directed to the pleasure appetite and subordinate to it.[20] To give some examples: In a game of tennis, the opponent is stronger than I thought. Faced with this challenge, my emotion of hope is aroused to move me to do whatever is necessary to overcome that obstacle. When successful, I'll be able to experience what the obstacle separated me from—the joy of winning or, when told by my physician that I need a serious operation, the emotion of courage (which follows the initial reaction of fear) moves me to submit. Once the surgery proves successful, I experience the joy of having regained good health.

In these two examples, my desire to win and to enjoy good health are served by the emotions of hope and courage. If, in the case of tennis, I had reacted with the emotion of despair of being able to win, I'd probably have renounced the desire to win and settled for the desire to learn as much as possible from my superior opponent. If I see one or two killers come at me with knives, my fear will move me to run as fast as I can to escape being harmed. If some person offends me or harms me in some way, my anger may move me to demand an apology which, when received, will be reason to enjoy having my self-respect restored.

Because of the subordination of the assertive drive to the pleasure appetite, the *main accent in the emotional life must naturally rest on the pleasure appetite* and not on the assertive drive. When the emphasis is shifted to the assertive drive, there is a disharmony of the emotional life, with potentially disastrous consequences to the psychological life. Later we shall have occasion to discuss this in greater detail.

Our claim that the pleasure appetite of human beings is more spiritual and intuitive—as compared with the more "rational" and mechanistic character of the assertive drive—can be understood only in the realization that we are not restricting sense pleasure to the meaning which is often

---

20. *See Summa Theol.*, Ia IIae, q.25, a.1: "The irascible passions both arise from and terminate in the passions of the concupiscible faculty."

given it: namely, to indicate simply and solely the gratification of the senses of touch and taste. In humans the intellectual pervades and elevates the entire sensory life, including the pleasure appetite. The most perfect and beautiful human emotions belong to this level of life and can be the source of the purest human happiness. What ultimately matters is *what* people strive for, not the striving itself. When persons choose that which is most proper to them as human beings, from all the possible objects which can stimulate their pleasure appetite, it will only be through the subordination of the assertive drive to the pleasure appetite that they can do full justice to their human nature.

The *predominance of the assertive drive*, on the other hand, leads to an extreme materialistic and mundane spirit and stifles emotional life. This is a frequent occurrence in modern times and is caused to a great extent by a premature development of the reasoning intellect before the emotional life has matured sufficiently. Since the assertive drive participates more in the functioning of the reasoning intellect, it will overstep its limits whenever the intellect exercises undue influence over a person's actions. This disturbance of the proper order of the psychological powers is the cause of emotional illness.[21]

Sensory Power of Movement

Following this discussion of the emotional life in general, one of its component parts—the sensory power of movement or motor system—warrants closer examination. This subject is usually mentioned only cursorily in philosophical anthropology, but, for a full understanding of the human person's psychological life, it is important to be familiar with this particular aspect and to recognize the various forms of motor reactions.

Limiting our discussion to the sensory power of movement (those movements which belong to the sensory order) we shall not discuss the powers of movement peculiar to the strictly physiological functions of the body, such as circulation and metabolism. These are of interest to us only insofar as they are affected and altered by psychological attitudes and emotional states, as occurs, for instance, in neurotic disorders.

By sensory power of movement we mean the sum total of movements which result from a sensory stimulus. Human beings respond to a particular sensory stimulus with a particular motor reaction. Although this is valid

---

21. See also p. 23, regarding heart and mind.

as a general principle, an analysis of the different sensory-motor manifestations will show that we must distinguish various forms of movement.

The first and most simple form of movement comprises the so-called *reflexes*. Here stimulation of an external sense (e.g., tapping the tendon below the kneecap with a reflex hammer) is followed immediately by a certain bodily movement (knee-jerk). In neurological terminology, the stimulus proceeds from the sensory nerve to the motor nerve via the sensory and motor nuclei in the spinal cord without passing through the brain. In psychological terms, the movement follows sense cognition without any intervention by the appetite. This is the most elementary form of sensory movement and therefore the first form to be found in the phylogenetic order of animal species. A snail shrinks when touched. In general these reflexes serve the most essential interests of self-preservation, self-protection, and procreation. They are of importance for the study of neurotic disorders only insofar as they are influenced by emotional conflicts.

In addition to these reflexes, there are *higher forms* of sensory-motor power, in which the motor reaction is not directly activated by the external sense stimulus but via the emotions. In neurological terminology, afferent sensory nerves conduct the stimulus to the brain and from the cerebral motor nuclei to the efferent motor nerves. It is customary to distinguish two forms of movement: psychomotor reactions and voluntary motor reactions.

Psychomotor reactions, of which the anatomical center is probably situated in the optic thalamus, are merely the natural spontaneous somatic expressions of the emotions: the happy person laughs, the unhappy one weeps, the angry person trembles and turns red or pale. All these external manifestations are best defined as natural expressions of the emotions. Psychomotor responses depend, as far as their manifestations are concerned, entirely on the somatic disposition: one person reacts in this way, another in that way; a woman reacts differently from a man (for instance, she is more disposed to weeping); the child's reaction differs from that of the adult. Differences in racial characteristics must also be considered. All in all, psychomotor reactions are highly individualized responses.

When we take a closer look at the psychomotor reactions we realize that there is more to them than merely the natural external manifestations such as laughing, crying, shaking, etc. In addition, there are always internal somatic changes which express the indivisible unity of psyche and soma. These particular psychosomatic reactions are not just muscle movements but are all the physiological changes which occur as the expression of the psychic (psychological) arousal in the body. In other words, *every emotion has a psychic component which is accompanied necessarily by a somatic component.*[22] An emotion represents a psychosomatic unit. The psychomotor reaction represents the material aspect; the psychic activity represents the formal or spiritual aspect. As long as the emotional experience lasts as a psychic event—and this is true of every emotion of both appetitive powers—there exist physiological reactions which are directed to the object of the emotion. These physiological reactions can be the secretion of internal glands, changes in size of the pupils, change in heart rate, elevation or lowering of the blood pressure, increased blood sugar level, and many others. Whatever their exact nature, however, the physiological changes associated with the emotions of the pleasure appetite serve the purpose of *optimal involvement in being moved*; and those associated with the emotions of the assertive drive that of *optimal intensity of movement or action.*

Voluntary motor reactions, on the other hand, are quite different from psychomotor reactions. While the psychomotor reactions constitute the emotion itself, the voluntary motor reactions are essentially distinct from it. Voluntary motor reactions are a response to the emotion—or for that matter to the will—for the purpose of obtaining the object of the emotion—or of the will.[23]

Voluntary motor reactions include not only what is commonly called body movements, walking, lifting, gymnastics, etc., but also those muscle movements which serve such highly specialized functions as speech and writing, for which there are separate centers in the brain.[24] In view of the fact that we can distinguish many differing aspects of voluntary motor reactions, there is reasonable doubt whether we can speak here of only one single power. We must confine ourselves to the task of defining the nature of the voluntary motor reaction and its relation to other mental functions.

22. Thomas Aquinas taught this by saying that every sensory appetite is accompanied necessarily by a *transmutatio corporalis.*

23. They are therefore a separate power, and whenever the *vis motrix* or *potentia locomotiva* is mentioned in philosophical anthropology, we must assume that voluntary motor reactions are meant.

24. We agree that it is not the presence of different organs, but rather the essential difference in objects, which is the deciding factor in the question whether or not there are several powers. Nevertheless, we are justified in suspecting that there is a formally different object; in which case we would have to postulate different powers, but it is outside the scope of this book to investigate this problem further.

It is clear that voluntary motor reactions proceed from the appetites—sensory as well as intellectual—when action is necessary in order to obtain that which is desired or willed. This motor power is related, not to the pleasure appetite, but to the assertive drive. This is because movement is a means to attain a sensory object, but an object is sought only by the assertive drive, following upon a usefulness judgment. It is absolutely necessary, therefore, that both cognitive and appetitive faculties be brought into action if movement is to follow. Naturally, this does not mean that this must be done on a conscious level; the actuation of the assertive drive can also take place automatically.

In other words, the psychological course of events is this: the emotions of desire and aversion actuate the assertive drive via the usefulness judgment for the purpose of directing itself to a means by which it can attain its goal; the assertive drive utilizes movement to effect its purpose. A practical application is presented in the following diagram.

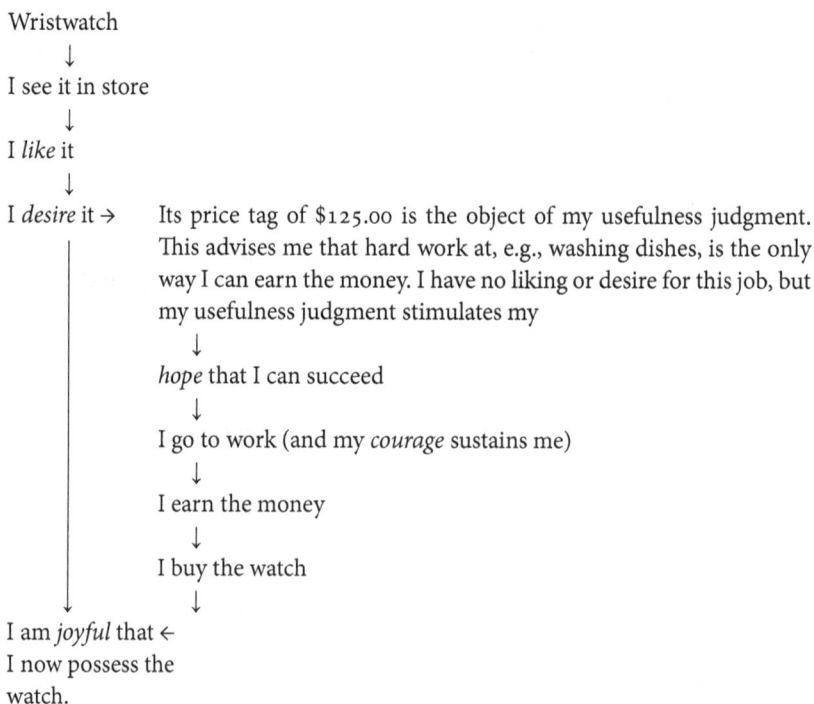

Wristwatch
↓
I see it in store
↓
I *like* it
↓
I *desire* it → Its price tag of $125.00 is the object of my usefulness judgment. This advises me that hard work at, e.g., washing dishes, is the only way I can earn the money. I have no liking or desire for this job, but my usefulness judgment stimulates my
↓
hope that I can succeed
↓
I go to work (and my *courage* sustains me)
↓
I earn the money
↓
I buy the watch
↓
I am *joyful* that ←
I now possess the
watch.

A pleasure emotion, elevated as it is in the human person by the intellect, may possibly engage the will directly for the purpose of voluntary motor reactions. This could occur when one is joyful and wants to express one's joy in song, dance or other signs of celebration. In such an occurrence there is no need for a utility judgment.

Before proceeding to our discussion of the intellectual dimension of the human person, we must stress the importance of a full and correct understanding of the purpose and function of the emotions or psychological motors. Its importance becomes particularly clear when one reflects on the fact that in the course of time the role of the emotions has been seriously misunderstood. Emotions have been feared, despised, considered suspect and accountable for the human person's "evil nature," and made the object of mortification, annihilation, suppression and repression. During the past few decades, reactions to this chronic failure to give emotions their proper due have become manifest in a variety of ways—some good, others bad and counterproductive. It is mandatory for the sake of society's mental health, or better its psychological wholeness, as well as for the prevention and treatment of emotional disorders, that the correct understanding of the emotions, by themselves, and in their relationship to the intellect and will, becomes general and widespread.

Intellect and Will

Human beings are human beings, not because of their plant-like and animal-like dimensions, but because they are gifted with an intellectual dimension. The intellect is a spiritual, immaterial power which enables human beings to know the universal meaning of things through abstract ideas. The very fact that they intend and point to the meaning of reality through these abstract ideas (e.g., the ideas of "character," "liberty," "motherhood," and so forth) makes it necessary for us to assume the reality of a spiritual power in human beings. If the object is immaterial, as in the case of an abstract idea, the object of which does not exist in a concrete form, the power, too, must be immaterial.

This does not mean, however, that intellect must be independent of matter under every aspect. Since the human intellect obtains its concepts by abstracting the essence or nature of material things from the data provided by the external and internal senses, it is dependent on the senses in its operation. According to the axiom of philosophical anthropology: "Nothing exists in the intellect that did not exist first in the senses."[25] First we

25. *Nihil est in intellectu quod non prius fuerat in sensu.*

have a sensory knowledge of concrete things. The external senses, central unifying sense, and imagination know sensory characteristics as they are in themselves; the usefulness judgment and memory know the useful or harmful qualities. The intellect abstracts from these sense images; it leaves the sensory limitations of color, form, location, and so forth out of consideration, and thus makes possible a universal concept which is free of matter or material limitations.

Even though the act of intellectual cognition is purely spiritual and performed without material organs, the intellect is dependent on the body for its operations. In humans a purely spiritual act without any material substrate is by nature impossible.[26] For this reason, the condition of our physical organs of perception is of decisive influence on our immaterial knowledge. Thus, the more perfectly developed our brains, the greater our knowledge; and conversely, any imperfection of the bodily substrate, whether innate or acquired, as in organic brain diseases, will affect the cognitive process itself. Yet this does not alter the fact that the act of intellectual cognition is itself spiritual or immaterial and can never be put on the same level with that of sensory cognition.

The intellect employs the data of sensory knowledge as the means of arriving at its knowledge. This implies that sensory knowledge is presented to the intellect to be illuminated, so to speak, by the light of the higher knowing power which penetrates all concrete limitations. We need only compare the sensory knowledge of even the most highly organized animal with that of a child in order to understand at once the fundamental difference between the two. Every art, every technical skill, every positive science is based on this illuminating operation of the intellect on sensory knowledge; only this operation makes art and science possible.

The task of the *theoretic* or *speculative* intellect is to discriminate between the true and the false; being engaged with knowledge for its own sake, its ultimate goal is demonstrable truth.

Because knowledge does not suffice in itself, the intellect has also another task, namely to distinguish between the moral good and the moral bad. The aspect of the intellect which accomplishes this task is called the *practical intellect*, since it knows things in relation to our appetites, and functions as the power for regulating the human person's inclinations and

---

26. It would be possible for God to infuse knowledge directly into the intellect of an individual, but knowledge thus acquired would be completely supernatural and in no way natural. Cf. *Summa Theol.*, Ia, q.84, aa.7 and 8.

the acts which follow those inclinations. What appears as pleasing to the sensory appetite will be judged in the light of the superior good which the intellect knows and values.

By means of the practical intellect, human beings know what is *morally* good and bad, and this makes it possible for them to enunciate prudential judgments as to how to behave here and now. This latter function constitutes the *conscience*, which guides all the person's actions directly. Through further reflection on this practical knowledge, human beings are able to formulate the general principles of morality in the practical science of ethics. This is a deeper explication of what is already known by their practical knowledge of conscience.

In addition to distinguishing between the speculative and practical intellect, it is possible to distinguish two different sources of knowledge within the intellect. One of them derives its knowledge from elaborating on the abstract ideas gleaned from the data of sense cognition, comparing, analyzing, synthesizing them, and so forth. Because this is in essence a process of reasoning, this intellectual power is called the *reasoning intellect*. Other terms are "*discursive intellect*" and "*ratio*" (reason).

The other element of the human person's intellectual power is the *intuitive intellect*, by which one collects and reads (*intelligere* comes from "*intus*" and "*legere*," which means: reading in or at a deeper level) the deeper meaning of reality, which cannot be represented by ideas or pictured by images. Another term is "*contemplative intellect*," because it receives its knowledge when being attentively present to God and His creation, His words as contained in the Scriptures, as well as the works of art fashioned by human beings.

In this connection it should be noted that we can speak of "the connatural knowledge of the heart" whenever the pleasure emotions—in their intimate relationship with the intuitive intellect—are elevated and transformed into psychological motors that completely support the contemplative intellect and loving will. It is precisely through this elevating effect that the human person's primary emotions, the pleasure emotions, become typically human. For this reason, we also call them the *humane emotions*. Whenever the heart is contrasted to the mind—as for example in the Scriptures—the *heart* is to be understood psychologically as the pleasure emotions elevated by and integrated with the intuitive intellect, the *mind* as reason in its close association with the utilitarian or assertive emotions.

Psychologically speaking, the heart in this sense could well be the spiritual power that spiritualizes the human person's intellectual dimension.

Since all knowledge is complemented by appetite, it follows that in a human being's intellectual life there must exist, in addition to the intellect which provides spiritual knowledge, a power which causes the human person to long for the immaterial goods known by the intellect. This *spiritual appetite* is as different from the sensory appetite as the intellect is from the sensory cognitive powers. By nature it is no more bound to matter than is the intellect, nor does it have a material organ. Its proper object is not the concrete sense goods which are the objects of the sense appetites, but the *universal good*; the good as such.

For this reason it is obvious that only one spiritual appetite exists. On the sensory level the two specifically distinct concrete objects—the pleasurable good and the useful good—require separate powers, but the universal good cannot be divided into classes because the aspect of universal good as such is present in every conceivable good. It follows, then, that the spiritual appetite is able to tend toward any concrete good, although not to a concrete good as such (which is the object of the sensory appetites) but insofar as the concrete good is recognized as falling under the aspect of universal good. *This spiritual power is called the will.*

From the difference in the objects of the sensory and intellectual appetites, it follows that there is also a profound difference in the manner of striving which proceeds from these two powers. The sensory appetites in and by themselves are compelled to act; since they are directed entirely to concrete objects, they will always begin to function when these objects are present. The will, on the other hand, is compelled to act only by the universal good, which can never be understood by the intellect in any other way than as good. The only object which is good in all respects is God. In every other object the intellect will be able to see the aspect under which it is not good. In these cases, the judgment of the intellect is not a compelling one and neither, therefore, is the movement of the intellectual appetite which follows the judgment.

Just as there is an intuitive and a reasoning moment in the human person's knowing power, so there is also a double element in the will: the loving will and the executive will.

The basic activity of the will is love. Love is the passion of the intellect. The *loving will* is a blind power which follows the enlightenment of the intellect. Just as the activity of the intellect comes to its perfection in a judgment about what really and objectively is, so the will comes to its perfection in accepting and approving what is insofar as it is. One approves the known being as valuable in itself, as worthwhile to be. What really and objectively is, is worthwhile to be appreciated and approved according to the level of its being. Therefore, the loving will is characterized by the activity of passivity. The core of love is: let it be, because it is good as is. Love is respect and adoration of the loved being. Love allows the being to be, and it enjoys its being.

Spiritual and objective love is not neutral and cold. It is disinterested in the sense of "it does not matter whether it is useful to me or not." The loving will follows the wondering intellect which is open to the mystery of being. It goes beyond the limits of what can be represented in images and ideas. Just as the intuitive intellect exceeds the boundaries of representation, so does the loving will, but the loving will is surrender where the intellect still hesitates. Unlike the reasoning intellect which brings the *knower* to perfection by interiorizing the known being, love is ecstatic. It goes out to the loved being and wills *its* perfection.

The second element in the will is the *executive will*. The intellect knows the being in its potentiality and all the possibilities which are hidden in its being. Love wills to advance the loved being according to its own dynamic inner forces towards its realization. The will strives for the fulfillment of the loved being. It is here that the will uses its power to realize those possibilities. However, just as the reasoning intellect is subordinate to the final contemplation of the truth, so the executive will is subordinate to the admiration of the loved being. The executive will comes to rest and finds joy in the advancement of the loved being.

Love, we said before, accepts and approves the known being according to the level of its being. The level of being which is proportionate to a human being is the other human being. It is especially the human person who has an innate need and desire to be approved as he or she is and to develop according to his or her own personality dynamics. To be and feel accepted and approved by others constitutes *a second birth, one's psychic or psychological birth*. Just as human beings are unable to give birth to themselves, neither are they able to accept and love themselves without the prior love of others. We receive our unique and specific full humanity from others. It is from this affirmation that we receive the strength to be *authentically human*, i.e., to give others in turn their unique and specific humanity.

The temptation to fashion ourselves, i.e., self-affirmation, is always futile. Ultimately it results in a narcissistic self-destruction and the destruction of others in the will to possess, the will to fame, and the will to power—three disparate ways to be loved, three forms of corruption of the will to be loved.[27]

Finally, we want to stress the *freedom of the will*. Intrinsically, no concrete object compels the will to act because there is no single concrete object that is infinitely good. Although the free exercise of the will may cease or diminish when extrinsic factors, such as a disproportionate influence of the emotions, force the intellect to make a judgment, this does not detract from the will's intrinsic freedom to choose. Normal persons have freedom of exercise of their actions and are therefore responsible for them. The freedom of the will to choose in persons with repressive disorders is the topic of Chapter VIII in this book.

After this explanation of the nature of the *spiritual appetite*, we must determine *its relationship to the sensory appetite*. Although these powers are fundamentally different, they are both used by human beings to pursue the good: the sensory good by the sensory appetites, and the universal good by the will. Both, however, are appetites belonging to human persons, and as the human person is a unity, there should also be harmony between the sensory and spiritual appetites. Since the concrete and limited good is a part of the universal and absolute good, it is by nature subordinate to it. In the final analysis, therefore, true human good is determined by the universal good, while the sense good is good for the human person only insofar as it falls under the universal good.

Consequently, it is in the nature of the human person's sensory appetite to function in accordance with the will. Thomas Aquinas expressed this forcefully with the words: "*It is the nature of the sensitive appetite to follow reason.*"[28] These are the distinctive, differing features of the sensory appetites of human being and animal: the animal knows the object only in its concrete sensory aspects and strives for it as such; but the human being, whose entire sensory life is subordinated to reason, can know the concrete object in its subordination to reason and pursue it as such.

27. For a more detailed discussion of "affirmation" and "self-affirmation" *see Feeling and Healing Your Emotions* by Conrad W. Baars, M. D., and also *Born Only Once* by the same author.

28. *Appetitus sensitivus natus est obedire rationi. Summa Theol.*, Ia IIae, q.74, a.3, ad 1 um.

If human beings were perfect by nature, this subordination would be fully manifest in their actions, and it would be impossible for their sensory life to desire anything which is in conflict with the universal good. However, we do not live in this state of perfection. Human nature has been disrupted—faith teaches that original sin is the cause—and we see the manifestations of this break in the relationship of the sensory appetites and the will. We constantly experience the arousal of sensory desires whose gratification would not be in harmony with our rational understanding of what is objectively good for us. When this happens, we must deny ourselves the gratification of such desires.

Yet this break in the relationship between the sensory appetites and the will is not complete. Although our nature has been damaged, it is still oriented in all things to that which is objectively right, and our emotional life always continues to be disposed to act, although imperfectly, according to reason.

This explains why even a fully matured and well-balanced person can have conflicts. Nevertheless, when reason denies the demands of the emotional life, the latter, no matter how great its resistance, will sooner or later become tranquil again and abide by the judgment of reason. Or, at least, there will be a balance between the two with reason providing the necessary guidance. It is important to note that this will not result in an abnormal psychological condition, for *it is the nature of the emotional life to be subject to reason*, and, therefore, it must naturally desist in its operation when reason has judged the concrete object of its inclination not to be a universal good. Even then, the emotional life attains the good toward which it is directed by nature; namely, the concrete good so far as it is reasonable.

On the other hand, there will be a defect in the psychic life if a sense appetite acts contrary to reason. This is not a defect as regards the sensory inclination itself, however, because the particular appetite will become quiescent once its goal has been attained. It is a defect in the relationship of appetite to reason, which is experienced as a feeling of discomfort and uneasiness. Hence, it is more than an intellectual awareness of the wrong that has been done; it is an actual feeling of incompleteness. This is the way in which well-balanced, mature individuals spontaneously react, and it forms the basis of the *feeling of guilt* which results from performing acts that are morally wrong. It is an experience of the psychological incompleteness of the human act.[29]

29. Here we touch upon the important distinction between the *intellectual awareness*

PSYCHIC WHOLENESS AND HEALING

The foregoing pertains, of course, to a fully matured and well-balanced person. In the case of a constitutionally determined abnormality in the relationship between the emotional and intellectual life, as we believe happens in some personality disorders, the subordination of the appetites to reason will be greatly diminished or completely lacking, depending upon the degree of impairment. The emotional life in such individuals will be directed to concrete sensory objects without adequate subordination to reason. This explains the irrational character of the emotional reactions of such persons; the reactions are merely responses to the concrete aspects of the object without benefit of intellectual considerations. At the same time, it explains why a person with a psychopathic personality is devoid of guilt feelings. Since their emotions operate independently of the natural need for conformity to reason, its absence in any given emotional reaction will not be experienced as a deficiency.

The same thing can be observed in persons with neurotic disorders, but in a completely different manner and as a result of entirely different causes. The emotional life of persons with neurotic disorders has a natural, innate tendency to act in accordance with reason, but it cannot actually do so because it has become distorted and is subject to abnormal tensions. In these persons, the emotional life has not developed harmoniously, but since their natural dispositions are healthy, it is possible to redirect their emotional life into normal channels. Once the psychological distortions have been removed and the abnormal tensions have been resolved, nature will again follow its course to maturity.

In view of the fact that the human person's sensory appetite is naturally directed to the object as it appears in the light of intellectual knowledge, we can point out other consequences of extraordinary significance. The sensory appetite of an animal is independent of any intellect and is therefore concerned only with the good of the animal itself. The nature of the concrete sensory appetite is such that it knows only the singular concrete object and tends toward it only as a good for the subject itself. It is therefore an *entirely egocentric appetite* which directs everything to itself.

---

of guilt, which is a function of practical moral judgment or conscience, and the *feeling of guilt* which is experienced in the sensory appetites. Both are normally present in the well-balanced person, but it is possible for an individual to have only the intellectual awareness of guilt without any sensory feeling, or to have a feeling of guilt which is not substantiated by any rational judgment. The successful treatment of patients will often depend upon the therapist's knowledge of these possibilities.

As regards the will, however, it is a different matter. The intellect and the will have as their proper objects the true and the good. Because the human being is a limited good, it is naturally proper for one to consider oneself as a part of the universal good. This is why human persons see their own good under the aspect of the universal good and desire it as such. They are not purely egocentric but seek the good for the sake of the good itself. For the same reason they seek the good of others, because this also contains the aspect of goodness. This is the psychological basis of the virtue of charity, which loves all creatures for the sake of God, the universal good.

When the object of the sensory appetite is considered in the light of the universal, the sensory life in this respect will come under the influence of reason and will more or less lose its egocentric character.[30] Moreover, it will also desire the good of others. This results in a noticeable elevation of the emotional life, in that it becomes more unselfish. This may be seen especially in the human person's sexual life. In contrast to the animal urge which seeks only the satisfaction of the appetite, the sexual desire of the truly mature person is transformed into an intimate expression of love. In other words, human sexuality only reaches its human fulfillment in human communication. The same is true for all other human emotions. Although they remain sensory appetites, they assume the highest and noblest human characteristics as a result of the natural influence of the intellectual appetite.

This concludes our discussion of the human psyche insofar as it pertains to the subject matter of this book. However, to prevent misunderstanding, we want to add one more comment. Although in the following pages we shall speak repeatedly of the operation of the various powers, we must always remember that these powers belong to the individual subject, the human person, who acts by means of them. It is always the person who knows, feels, and moves in, through and by the operation of his or her powers. *The whole person, not the power alone,* knows, feels, and moves.[31]

---

30. Cf. *Summa Theol.*, Ia IIae, q.30, a.4.

31. *See* Appendix A for a discussion of the Human Drives underlying the powers and functions of the human psyche.

CHAPTER II

THE REPRESSIVE PROCESS

Whereas God always forgives
and man sometimes forgives
nature never forgives—when
one thwarts nature,
nature rebukes, retaliates,
strikes back.

Anonymous

Emotions in Conflict

HAVING EXPLAINED THE NATURAL relationships of the various psychological powers in the healthy integrated person, we shall now discuss the
emotional deviations which may develop. This discussion shall be confined
to acquired deviations, because constitutionally determined deviations, as
in psychopathic personalities or personality disorders, and abnormalities
of the emotional life which are the result of cognitive dysfunction due to a
general medical condition, do not pertain to a discussion of this nature. We
shall restrict ourselves to a study of the cause and development of *repressive
disorders*.[1]

1. We have described the neurotic disorder which is not the result of repression—

THE REPRESSIVE PROCESS

The idea that certain neurotic disorders develop as a result of *repression* has been generally accepted in psychiatry, thanks to the brilliant investigations of Freud. Fundamentally, this kind of disorder is the result of two factors: an emotion which arises in the psyche and a force which opposes and represses this emotion. The emotion does not, however, disappear completely as a result of this repression; having been *buried alive*, so to speak, it continues to exert its influence in the subconscious life and manifests itself in symptoms which may be called pathological. We shall now evaluate this in the light of philosophical anthropology as discussed in Chapter I of this book, and give our reasons why we disagree with Freud's conclusion that the *superego* constitutes the repressive force in neurotic disorders. It is our contention that the repressive conflict takes place among the emotions themselves, and not between an emotion and the superego force.

When we speak of a conflict between emotions we are not referring to the fact that one's emotions may be stimulated consecutively by different and contrasting objects. This follows logically from the limitations of human knowledge. Every human emotion is aroused by an object. Since many may value an object first as pleasing and later as displeasing, it follows that one emotion may be replaced by another. As there is no actual clash between these emotions, however, there is no question of a conflict. It merely amounts to a change of disposition in the emotional life.

Properly speaking, a conflict results when two opposing emotions are present simultaneously in regard to one and the same object. The appetite is moved by the object either as good and pleasing, or as bad and displeasing. If it is pleasing, it necessarily results in a tending toward the object; if it is displeasing, it results with equal necessity in a tending away from it. Moreover, an object cannot be considered good and bad under the same aspect.

To be able to speak of a conflict, it is necessary that two or more appetites are aroused by the same object. In this way, each appetite will respond to the object from a different aspect. The object in question can be pleasing for one appetite and at the same time harmful for another. Hence, there may be a simultaneous movement toward and away from the object.

As we have seen, there are three appetitive powers in human beings: two sensory appetites (the pleasure appetite and the utility appetite or assertive drive) and, above them, the intellectual appetite or will. Conflicts,

Emotional Deprivation Disorder (formerly called *deprivation neurosis*)—in *Healing the Unaffirmed: Recognizing Emotional Deprivation Disorder*, by Conrad W. Baars, M.D. and Anna A. Terruwe, M.D., Rev. ed. Suzanne M. Baars and Bonnie N. Shayne, eds., Staten Island, NY: Alba House, 2002.

therefore, may develop in two possible manners: between the sensory appetites and the will, or between the sensory appetites themselves.

As to the first possibility, it may happen that an object which appeals to the sensory pleasure appetite is not considered as good by the intellect and thus not willed. For example, a diabetic who has a great liking for sweets may experience a purely sensory craving for candy, but reason and will deny the gratification of this desire. Conversely, a person may have an intense dislike for cod-liver oil yet be willing to take it since reason says it is good for one's health.

Similarly, a conflict may arise between the sensory assertive drive and the will. Persons may reasonably will something of which they have a great fear, such as a surgical operation to prolong their lives. On the other hand, they will refrain from an action even though they experience a natural urge to use every means to perform it, as when someone refrains from revolting against unjust oppression. Every individual experiences this kind of conflict from time to time. It is the result of defective subordination of emotional life to reason and will.

In addition to this group of conflicts, another group results from the contrasting emotions of the pleasure appetite and assertive drive in regard to the same object. Such conflicts originate when the pleasure appetite desires something as good and pleasurable, while at the same time the assertive drive seeks to avoid it as harmful. Thus, a person may experience a sexual desire and at the same time be afraid of the object of this desire, or, what amounts to the same thing, be afraid of the sexual desire itself. Likewise, the reverse may happen; something is experienced as unpleasant by one appetite but is pursued as useful by the other. This may be seen, for example, in a religious novice who is determined to become a saint and, with that goal in mind, practices mortification; for example, by self-inflicting pain.

The possibility of this kind of conflict is due to the fact that in human beings the assertive drive does not blindly follow an instinct which in animals is directed entirely to sense objects. The assertive drive is stimulated by one's usefulness judgment. Because of the influence of the intellect, this power is able to form a particular judgment regarding the usefulness and harmfulness of objects, and this judgment is not determined solely by the ability to attain a certain concrete sense good. For this reason, humans alone, and not animals, can have conflicts which are of decisive significance in the origin of repressive disorders.

Now that we have recognized two possible kinds of conflicts, we shall discuss each one separately and in more detail.

Conflict between Sensory Appetites and the Will

When we discussed the relationship between sensory appetites and the intellectual appetite, we saw that a conflict between sensory appetite and intellectual inclination does not of itself lead to an abnormal psychological condition. As the sensory appetites are by nature subject to reason, it is only natural for them to follow it. When a sensory appetite for an object is contrary to the attitude of the will towards the same object, its lack of gratification or renunciation by the will is the natural fulfillment of the appetite,[2] just as much as it would be its actual attainment, and hence this situation could never produce an abnormal relationship. Consequently, repression is impossible when there is a proper guidance by the intellect and will—there can be no question of a subsequent neurotic disorder.

It also follows from this that the rules of *natural law*, provided they are properly understood, can never exert a repressing action, for natural law teaches one how to act according to reason in every circumstance. Hence, in the natural order, moral acts correspond to reasonable acts, for if persons are to attain the good that is proper to them, they must conduct themselves as human beings, that is, as rational beings. By acting according to reason, their actions are morally right, because the rules of morality are merely formulations of what is intrinsically rational.

When we spoke of the emotional life being guided purely by reason and will, we did so on purpose, for it may happen quite easily that the guidance is not solely by reason and will but is partly rational and partly sensory. Inasmuch as they concern concrete singular acts, rational motives always reverberate in the usefulness judgment. Whenever this sensory power is activated, it is inevitable that the appetitive power which corresponds to it—the assertive drive—will also be set in motion. This does not present any difficulty as long as this appetite retains its natural subordination to the intellectual appetite, for in that case its action will be completely according to reason and will, and the natural order will be maintained. When the sensory appetite does not actually observe the natural subordination to the intellect, however, its action will not stay within the limits of reason but

2. This is so because every emotion and thus every desire has a "built-in" tendency to be guided by reason, even if this means its nonfulfillment as such.

will proceed beyond them. When that happens, emotions of the pleasure appetite, when aroused, will no longer be guided by reason and will, but, partially at least, by the assertive drive. This results in a conflict of the second group where, as we shall discuss presently, repression does take place.[3]

When Freud, therefore, attributes repression to the action of certain norms, whether moral or social, which by their censuring action cause an emotion of the pleasure appetite to be unacceptable, he is correct when the moral norms are interpreted by the individual in a sensory, nonintellectual fashion (as, for instance, children always do). He is not correct, however, when the moral norms are understood as they truly are; namely, as rational rules which appeal to intellect and will. *Freud did not make this distinction.* It may be assumed that he was not even aware of it. Observing what he considered to be the pathological effects of the norms of morality, it is understandable that he failed to attribute them to the incorrect interpretation of these norms.

Conflict between the Sensory Appetites

In the conflict between a sensory and a rational appetite, there is no unnatural repression because the emotional life is by nature subordinate to reason and thus directs itself to reason in a natural manner. We do not find such a natural solution in the case to be discussed now, namely, in the conflict between an emotion of the pleasure appetite and one of the assertive drive. We are dealing here, for example, with a desire for a pleasurable object, but the desire is considered harmful by the usefulness judgment, which for some reason or other is misinformed, and arouses a corresponding emotion—for instance, fear—in the assertive drive.[4]

---

3. This course of events is the cause of many neurotic disorders which originate in childhood. The child understands the ideas and rules of morality in a childish way, which means that the emphasis is on sensory knowledge. Such knowledge predominates in the child. Consequently, these ideas and rules strongly influence the child's assertive drive which may react, for instance, with fear. If educators do not guide this fear into the proper channels with the utmost understanding and reason, it will not fail to exert an excessive influence with all the ensuing psychological consequences. The same situation is found in adults whose emotional life is abnormally sensitive. Persons with neurotic disorders, reminded of their duty of reasonable self-control, will inevitably proceed to control themselves in an unreasonable manner, and thus repress and further aggravate their disorders.

4. The reverse may also occur. The pleasure appetite rejects a sensory evil which is sought as useful by the assertive drive, e.g., energetically inflicting suffering on oneself in

We have already explained that the pleasure appetite is not subordinated by nature to the assertive drive. On the contrary, the assertive drive assists the pleasure appetite in attaining its goal. However, human beings do not possess the blind drive of the animal's assertive drive toward each and every obstacle which stands between it and the object which appeals to its pleasure appetite.

Because of a misinformed usefulness judgment, it is possible for a human being to consider a desire for a pleasurable object as harmful, and thus to arouse in the assertive drive, for instance, the emotion of fear. In the case of a conflict between the emotions of these two appetites—desire and fear—the sensory life does not possess any natural means of solution. Consequently, neither the desire nor the fear can be stilled, as happens when reason provides the necessary guidance. Both emotions continue their active inclinations.

What happens in such a case? There are two emotional currents in relation to one and the same object. They are at odds with each other. As they are restricted—according to our hypothesis—to the sensory life, so that the conciliatory action of reason is precluded, the more powerful emotion of the two will win out over the other. If it happens to be the emotion of fear, as is usually the case, then the desire will not attain its object. If the emotion of desire prevails, on the other hand, it will obtain the desired satisfaction by momentarily overcoming the repressive action of the fear.

What will happen to the emotion of desire when it has lost out in the struggle? If it does not succeed in attaining its object, it will not find peace. It does not attain its object, either as a purely sensory object, because it is exactly as such that it is rejected by the assertive drive, or as a rational-sensory object, because the repression prevents the intellect from considering the object in the light of reason. This emotion, therefore, does not attain its natural fulfillment and must continue to exist in a state of tension. It keeps on desiring without ever being able to attain its object so long as the other emotion, fear, remains stronger, and thus prevents the desire from running its proper and natural course.

Here we are faced with a situation in the emotional life which is completely abnormal. Every emotional arousal temporarily disrupts the psychological equilibrium, but balance is restored as soon as the object has

---

order to achieve a spiritual goal. Since this situation is analogous to that explained in the text, we shall confine ourselves to the discussion of the desired pleasurable good which is rejected by the assertive drive.

been attained or freely renounced under the guidance of reason. When this does not materialize, however, the state of imbalance becomes chronic and results in a psychologically abnormal condition.

At this stage we must take a closer look at the condition which results from repression, for this condition is the *beginning of a neurotic disorder* and of all neurotic manifestations. Without an adequate understanding of the nature of the psychological condition caused by repression, we cannot explain these manifestations.

We have seen that the repressed emotion, buried alive as it is, so to speak, continues to exist in a state of tension. It keeps on acting, tending toward something that it cannot attain. In doing so, it seeks some means of escape in order to find peace. As we shall see in the next chapter, this activity may manifest itself in different ways. At present, however, we confine ourselves to drawing attention to the *active character of the repressed emotion.*

Furthermore, it is of the utmost importance that we realize that the action of the repressed emotion is *removed completely* from the control of reason and will. Clinically, this is clearly demonstrated when the repressed emotion manifests itself in a so-called somatic conversion; for instance, a psychogenic paralysis. It is out of the question that the will can influence it to any extent. Only proper psychotherapeutic intervention in the disturbed processes of the emotional life can change this effectively.

The matter is equally clear in the so-called obsessive-compulsive symptoms, as, for instance, in the case of a person who, as the result of a repressed sexual desire, has a continuous compulsive urge to look at women's breasts. Its compulsive character is manifested in the fact that all efforts to stop this, rather than improving the matter, make it worse. If this urge were subject to guidance by reason and will, its continued denial would lead after a time to the *formation of a habit*, so that the urge would respond to the guidance of reason with increasing facility. This, however, does not occur; instead, the compulsion becomes stronger as a result of continued denial.

Medically speaking, it is a proven fact that *repressed emotions cannot be controlled by reason and will.* For us, however, the question is whether this can be explained by the interpretation of repression in the light of philosophical anthropology. We are of the opinion that it can.

What happens in repression? The pleasure appetite is governed, not by reason, but by the repressing emotion so that in the act of repression the use of reason is momentarily suspended. The repressed emotion, however, continues to exist in a state of tension because it *wants* to be guided by reason. When this tension becomes more pronounced, the repressing emotion comes into action and the repression is repeated, and once more reason has no chance to intervene because the action of the repressing emotion precedes that of reason.

To put it differently, the repressing emotion has been *wedged* between the repressed emotion and reason. Thus, the action of the repressed emotion remains outside the sphere of control by reason and will. Only when the repressing emotion recedes and normal psychological conditions return will guidance by reason again become a possibility. So long as this remedial process has not taken place, the condition remains the same: reason and will are unable to influence the repressed emotion and no intellectual considerations will be able to prevent the consequences of its activity in the emotional life. We must look at the repressed emotion as a *foreign body* in the psychic life because the essential characteristic of the human person's emotional life is that the emotions can and need to be guided and directed by the intellect and will. It acts in the psychic life as independently and as persistently as a malignant tumor in the body tissues.[5]

It is also necessary to remark that the presence of the repressed emotion may be more or less conscious. We have seen that its activity passes beyond the guidance of reason and will, yet the question of voluntariness is not identical with the question of whether or not the person is aware of an emotional arousal. Being conscious of the presence of such arousal in the emotional life is a matter of observing what takes place within oneself. Voluntariness, on the other hand, concerns the control of the emotional arousal by the will. These are two entirely different things and must be sharply distinguished.[6] An emotional arousal may be present more or less consciously even when it is not voluntary.

Whether or not this arousal is conscious depends on the intensity of the repression. The emotion is made up of two elements: first, the feeling itself, which is aroused by the object as represented by the senses and especially the imagination; second, the psychomotor reaction, the somatic arousal aimed at optimal involvement with the object. When the repressing emotion attacks this emotion, it may only *prevent* the psychomotor reaction, or

---

5. *See* "Freedom of the Will in Repressive Disorders," Chapter VIII.

6. Failure to make this distinction is often the cause of difficulties in patients. They say: "I know what I do, therefore I do it voluntarily." This conclusion, however, does not follow. Persons with psychotic disorders often know that they do certain things, yet one cannot say that they have freedom of the will.

it may also attempt to efface the image that aroused the emotion. When only the psychomotor reaction is prevented from occurring, the consequences are much less serious than when the repression also attacks the source of the emotion. In that case, the image disappears from consciousness and the awareness of the emotion also disappears; the repressing emotion prohibits the imagination from reproducing images, with the result that they disappear, as we say, from memory. It follows from this that the psychological action of the repressed emotion, as we have already indicated, will also be more unconscious and the neurotic disorder therefore proportionately more severe. It is evident that there are *degrees of intensity of repression*. It is likewise evident that an originally mild repression may in time become steadily more intense and may obliterate the image more and more.

We must also conclude from our discussion that there are *two kinds of repression*. In one, an emotion of the pleasure appetite is repressed by one of the assertive drive, so that the former does not attain its goal. In the other, the pleasure emotion wins out while the assertive emotion fails to be satisfied. The first kind is more prevalent and is usually the only one discussed. When Freud speaks of the repression of the libido he obviously has only this particular kind in mind.

The other kind of repression, however, is nonetheless real, as in people who have a great fear of everything sexual but in whom the sexual urge nevertheless repeatedly gets the upper hand. Whenever this happens there is a *momentary suppression of the fear* and this process is as unnatural as the repression of the sexual urge by fear. Evidently, this process will also lead to a neurotic disorder, though in a somewhat different manner. For the sake of convenience, however, we shall omit this distinction and discuss only the first kind of repression.

Finally, it must be realized that we have discussed only the relationship between the repressing and the repressed emotions. It must be remembered, however, that the repressing emotion is often partly under the influence of reason, as we have already mentioned. Yet, because we are considering the emotion precisely in its irrational activity, this does not change the fact of the repression. We shall soon see that this fact is of great importance in the unraveling and treatment of the conflict.

Repressing and Repressed Emotions

Having discussed the nature of the repressive process, it remains to be seen which emotions can have a repressing action and which can be repressed.

In discussing which emotions are able to exert a *repressing* action, we recall how the predominance of any of the emotions of the assertive drive is determined by the particular disposition of the person in regard to the intended object. If a person is so disposed as to feel capable of overcoming an obstacle or confronting a threatening evil, his attitude will reveal courage and daring; he will do what must be done with energy and boldness in order to obtain what he wants. If, on the other hand, he feels inadequate in the face of difficulties and dangers which stand between him and the desired good and pessimistic concerning its ultimate attainment, he will experience fear or despair in regard to the task at hand and will seek to avoid the difficulty or danger.

There are two possibilities in regard to these two basic responses of the assertive drive, depending on whether the usefulness judgment has been formed correctly or incorrectly. For example, we may speak of a correctly formed usefulness judgment in a medical student who sees as a worthwhile and useful obstacle the many years of hard work and unavoidable sacrifices which separate her from her goal of being a medical doctor. Regardless of whether her assertive drive is optimistically or pessimistically inclined, it is subject and responsible to a natural and proper regulation by reason without development of undue tension or anxiety.

However, when, as a result of faulty or misleading instructions, an individual has been led to believe that something is harmful when actually it is a concrete good for the individual and therefore pleasurable, then the *usefulness judgment has been formed incorrectly*, and the stage will be set for a neurotic development. For example, if a man experiences the pleasurable sensation of a sexual urge, but has been led to believe that such an urge is harmful in itself, then his usefulness judgment will tell him not to permit this urge. To this he may respond in either of two ways: he may react confidently and assertively, feeling that he is capable of conquering the urge, or he may become fearful because he is afraid that he will not be able to control it. In either case, there is no normal subordination of the emotion of the assertive drive to reason; it acts beyond the control of reason and will. No matter how one responds, the emotion of the assertive drive proceeds to determine one's attitude in regard to the pleasurable sexual sensation which the particular reason has judged as harmful. In one case, the individual will repress the urge with energy, in the other, with fear. The goal is the same in either case, namely, to escape from the pleasurable but unacceptable sexual urge. However, the psychological attitudes are quite different in each case; in fact, one may say they are opposed to each other.

Thus, two possible ways of repression must be distinguished in regard to the repressing emotion: *repression by energy* and *repression by fear*. As we shall see in the next chapter, these result in two completely different clinical pictures. At the moment we shall discuss only the principle involved.

We could ask ourselves still another question, namely, whether we ought to distinguish additional repressing emotions. In the first chapter, we learned that there are several emotions in regard to the obstacle which separates us from the desired object and in regard to the threatening evil. In one state of mind the sense knowledge of the possibility of overcoming an obstacle is accompanied by a feeling of hope or energy; the possibility of staving off danger, by a feeling of courage or daring. In the other state of mind, however, one despairs of the possibility of surmounting the obstacle and is fearful of not being able to stave off the danger.

Although these distinctions are based on fact, they have no bearing on the subject under discussion here. Both dispositions in regard to what is useful or harmful result in identical emotional reactions: a hopeful and energetic person is also courageous; a fearful person tends to despair. As far as the repression is concerned, there is no reason, therefore, to make further distinctions. It is safe to state here that a *repression will always occur* as the result either of *energy* or of *fear*, with the understanding that these terms also apply to the other closely related emotions.

In discussing which emotions can be *repressed*, it is necessary to consider them first according to their specific natures and then according to their objects, because each individual emotion has a different object.

The Repressed Emotions According to Their Specific Nature

Before continuing, it must be stated that all the emotions of both sensory appetites described in the first chapter may occur in different degrees of intensity. The gratification of a concrete sensory desire, eating candy for example, is vastly different from the enjoyment of beautiful music. This, however, does not change the character of the emotion itself.

In asking which of these may be repressed, the emotions of the pleasure appetite must be considered first. Although all of these must be considered—those concerning a sense good as well as those concerning a sense evil—there can be no doubt that the ones aroused by sense goods are repressed most frequently. In desiring a good, the elementary arousal in the psychological life, the child encounters its first restraining orders. Nevertheless, repression of emotions concerned with a sense evil also occurs. For example, we all know of the compulsory "little sacrifices" sometimes demanded of children by well-meaning but uninformed educators. The same is true of people who want to be strong and force themselves to ignore every suffering, not to mention the exaggerated asceticism practiced at times by some people.

Furthermore, there is a *regular sequence of the various emotions* in each pleasure appetite: from liking or love to desire to joy, and from dislike or hate to aversion to sadness. This development has a somatic counterpart in the psychomotor reactions. The repression can assail each stage of this development and will be most penetrating when even the primary emotions of love or hate themselves are repressed. When that happens, the emotional life is attacked in its very foundations and twisted out of shape so thoroughly that in the people in whom this occurs, all feeling seems to be dead, and only cold intellectual control remains.

The emotions of the assertive drive may also be the object of repression. We have already said that this occurs sometimes in a conflict between an emotion of the pleasure appetite and one of the assertive drive when the former wins out and persists. In such cases the repressed emotion of the assertive drive continues to exist and function in the state of repression. For example, an intensely sensuous but also very fearful young woman had fallen in love with a young man who repeatedly tried to seduce her. Although she became very fearful every time this happened, she was never able to resist for long, and suppressing her fear temporarily, she gave in to the demands of her boyfriend. Afterwards, however, the fear which had been repressed would make itself felt with renewed intensity.

There is, however, still another possibility; namely, a repression of an emotion of the assertive drive by another emotion of the same appetite.[7] This emotion is then considered harmful, and as such becomes the object

7. At first glance, this may seem to contradict our earlier statement that an object cannot be considered both good and bad, or both useful and harmful, under the same aspect. This immediately becomes obvious when we consider the example of persons who are afraid of their own anger. Here their fear is not aroused by the object of their anger, but only by the emotion of anger itself. For all practical purposes, this conflict has the same consequence, namely repression.

of repression. For instance, in people who do not want to be fearful or do not want to reveal their fear, the fear may be kept in check by an act of energy. Conversely, sometimes, in people who want to be strong, an overwhelming fear represses the energy. It may even happen that an emotion of the assertive drive is repressed by the same emotion of the same appetite. Thus, one may be fearful of one's own fear or may want to check one's own energy by force. The latter is seen repeatedly in individuals who have always controlled themselves too rigidly and, having developed insight into their mistaken way of life, then want with all their might to bring about the needed improvement.

Perhaps the most frequently occurring repression of one assertive emotion by another is that of the emotion of anger by the emotions of fear or energy. Failure on the part of educators to make a clear distinction between anger as a feeling and anger as an act, and the widely held belief that "anger is a capital sin," have been at the root of many a child's repression of anger. Certain forms of behavior have had, and continue to have, an equally pernicious influence on a child's attitude toward anger. For example, parents beating the child in blind anger; the child's observation of angry, abusive fights between its parents; the child's desire to escape by exemplary behavior the fate of its older siblings who are constantly victimized by their parents' uncontrolled angry outbursts, and so on.

The widespread repression of anger in our society deserves serious study since its consequences are many and varied, more so than those of the repression of sexual feelings ever were. An accurate understanding of the function of the emotion of anger as well as of the mechanism of repression is an absolute must for the successful treatment and prevention of neurotic and psychosomatic disorders caused by its repression. Without this understanding pop-psychology, in its attempts to attack the prevailing ignorance about anger and aggression, threatens to create new psychological disorders, just as sex education in the schools has done in its fervor to make all children the beneficiaries of its concept of "sexual health."

The Repressed Emotions According to Their Objects

In order to understand the significance of the objects of the emotions in the development of neurotic disorders, it is necessary to recall our discussion of innate drives and acquired inclinations. We stated that the differentiation between biological and human inclinations has great psychological importance. Since the basic innate drives are served most directly by the biological inclinations, it follows that their repression will also have the most profound consequences on human emotional life, related as they are to the most fundamental human goods. It is not at all surprising, therefore, that the *repression of the sexual feeling*, more than any other repression, will lead to the development of a neurotic disorder. Repression of the drive for food and drink occurs, of course, but only to a limited degree,[8] for the simple reason that one cannot exist without satisfying this drive. However, repression of the sexual feeling, in itself and also as it develops in the infantile gratifications of the sense of touch,[9] is such a frequent occurrence and has such far-reaching consequences that it is advisable to consider it as a possibility in every case of a neurotic disorder. This is why Freud concluded that repression of the infantile sexual drive is the cause of all neuroses. We believe, however, that it is the cause, not of all, but of many neurotic disorders.

On the other hand, a *repression* of the fundamental human inclinations, especially *of the assertive emotions* which serve these inclinations, with the resulting intensity of their continued activity in the unconscious, ranks in order of importance only second to the repression of the biological inclinations, e.g., the sexual feeling. Here we need only think of the reaction that may be caused in a boy as the result of a conflict with his domineering father, or in a girl whose mother continually frustrates her by an overprotective, smothering attitude which does not allow the girl to demonstrate and test her capabilities.

In the first chapter, we distinguished, in addition to the fundamental human inclinations, those inclinations whose gratification contributes only incidentally to a person's happiness. We stated that the number of these incidental human inclinations is endless because one's sensory life may be

---

8. This may occur in children whose parents are too strict in condemning all use of candy and also in women who suffer from *anorexia nervosa*. In its extreme form it often results in death.

9. The sexual drive gradually differentiates itself during the adolescent's period of growth. During puberty the sexual drive normally awakens and begins to seek its object, progressing from the undifferentiated object to the natural heterosexual partner. Even prior to puberty, there is a process of development, although not of the sexual desire as such—the child is not yet mature enough for this desire—but of the gratifications of the sense of touch that are prompted by the infantile sexual drive. We believe that Freud would have been more correct to call his oral and anal erotic stages not sexuality but sensuality influenced by the procreative drive.

attracted by an infinite number of goods.[10] Here we want to add that these inclinations do not develop into a neurotic disorder if repressed. In general, the goods which arouse these incidental inclinations have too little meaning for the personality itself to be able to produce a disorder. Undoubtedly, there are few who do not encounter conflicts and repressions at some time during their life in regard to these inclinations, but unless persons already have a neurotic disorder, they will usually have no trouble in dealing with these conflicts without pathological consequences.[11] If these people already have a neurotic disorder, however, repression of those incidental inclinations will aggravate their disorder.

Our differentiation between fundamental human inclinations which concern the inner growth of the human person and those which concern incidental objects has, however, still another important bearing on our understanding of neurotic disorders. Since the former originate in one's very nature, it follows that they necessarily belong to the very essence of the human person. The latter, on the other hand, depend for their character and intensity much more on external circumstances, education, milieu, culture, and similar factors. For their activity to be psychologically sound, these latter inclinations must never be allowed to repress the inclinations for objects required by one's inner nature or to prevent them from attaining their fullest expression. If they do, they will foster the growth of a neurotic disorder. It seems to us that nowadays *excessive cultural demands* produce this effect repeatedly: the healthy natural personality is smothered by incidental matters and thus becomes abnormal.

In summary, the biological inclination, especially the sexual feeling, must be considered to have the greatest significance in the development of a neurotic disorder; next in importance are the specifically human inclinations which concern the unfolding of one's inner personality. Particular inclinations for incidental goods have only secondary significance.

10. *See* page 4.

11. It would be more likely for these people to develop what we would call "pseudo-neurotic reactions." Even individuals without neurotic disorders are sometimes psychologically unable to control certain situations but react to them with neurotic symptoms which disappear as soon as the situation has changed.

Psychological and Somatic Upheaval

In the preceding pages we explained the nature of the repressive process and also briefly treated its mode of action. We must now take a closer look at this process and its consequences. In order for our study to be complete, it will be necessary to discuss: 1) the activity of the repressing emotion, 2) the activity of the repressed emotion, and 3) the clinical consequences of these activities.

The Activity of the Repressing Emotion

In the investigation of the activity of the two emotions involved in the repressive conflict, we shall start with the repressing emotion. Here we can ask ourselves three questions. First, in what manner is the repressing emotion able to assail the emotion which is to be repressed; second, what is the relationship between these two emotions after the repression has taken place; and third, what further course does the repressing emotion take?

The pleasure emotion which is going to be repressed is a psychological phenomenon consisting of several stages. The emotion arises, grows, and increasingly tends to the attainment of the object, finally beginning to employ the means necessary to attain it. To do this, as we have seen in the first chapter, the assertive drive is set in motion.

It is evident that the repressing emotion can attack the pleasure emotion in any of these stages. First of all, it can confine itself to the last stage and merely prevent the use of means to attain the object. It is also possible to assail the pleasure emotion itself, either in its formation and growth or in its very existence as such. The deeper the attack of the repressing emotion, the more absolute the repression will be.

The action of the repressing emotion is least intense when it merely prevents the assertive drive from attempting to attain its goal. This course of events can be an entirely normal one, for when someone has intellectual reasons for not giving in to a sensory desire, the refusal will take place in this stage. In that case, reason judges that a certain desire must not be gratified; consequently, the assertive drive which then functions under the direction of reason and will, precludes further action by the pleasure appetite. This is an entirely normal process.

Only if the refusal is *not based on reasonable motives, but on feelings,* does it become a repression, for in that case one emotion attempts to force another, and this is unnatural. For instance, it may happen that a person experiences strong sexual desires, yet never dares to have sexual intercourse because of fear and not because of rational motives. Here repression does take place. However, when the repression occurs in this particular stage, the psychological consequences will not be very serious because the emotion itself retains its natural value. Even though the tension is not resolved, the emotion as such is not distorted.

When, however, the repressing emotion goes beyond merely preventing attainment of the goal, the emotion itself is assailed. It does not wait, as it did in the former instance, until the pleasure emotion requests its cooperation in employing the means to attain its goal. It assails the emotion of the pleasure appetite before it can entice it, so to speak, into lending a helping hand; it assails it in an earlier stage and will not even permit it access to the psychological life. Evidently, the refusal here is much stronger. The emotion itself is considered as an evil to be shunned or a danger to be avoided.

In this case, again there exist two possibilities. Either the pleasure emotion has an opportunity to develop somewhat before it is repressed, or it is refused access into consciousness from the very beginning. In the former case, the emotion is aroused in a normal manner, but as soon as it becomes stronger and begins to tend toward its goal, it is blocked, pushed back and held in check. In the latter case, the refusal is so prompt that even the vaguest stirring of the emotion is repulsed, with the result that it can never develop, and the person believes that it no longer remains.

In either case, the result is that the somatic aspect of the emotion, which we have called its *psychomotor reaction, no longer develops* or does so only partially. In the former case, since the emotion is permitted access to some degree, the psychomotor reaction develops somewhat; in the latter case, however, it does not develop at all because the emotion is repressed completely. Thus the natural, spontaneous physiological manifestations of the emotion are lacking, and in their place a forced attitude appears which is determined by the repressing emotion. In this kind of repression the individual no longer makes a natural, spontaneous, and sincere impression. This will not be absolute if the emotion has developed somewhat before it is repressed—one will more or less sense the inhibition and inner struggle; but if the emotion was absolutely prevented, there will be no trace of the natural physiological changes associated with the repressed emotion.

At this point we must ask how the repressing emotion achieves this effect in these cases. It does so only *through repression of the cognitive image.* An emotion is always associated with previous knowledge. One is aroused toward that which is known, even on a sensory level. As long as the cognitive image exists, the arousal can follow. Therefore, if the repressing emotion wants to subdue the pleasure emotion, it must make the cognitive image disappear from the imagination—and that is what happens.

When the pleasure emotion has an opportunity to develop somewhat, the interference by the repressing emotion turns the mind away from the object so that, consciously at least, the inclination is eliminated. It continues to exist, of course, as a tension, but the subject no longer realizes that the tension concerns that particular object because the object has disappeared from consciousness.

The same thing happens when the pleasure emotion is assailed in its very first stirring, but in a much more radical manner. The repressing emotion not only forces an image out of the imagination, but it forbids the imagination to reproduce any images of a similar nature. This results not only in a temporary unawareness of the corresponding emotion, but eventually the *repression of the emotion becomes habitual.* This may progress so far that the subject no longer recognizes that emotion as related to a given object; he or she has the feeling that it has completely disappeared. This, of course, is not actually the case; the emotion still exists in the form of tension and only the awareness of the striving for the object has disappeared. This, obviously, is an extreme occurrence. As a rule, some degree of arousal will continue to manifest itself in some form or other. This is particularly true of the sexual urge, which is rooted so deeply in human nature, although it may often happen that the sexual urge in the strict sense of the word no longer arises to the level of consciousness.

In these extreme cases repression may act in still another way by causing an *attitude of reserve* in the subject in regard to impressions from the external senses. When such persons do not wish to allow certain emotions to be aroused, they will be readily inclined to shut themselves off from the outside world, at least in the sense that they want to prevent certain impressions from forming, if this is at all possible. Frequently, the repressing process will be intensified, especially if it concerns emotions regarded as sinful or dangerous because of the educators' excessive emphasis on moral precepts. This leads to a fear of seeing, a fear of reading, a fear of being seen, a fear of associating with others, and many other fears. The extent of this development depends entirely on the intensity of the action of the repressing factor. In extreme cases, it will lead to absolute *withdrawal*, simply out of fear of experiencing any emotion. In less serious cases it develops into a strange and unnatural attitude which precludes establishing a normal rapport with others.

Shutting out the outside world results in a more pronounced egocentricity. Persons with neurotic disorders are already preoccupied with themselves as a result of the neurotic process, and since the natural inclination to find diversion outside themselves is thwarted, their illnesses will be further aggravated.

Our next question concerns the *relation between the repressing and repressed emotions* after the repression has taken place. Again, two possibilities present themselves: first, after having been repressed, the repressed emotion may be free to go its own way without interference by the repressing emotion; second, the repressing emotion may pursue the repressed emotion in its subsequent operations.

To explain this difference, we must realize that it is to be expected from the very nature of repression that the repressed emotion in its initial state will experience the influence of the repressing emotion, which prevents it from reaching its goal and forces it to seek an outlet elsewhere. Sometimes, however, the *repressed emotion continues to function without hindrance* once this repressive process has been terminated. In such cases, the repressing emotion is no longer concerned, so to speak, with the repressed emotion and is no longer discernible in the clinical manifestation of the repressed emotion. This may be seen, for example, in the conversion symptoms which are merely the expression of the repressed and inadmissible emotion; the repressing factor is not involved in these symptoms and cannot be discerned in them. The same is true for psychological symptoms; for instance, a young woman who has repressed a sexual urge will freely indulge in flirtatious conduct without showing the least trace of fear.

The situation is completely different when the *repressing emotion continues to pursue the repressed emotion* and does not allow it to express itself freely. Here, too, symptoms appear sooner or later, because the repressed emotion remains active and restless, but the repressing emotion leaves its mark on all those symptoms and gives them a different character. Thus, the symptoms of a young woman who has repressed the sexual urge will also manifest the activity of the repressed urge, but these symptoms will never be spontaneous and free of tension; rather, they will arouse and manifest fear. For this reason, conversion symptoms do not occur in these cases. The conversion reaction presumes a continued but entirely unconscious activity of the repressed emotion, which is absolutely impossible if fear is constantly concerned with these symptoms.

In analyzing these observations, we must conclude that the repression is less thorough and less consistent when the repressed emotion is free to go its own way than when it is pursued by the repressing emotion. At first glance, one would be inclined to claim the opposite, particularly in the conversion reaction, since this offers such a dramatic clinical picture, but this is not correct. The conversion symptoms are able to develop precisely because the repression is confined to the act of repression and does not pursue the repressed emotion any further. The very act of repression is the reason why the further activity of the repressed emotion is not subject to the control of the intellect, for the repressing emotion, as we have seen, *has been wedged between the intellect and the repressed emotion as the direct result of the act of repression, and hence reason cannot touch the repressed emotion.* Not only this, but since the repressing emotion does not persist in its repressive action, the repressed emotion is able to do as it pleases in the psychological life.

In the other type of repressive disorder, however, the repressing emotion continues the pursuit of the repressed emotion in a much more consistent manner. Why the repressing emotion acts more persistently in one person than in another to the extent that they cause the difference in action and, consequently, in development of the various types of neurotic disorders, depends on differences in the personality structure of the individual. It is not merely the strength of the repressing emotion which determines the extent of the repressed material, but rather its penetration into the psychological life. In this respect, it seems to us that the individual's intellectual nature must play a decisive role. For it is only through the usefulness judgment and the intellect which the emotion serves that the person becomes aware of the psychological manifestations. Consequently, the better the intellect and the deeper its introspective power, the greater the awareness of the continued activity of the repressed emotion and hence the need for a continued repression.

In regard to the third question concerning the further activity of the repressing emotion, it may be said that every repression has a tendency to grow and spread in two directions: first, in *intensity*, by strengthening the roots of the process, and second, in *expansion* by spreading to other objects.

Every repressive process gradually becomes more deeply rooted in the psychic life. *It never stops at a single repression.* Once a certain pleasure object has been declined by the assertive drive, it will be declined again and again. Besides, as we have said before, the repressed pleasure emotion persists in the form of tension and continuously pushing in the direction of its object, repeatedly brings about the declining reaction of the repressing emotion. Moreover, the first repression increases the disposition to additional instances of similar activity: every subsequent repression requires less effort, as is true in the acquisition of any habit. As with many psychosomatic activities, this can ultimately lead to a completely automatic process: one represses as a matter of course, immediately and without being aware of doing so.

Except for very young children, the initial repression must have been the result of a conscious recognition of something—which is actually a good—as harmful and its conscious repudiation. This awareness gradually diminishes until it practically disappears altogether, if the repression continues long enough and becomes second nature. In such cases, these *persons no longer realize that they are repressing* or to what degree they are repressing. In treatment, they often become aware of this only when the repression ends at a certain moment and they see, to their great amazement, that even in their treatment they had been repressing. At times the development of such an autonomously functioning mechanism of repression does not even require that much time. It may develop rather suddenly, as when the repression is very decisive and forcible.

Thus, the repressive process is rooted more and more deeply in the psychic life. As a matter of course, its action on the repressed emotion will at the same time tend to progress with evermore profound consequences. However, the degree to which this happens depends to a great extent on the psychological disposition of the individual. It can be stated in general that the more intelligent the patient, the more deeply the repressive action will penetrate and the more profound the pathological disturbance will be.

In addition to this growing intensity of repression, an *expansion* of the repression also occurs which results in an automatic enlargement of the object which the individual represses. This expansion can be caused in two ways: first, because of a *similarity* between the new object and the repressed object. As the result of this similarity, which is nothing but a simple association, the new object calls up an image of the old one. This leads to a reactivation of the repressing emotion, which will then repress not only the old object but also the new one, because it is associated with the repulsion brought on by the former. The fear of sexual matters, for instance, may lead to a dread of a variety of things which resemble them to some degree and therefore bring them back to memory.

A second, and in our opinion, even more important cause of the expansion of the object is *intellectual interpretation*, for whenever one rejects a certain object, it is possible to realize the reason for this rejection. In that case, however, it is logical to also reject all other objects which present the same reason for being unacceptable. The repressing emotion will assail all things which are recognized by the intellect as possessing such reasons for being unacceptable. For instance, when a man represses feelings of a sexual nature because he thinks that they are sensual or too sensual, he logically proceeds to repress all sensual feelings—first, the pronounced sensual feelings of touch and taste, and finally all feelings. This example explains the tremendous importance of the intellectual expansion of the object in the enlargement of the repressive process.

These two causes of object expansion will not be equally active in every person. Generally, the first cause—that of association—will occur more often in persons of lower intelligence. It functions in the imagination without participation of the intellect. Intelligent people, who control their sensory cognitive life, are much less disposed to an activation of their repressing emotion as the result of a single accidental similarity. On the other hand, intellectually determined expansion plays a much greater role in these people. The more intelligent a person, the greater his or her reasoning power and the greater the danger of this form of object expansion. In such people, the repression will often dominate their entire way of life because the *intellectually determined expansion is more inclusive than that of association*. Consequently, the intellectual "complexes" are more serious than the associational ones.

Activity of the Repressed Emotion

Now that we have studied the varied activities of the repressing emotion in different types of individuals, we must make a similar study of the repressed emotion. Since it has been prevented by the repression from attaining its goal, it does not find a natural solution and continues to exist in a state of tension. In other words, it continues to be active to a certain degree.

We must state at once that this activity lacks all control and guidance by the intellect. The repressing emotion has come between the intellect and the repressed emotion, and it prevents reason from regulating the activity of the repressed emotion so that it becomes autonomous and, as such, *acquires an obsessive-compulsive quality*.[12] It is something that cannot be helped, something that the individual must contend with. Although the subject can attempt to stop the activity, this can only be done by means of further repression which, of course, only aggravates the pathological condition.

The many varied obsessive-compulsive symptoms that may occur result from the fact that the repressed emotion, like every manifestation of the sensory life, is a psychosomatic unit and therefore possesses two aspects: that of the psyche and the soma. Since it is plausible to assume that the activity of this emotion may become manifest psychologically as well as physically, both possibilities must be investigated and analyzed.

Psychologically the repressed emotion can be understood as an inhibited, restless tendency toward a certain sense object.[13] The inclination toward this object persists either consciously, semiconsciously or subconsciously depending upon the intensity of the repression. It will force itself in that direction stubbornly and persistently. Since the object itself, however, has been blocked, only the inclinations in the direction of the object remain. These inclinations vary to the degree that they are affected by the repression. This may be illustrated by a simple example.

A man represses his sexual urge and therefore does not obtain relief of his sexual tension. The urge continues to exert itself in the same general direction and manifests itself, for example, in the desire to look at nudes or to read off-color stories. We repeat that since these urges have a compulsive character, they do not permit the person any rest; the man is compelled to look and to read. These matters demand all his attention, no matter how he is otherwise occupied. He cannot help doing these things even when he morally disapproves of them. These compulsive tendencies may reveal themselves in the imagination as well as in the external senses and the motor system. In the imagination they are observed in the form of obsessive ideas and dreams, in the external senses as compulsions to see, to touch, or to hear, and in the motor system in certain compulsive movements or in the urge to speak or write certain words, and so forth.

12. *See* "Freedom of the Will in Repressive Disorders," Chapter VIII.

13. We remind the reader that we limit ourselves to a discussion of this particular emotion for the sake of convenience. It is equally possible for the repressed emotion to be an aversion to a sense object. In that case the same reasoning applies, with the necessary changes.

As far as the activity of the repressed emotion is concerned, the immediate result of the repression is the development of obsessions and compulsions in the direction of the repressed object. It is also possible, however, that the repressing emotion will not even permit this kind of obsession or compulsion and will eliminate them from consciousness through repression. Naturally, the tension persists and seeks to discharge itself in other ways. This may be done through association with objects possessing some resemblance to the forbidden urges.

Freud discovered this psychological mechanism and described it as *symbolism*, meaning that a certain image or a certain act is a symbol that represents a forbidden image or takes the place of an inadmissible act. For example, a young man represses a strong dislike for his father; later he violently dislikes and opposes every form of authority. A repressed, unsatisfied sexual urge may manifest itself in an uncontrollable compulsion to eat candy or in an abnormal desire to collect things. A repressed love of self may lead to a pathological need for recognition and appreciation. Symbolism may be revealingly expressed in dreams which are therefore important therapeutic means for investigating the nature of repressed emotions.

Finally, the psychological vexation and tension of the repressed emotion may also try to become quiescent, not in some specific symbol, but in a different form of sense gratification. Such sense gratification may be sought in any area of the sensory psychic life; not even the noblest, intellectually most refined areas are excluded from this. So, for instance, a repressed sexual urge may lead to a highly active scientific career; more frequently yet, it leads to a pathological search for gratification in religious experiences.

The activity of the repressed pleasure emotion extends itself even further. Until now, we have only seen how its tension can persist in the area of the pleasure appetite itself. It is also possible, however, that it will affect the emotions of the assertive drive. To understand this, one must remember that the assertive drive is set in motion by the pleasure appetite which, in desiring a sense object, automatically causes the assertive drive to search for means to obtain this object. It is obvious, therefore, that a persistent abnormal tension in the pleasure appetite also cannot fail to activate the assertive drive and bring it into a certain state of tension. However, this tension is not allowed to attain the object to which it is directed by nature, for repression has eliminated this object, but it is more or less suspended in air, searching for an object. In other words, this leads to a *greater irritability* and *excessive activity* of the assertive drive.

It is here that we find the explanation of the well-known clinical observation that a repressed sexual urge may provoke fear (*scrupulosity*, for instance) or lead to an extraordinary activity. Which of these two emotions of the assertive drive will prevail depends on the disposition of the individual. If fear is the stronger emotion, it will become intensified; if not, the energy will become greater. Usually, the dominating emotion is also the repressing emotion, so that we witness the remarkable fact that the *repressed emotion reactivates the repressing emotion*. It becomes a vicious circle which automatically aggravates the disorder.

In addition to the psychological manifestations resulting from the repressed emotion's continued activity, we must study the purely *somatic manifestations*. One example of these manifestations are *conversion reactions*. This term is not entirely appropriate, as it suggests the conversion of something psychic into something somatic. This is not accurate because every emotion is psychosomatic from its very inception, but since the term is now generally accepted we will use it here.

Just as the psychological element of an emotional reaction may be described as a tension in the psychological life, so the somatic element may be said to be a tension in what we call the psychomotor reactions. When an emotional discharge is interrupted in its course in an abnormal manner, the somatic tension persists, as does the psychological tension, and it may express itself in abnormal psychomotor reactions. The somatic tension will attempt to manifest itself in the same manner as the psychological tension. We should not forget, however, that since it is the total person who experiences a certain feeling, the entire body is involved in psychomotor activity, even though the feeling will usually manifest itself in one specific part of the body. If abnormalities develop, they may result in repercussions in every part of the body, the motor system, the sensibility, the senses, and even the internal organs. It depends entirely on individual factors where these changes will take place. It suffices to state here that the very fact of this change finds its explanation in the nature of the repressed emotion.[14]

The occurrence of bodily conversion symptoms has been ascribed to the defective overflow of the emotion into the psychomotor system. In our

14. In this connection it should be recalled that although we usually speak of desire, the opposite emotion of aversion is also included. With this in mind, some manifestations, such as paralysis, are more easily understood when applying the explanations in the text. So, for instance, the nun who has an intense, though unconscious, dislike of cloister life is suddenly unable to walk. The body then expresses what is consciously not admitted.

opinion, there still exists, however, another way for conversion symptoms to develop, namely, through the voluntary motor system. An emotion not only possesses its own psychomotor activity by which it tends toward its proper object, but it is also able to activate the voluntary motor system for the purpose of achieving its goal. This again constitutes a somatic aspect of the psychological activation of the assertive drive. This means that the repressed emotion will also choose bodily states as means for attaining its goal. For example, a man who feels the desire to escape from a danger chooses to do this by means of a paralysis, or a woman who has an emotional need to attract attention develops psychogenic seizures. The fact that the body obeys the unconscious desire in these cases may be explained by the intimate relation between psyche and body. We shall see later, however, that this indicates the existence of a particular type of constitution.

It appears to us, then, that there are *two kinds of conversion*: that in which the bodily symptom is a manifestation of faulty psychomotor activity, and that in which the symptom has been unconsciously chosen as a means for attaining the desired goal. Since psychomotor activity and voluntary motor activity can work together, it is to be expected that this can also happen in conversion reactions. This is well illustrated in the case of a young woman with a hysterical neurosis[15] who had a pathological crush on her family physician. This manifested itself in her psychomotor activity by exaggerated sentimental and flirtatious mannerisms in his presence. The voluntary motor system was utilized for the purpose of attracting the doctor's attention by such unconscious efforts as simulated illnesses, false pretenses, lies, and so on.

Clinical Consequences of the Activity of the Repressing and Repressed Emotions

Although we have already discussed some of the more specific clinical symptoms which may result from repression, we want to add a description of the more *general symptoms occurring in all repressive disorders*. They are the manifestations of the disruption of the proper relationships between

15. Editors' Note: The American Psychiatric Association removed the term "hysterical neurosis" from its more recent editions of the *Diagnostic and Statistical Manual of Mental Disorders* (*DSM*). Disorders that would have been classified as hysterical neuroses in earlier versions are now classified in categories such as *somatic symptom and related disorders*. To avoid confusion, we have left this term in some sections of this revised edition. (*DSM-5*, Arlington, VA,, American Psychiatric Association, 2013).

the emotions themselves and between the emotions of the intellectual life. When the natural equilibrium has been disturbed and not restored, this disturbance will consequently reveal itself in the psychic and somatic aspects of the emotion.

The *psychological disturbances* caused by repression especially manifest themselves by a certain *unrest* which pervades the psychic life. Initially, this state of unresolved tension is hardly noticeable, but later, when the acts of repression multiply, it develops into an unrest which dominates the entire psychic life. One becomes nervous, tense, restless; one is unable to concentrate on any particular thing; one becomes agitated. Usually the tension first manifests itself in the imagination, as this psychological power is most directly under the influence of the emotions, but eventually it spreads to all the sensory faculties and even to the motor system. Thus nervous people cannot sit still. Their internal tension seeks a way to express itself, but being restrained intentionally, it makes its own way unconsciously.

Another psychological effect of the repressive process is a lessened degree of resistance to emotional stimuli, and concomitantly a *heightened sensitivity* and *irritability*. Human emotions should be regulated by the intellect, which automatically provides every stimulus with its correct value and controls and tempers the emotional reaction. When repression has taken place, however, which *ipso facto* removes the emotional life to a certain extent from influence by the intellectual life, this regulatory action of the intellect is decreased, so that one's emotions are less restrained. Here, too, it is to be expected that this effect will begin to show itself only gradually. With continued repression, however, it inevitably appears in every person with a neurotic disorder, although in each one in a different and highly individual manner.

The *somatic symptoms* attributed to the repressive process comprise the common complaints of individuals with neurotic disorders: *fatigue, headache, insomnia, backache,* and many others. The presence of these symptoms usually indicates repeated repressions over a prolonged period of time. However, we know of persons in whom every act of repression is followed by acute fatigue. The extent and manner in which these somatic symptoms present themselves depends entirely on the individual constitution; some symptoms occur in one person, some in another; some develop early, others late or not at all.

Disturbances in *bodily functions* may also occur. Unmarried men, for example, who strongly repress the sexual urge, will after some time no longer have nocturnal emissions. Women in similar circumstances may undergo marked changes in menstruation. Even the whole body may feel the influence of the repression, and begin to show the pressure under which the emotional life operates. The *posture*, for instance, becomes bent or stiff, and the *facial expression* tense. We know of several persons who, in spite of plentiful food, remained *thin* as long as the repression lasted, but whose physical condition improved visibly as soon as treatment eliminated the repression. It is possible that research in the fields of neurobiology, neuropharmacology, and depth electroencephalography will shed considerable light on this subject, especially on the effect of repression on the hypothalamus, which not only regulates endocrine and autonomic functions but also represents, as is generally assumed, the subcortical center for the integration of emotional responses and their psychomotor reactions.

The somatic consequences of the repressive process are particularly evident in those cases in which the repression interferes with the incompletely developed emotional life of the young. In these childhood repressions, it may be observed repeatedly that repression of sexual feelings also prevents or *retards bodily growth*; for example, the onset of the menses, nocturnal emissions, the development of secondary and sometimes even the primary sex characteristics.

The following case will serve as a good although perhaps rather extreme illustration of the foregoing. We once treated a young man who from childhood had been impressed with the obligation of avoiding sin. At the boarding school to which he had been sent when he was twelve years old, the emphasis in spiritual training was placed on the avoidance of sins of impurity and the rejection of everything physical and sensuous. As he was not given any sex education, he was still psychologically a child when he entered the novitiate of a religious order. When, after a few months, he realized that he was not suited for the religious life, he left the novitiate, convinced more than ever of the need to reject all sensuous matters. He enrolled at a university to study law, but felt so uneasy among the other students that he soon began to live and study in seclusion. When he came to us at the age of twenty-five, he had the secondary sex characteristics of a child and his knowledge of sexual matters was practically nil. He had never experienced nocturnal emissions or penile erections. But all this was gradually corrected during the course of treatment, and eventually he was able to lead a happy married life.

CHAPTER III

TYPES OF REPRESSIVE DISORDERS

The magnanimous man rejects useful things for his goal because they are
subordinate
to what is good and pleasurable.

Aristotle, *Nicomachean Ethics*

HAVING PRESENTED A THEORETICAL discussion of the action of the repressive process and its development and of the nature of the repressing and repressed emotions, it now becomes mandatory to submit these ideas to the test of the data presented by clinical knowledge of repressive disorders. Here we are faced, first of all, by the generally accepted clinical distinction between hysterical neurosis[1] and obsessive-compulsive neurosis[2] and, hence, by the question of whether these distinct clinical syndromes can be explained in the light of our theories. If so, the difference between these

---

1. Editors' Note: An obsolete diagnostic term. *See* Chapter II.

2. Editors' Note: The authors understood the term *obsessive-compulsive neurosis* in a broader fashion than the current *DSM* diagnostic category of *Obsessive-Compulsive Disorder*. The *DSM* diagnosis is based on observable symptoms, while Dr. Terruwe and Dr. Baars based their diagnosis on the underlying repressive process that takes place. In this revised edition, we have changed most of the authors' references to obsessive-compulsive *neurosis* to the term obsessive-compulsive *repression* in order to preserve this understanding.

syndromes must be the result of a distinctly different action of the repressive process.[3]

We have already explained that there are two possibilities as far as the repressive process and its continued action are concerned. It may happen that after the repression has taken place, the repressing emotion allows the repressed emotion to do as it pleases, without bothering it any further. As a result, the *repressed* emotion will be most pronounced clinically. Alternately, it may happen that the repressing emotion continues to influence the repressed emotion and to obstruct its further activity. In that case, the clinical picture is determined much more by the *repressing* emotion.

It seems to us that this twofold manner of action by the repressive process is the cause of the existence of these two clinically differentiated neurotic syndromes. In hysterical neurosis, the clinical picture is determined chiefly by the repressed emotion; in obsessive-compulsive repression, it is determined by the repressing emotion.

The Hysterical Neurosis

The continued post-repression activity of the repressed emotion—which we believe to be the main determining factor of the *hysterical neurosis*—is not, according to the nature of the neurotic process, amenable to control by the intellect or will. Consequently, its manifestations, except for those which are actually repressed, experience little or no obstruction from the repressing emotion. Because of this lack of regulation and modification by reason, the repressed pleasure emotion reveals itself to an extraordinary degree in the display of an emotional attitude which is generally sensed by others as pathological. These patients, however, are not at all aware of

---

3. It is true that the so-called neurasthenic neurosis is also distinguished clinically. However, neurasthenia is an illness which at present is generally considered to have a primarily somatic basis; it consists of a general weakness of the nervous system. Neurasthenic patients have little constitutional resistance against emotionally taxing situations. They quickly become abnormally fatigued, are excessively sensitive to stimuli, and collapse quickly whenever called upon for something that is beyond their powers. In addition, they often have bodily complaints: headaches, gastro-intestinal upsets, insomnia, and the like. Yet not all of these symptoms are psychogenic. The neurasthenic constitution is a fertile soil in which conflicts may easily grow. Because of the labile constitution, these conflicts will usually exert a profound influence, but they have to be distinguished from neurasthenia as such. For this reason we shall not discuss this illness. [Editors' Note: This diagnostic category is obsolete, but has been left unchanged to illustrate the authors' thinking.]

what is taking place and would be the last ones to consider their conduct as pathological, if their *bland indifference* did not prevent them from taking a closer look at themselves. A few examples will clarify what we mean.

Early in life a young woman of a very sensual disposition had become afraid of the sin of impurity and this fear had grown into an intense fear of everything sexual. For instance, she did not want to marry and still had not done so at the age of thirty-five, even though she did have plenty of opportunities. She even avoided every contact with unmarried men because such contact presented the possibility of eventual marriage. She had, on the other hand, an intense need for erotic gratification. This was quite evident from her appearance which, in spite of herself, attracted many men. She purposely rebuffed bachelors, but she did not have any fear of men with whom marriage was out of the question—at least in those days—such as married men or priests. Accordingly, she was less reserved in her contact with them. At times she was even very affectionate, which occasionally led to difficulties. She immediately resisted every man who tried to take liberties with her and if anything happened, she lived in terrible fear. Inwardly, the repressed craving continued to exert its influence by repeated masturbation which she tried her best to suppress out of fear, though in vain. Although the facts spoke for themselves she did not have the slightest insight, and she rejected every attempt to make her realize what was going on.

Another woman, unmarried and forty years of age, had remained entirely infantile in her psychosexual development. As everything pertaining to sex had been pushed completely out of consciousness during her childhood, she had in this respect not yet reached the stage of puberty. Although she never had known any conscious sexual feelings, she nevertheless experienced an abnormally intense need for affection. This need was tinted sexually to such a degree that she was considered a "dangerous" person at her place of work, and although this label was completely undeserved, it was typical proof of the air of sexuality which she unconsciously radiated. Her need for affection caused her constantly to do things which she thought would gain her the attention and affection of those individuals on whom her need had focused itself. For instance, there was no end of little gifts and favors, even to the point of absurdity. In this manner she practically forced herself upon others, yet although she achieved the opposite of what she desired, she was unable to act differently. She simply begged for a caress and the need for it dominated her entire life. At last this need became so intense that she could no longer perform her work. She then continued to live for herself, egocentrically directed everything to herself at the cost of many conflicts, and was fully absorbed in her desire to become attractive and desirable.

In both of these cases we are dealing with true hysterical neuroses in which the repression of sexual feelings led to a pathological condition. A similar condition results when, instead of the sexual feelings, the emotions which serve the drive for self-realization are repressed. Whether in men or women, the repressed assertive emotions will make themselves manifest in a pathological need to be recognized, an over-sensitiveness to all kinds of real or imagined slights and setbacks, and a need to force oneself into the forefront. Repressed assertive emotions manifest themselves in the clinical syndrome of hysterical neurosis as much as flirtatious behavior does in the two previously mentioned women who had repressed their sexual feelings.

Although in the hysterical neuroses, in general, the repressing emotion allows the repressed emotion to do what it wants, it may at times become active enough to prevent its undisguised expression, so that the repressed emotion is forced to manifest itself via another route where the repressing emotion does not put any obstacle in its path.

This gives rise to the so-called *conversion reactions*. Conversion reactions may affect every area of the sensory life: the sensibility, the voluntary motor system, the external senses, the vaso-vegetative system, the consciousness, and others. No matter where they become manifest, neither reason nor the repressing emotion has any influence over them.[4]

A good example of a conversion reaction affecting the voluntary motor apparatus was seen during World War II. One day in the winter of 1944–45, when the city of Nijmegen was in the front lines of both the Allied and the German forces and shells were exploding continuously, a roofer

---

4. As a possible substitute for the common classification of conversion reactions based on clinical and neurological data, the following, which reflects Aristotelian-Thomistic concepts of human nature, is merely a suggested outline.

    I. Conversion reactions affecting the vegetative order: pimples and blisters, stigmata, skin hemorrhages, vomiting, diarrhea, etc.

    II. Conversion reactions affecting the sensory order:

        1. External senses: blindness, tunnel vision, deafness, anesthesia, analgesia, etc.

        2. Internal senses: *Sensus communis*: impaired sensory consciousness, twilight states, confusion, trance states, "fainting" spells. Imagination: hallucinations, illusions. Memory: amnesia.

        3. Appetites: transference feelings.

        4. Motor system: pareses and paralyses, aphonia, astasia-abasia, etc.

    III. Intellectual order: none.

was admitted to the emergency room of the hospital there because he had been hit by shell fragments. Examination showed that it was not serious; all he had was a superficial wound of the upper arm. We congratulated him on being so lucky, dressed the wound, and advised him that in a few days he could go back to work again. After a few days, however, he returned to the hospital with his arm totally paralyzed. From our examination it was clear that his paralysis had no organic cause, and certainly was not due to the superficial wound sustained a few days earlier. We suspected at once what the psychological cause might be: being a roofer in those times was dangerous work as he had no protection from exploding shells. As his injury had activated his fear, he was naturally not eager to resume that kind of work. When we advised him that we were not sure whether that kind of job was the right one for him, he brightened up immediately. As a result of this therapeutic approach, the paralysis disappeared, and our roofer became a streetcar conductor. He was never again bothered by his arm.

The repressing emotion does not assume a prominent place in the clinical picture of hysterical neurosis. When, for instance, repression occurs as the result of fear, that fear will most likely be manifested in the personality, but not in the pathological conversion symptom as such. The women in the aforementioned examples will not manifest any trace of fear in their flirtatious conduct. A psychogenic paralysis seems to be an emotionally isolated occurrence and lacks any identification with the repressing emotion. As far as the clinical picture in either of these two cases is concerned, it does not make any difference which emotion—fear or energy—caused the repression; the pathological effect is the same. It is no use, therefore, to distinguish between the different repressing emotions in these cases, for they have no bearing on the hysterical syndrome.

It is our opinion that the appearance of this type of neurotic disorder is closely related to a diminished degree of penetration of the emotional life by the *intellect*. If the intellect had a greater influence on the emotional life, it would be much less likely to allow the repressed emotion to function on its own. In that case there would be a much greater awareness of what is going on in the emotional life and, thus, less chance for the repressed emotion to do as it pleases in such a completely unconscious and autonomous fashion as occurs in conversion reactions.

Practical experience has prompted us to make the same conclusions. In our psychiatric practice, persons with hysterical neuroses usually do not possess a sharp and penetrating intellect.[5] We even get the impression that if such a person has a good intellect, the neurotic disorder usually is associated with a somewhat psychopathic constitution.[6] This again is easily understandable. The emotional life of a person with a psychopathic personality is already less subordinated to the intellect and thus is more independent. Consequently, in the case of repression it will be much easier for the repressed emotion to do as it pleases without any restraint, either directly by the intellect itself (which has already been eliminated), or by the repressing emotion (which, as an emotion of the assertive drive, lacks the direction by the intellect seen in a person with a psychopathic personality.)

This rule is not without exceptions, however. We know of a few persons diagnosed with a hysterical neurosis who possess a good intellect, yet could not be said to have a psychopathic constitution. In these cases, however, one could not speak of enlightened control of the emotional life by reason since these persons had had little opportunity to develop their intellectual capacities and possessed a primitive emotional life. Thus, not only the intellect as such matters, but also the degree to which the intellect is inclined to concern itself with matters pertaining to the emotional life. It could well be that the more frequent occurrence of hysterical neuroses in women than in men is due to this fact. The emotional life of the woman is more autonomous and spontaneous than that of the man, and such hysterical manifestations would therefore occur more readily in women.

Quite the opposite of the hysterical neuroses are the obsessive-compulsive repressive disorders, which are determined clinically by the *repressing* emotion. Here, the repressed emotion does not function, or only slightly so, independently of the repressing emotion. Although the repressed emotion retains an active function—this is inherent in the repressive process—it is always colored by the repressing emotion which predominates in the clinical syndrome. This evidently will result in a clinical syndrome which differs according to the emotion which brings about the repression. As there are two such emotions which can bring about a repression, namely, fear and energy, there must be two different syndromes. These are:

a) *fear-based repression* (see anxiety neurosis—Appendix—B);

b) what we call *energy-based repression*; and

5. The best examples of conversions are seen in persons who are mentally impaired.

6. *See* A.A.A. Terruwe, M.D., *Psychopathic Personality and Neurosis*, translated and edited by Conrad W. Baars, M.D. and Jordan Aumann. O.P., S.T.D. (New York: P.J. Kenedy & Sons, 1958).

c) a combination of these two syndromes—*camouflaged fear-based repression.*

Fear-Based Repression

The repressing emotion of fear is so prominent in the syndrome of fear-based repression that it places its mark on the entire personality. Fear is a natural emotion that arises as soon as a person is threatened by danger. In fear-based repression, however, the fear pervades the psychic life so intensely that it is aroused not only in the presence of an actual danger, but even at the slightest possibility of danger or when danger is anticipated where none exists. Persons with fear-based repressive disorders live in perpetual fear that danger may befall them.

Fear, therefore, is the characteristic sign and symptom in this form of repressive disorder. It represses other emotions which, as we have already mentioned, continue to exert their action in the subconscious life. Yet, the repressive process as such is not the pathognomonic element of this neurotic syndrome, for it is common to all neurotic disorders. Typical of this disorder is its outward characterization, not by the repressive process or the repressed emotions, but by the fear which set the repressive process into motion. Therefore, in the discussion of the pathognomonic feature of this disorder, we do not consider the repression or the repressed emotions, but concentrate solely on the fear.

In trying to determine the cause of this fear, it becomes clear that in the person with a fear-based repressive disorder it is *acquired* and not innate.[7] It may develop in an entirely normal and not excessively fearful child. When something has aroused fear—and this is especially true for the childhood years—and this fear has not been resolved or guided into the right channels, it will begin to repress other feelings and emotions. In that event, the fear begins to grow both in *extension by enlarging the object*, and in *intensity by taking deeper root* and also because the repressed emotion

7. In this connection it should be stated that a person's excessive fearfulness is not synonymous with having a fear-based repressive disorder. The latter state implies that emotions have been repressed and although this may happen easily in the presence of excessive fear, it does not mean that it is unavoidable. This is the reason why very fearful children are not necessarily neurotic, although such an emotional state readily leads to the development of a neurotic disorder. For more detail on this subject *see* Chapter VI.

reacts again on the fear. Ultimately, the psychological life will be seriously and at times completely dominated by fear.

The fact that the excessive fear in a fear-based repressive disorder is an acquired abnormality does not preclude a natural predisposition for the presence of such an abnormal fear. On the contrary, persons with weaker constitutions are less able to cope with difficulties. If they are aware of this defect, there is more likelihood that they will suffer from this form of disorder. Ordinarily, fear-based repressive disorders occur more readily in women than in men, but they will be less severe in women than in men. Moreover, there are certain types of both men and women who, as the result of a general asthenia, seem to be predisposed to develop fear-based repressive disorders.[8]

In fear-based repression, this fear will reveal itself in *somatic* and psychological manifestations. As far as the former are concerned, the psychomotor reactions of the fear will become chronic. An acute attack of fear may produce disturbances of heart beat (palpitations) and circulation (blushing or turning pale), secretory and excretory disturbances (urge to urinate and defecate, perspiration), pupillary dilation, tremors and shivering, speech disturbances (incoherent or illogical speech, loss of speech, and in more serious cases stammering), or insomnia. When fear rules the emotional life of such a person, these symptoms become more or less chronic. They are continuously present or at least appear at intervals for the slightest reason. Which symptoms will be present, and to what degree of intensity, depends, of course, on the individual constitution.[9]

As far as *psychological* manifestations are concerned, neurotic fear will be expressed in all kinds of irrational fear reactions. One fears all sorts of things that a normal person does not even consider. One is afraid of sins when sins could not possibly have been committed. One worries about bad confessions which have already been repeated a hundred times. One frets about the most remote consequences that might possibly follow a certain act. One fears people and sees threats everywhere. One is afraid that nothing will be accomplished and that everything will go wrong. The most sympathetic help is seen as a danger. In short, everything is overshadowed and

8. This is called a psychasthenic constitution, as seen in the psychasthenic syndrome of Janet. [Editors' Note: This is an outdated term which Pierre Janet used to identify a neurosis characterized by obsessions, compulsions, feelings of inadequacy and incompleteness, among other things.]

9. Tics, too, may be the result of fear, although, in our opinion, of a fear which has been repressed. *See* section below on camouflaged fear-based repression.

determined by fear. How pathological the emotion is will be evident from the complete lack of any reasonable relationship between cause and effect.

A fear-based repressive disorder, however, does not manifest itself only in irrational fear reactions. Fear pervades all spheres of the psychic life. It influences thinking and the imagination; it influences motor activity. It interferes with the thought processes, leading to doubts which turn into indecisiveness when there is a need to act. Fear undermines every certainty and always leads to hesitation.

Even greater is the influence exerted by fear on the *imagination*; this is to be expected, as the imagination is closely associated with the emotional life. This influence of fear on the imagination leads, in turn, to a further effect on the dream life, which has an important bearing on diagnosis and therapy. Both the repressed emotion and the repressing emotion manifest themselves strongly in *dreams*, first in the form of symptoms of fear and then in the manner in which the fear modifies the repressed feelings. This provides us with an excellent method of determining the degree of progress during the therapeutic program.

Fear, furthermore, influences the external senses by making them excessively sensitive. The extreme tension of persons with fear-based repressive disorders makes them discern the slightest differences in the stimulation of all their senses as long as it concerns objects which in any way may be affected by this fear. Finally, it is important to realize that fear exerts a marked influence on motor activity. This may result in restlessness and agitation or in blocking and retardation. This depends, again, on individual constitution.

Both the intensity and the compulsive quality of the effect of fear on these various spheres of the psychic life may vary. It reaches its most extreme degree in the so-called *phobias*, when persons become completely obsessed by their fear regarding certain acts, circumstances, or events. It is not necessary to mention here the different types of phobias; they may involve any object of human interest and activity.

Furthermore, a person may suffer acute exacerbations of fear which may change to *outbursts* of *anger*. Although these attacks sometimes appear to be of a hysterical nature, they are not all hysterical. Rather, they are a sign that these people still possess some resistance against the fear, that they do not yet want to give in to the fear, and in this respect angry outbursts may be considered as a favorable sign and treated as such.

Once the fear no longer meets with any opposition, a state of *depression* is inevitable, for then these patients finally feel the danger which has threatened them for such a long time to be unavoidable. They then lose any remaining vestige of courage and desire to live, and despair and dejection, with all their consequences, dominate their psychic life.

Energy-Based Repression

Energy-based repression is different from fear-based repression in that repression takes place not through fear, but through its opposite emotions of courage, daring, fearlessness, energy, or whatever one wants to name them. The repressing emotional energy is so prominent in this form of neurotic disorder that it places its stamp on the person's whole personality. Again, as in a fear-based repressive disorder, it does not matter what kind of emotions are repressed, for the characteristic feature of this disorder is the all-pervading action of the energy.

Not every excessively energetic person, however, can be said to have an energy-based repressive disorder. We made a similar remark in the section on fear-based repression, but here it has even more significance. There are many individuals in whose psyche energy assumes too prominent a place, so much so that other emotions may suffer as a result; yet one cannot speak of these persons as having a neurotic disorder. Otherwise, a great number of highly successful and energetic people in our society would have to be counted, and incorrectly so, among this group.

The reason that these highly successful persons do not develop an emotional disorder may be due to the fact that in them the excessive energy rarely leads to a repression of those emotions which we consider to be particularly apt to produce a neurotic disorder, namely those which serve the procreative drive and the drive for self-realization. Persons who force their way up in the socio-economic milieu usually are able to give full expression to these particular emotions and feelings, while any repression in these people will often concern less essential, more refined feelings and emotions. The latter repression, however, in people who are not neurotic rarely leads to the development of this emotional disorder.

These remarks are not meant to convey the impression that such a basic approach or attitude in life would not leave its mark on the individual, or that these resolute and strong-minded persons are spiritually mature and well-balanced. Far from it. The higher, more refined emotions will more likely remain atrophied in these persons. They are so occupied with material things that there is no room for finer human sentiments, and although they are not neurotic, they neither possess nor experience the full expansion of the human personality. As a result, they are unable to sense the emotional needs of others and to establish rapport with them. The strong-willed husband will be incapable of understanding his wife and will repeatedly hurt and disillusion her in spite of his best intentions. The meaning of love's tenderness escapes him entirely. Notwithstanding his concern for his children, he becomes for them a domineering father who only radiates coercion and inspires resistance, and hence repression. He may not have a neurotic disorder, but the man with excessive energy readily causes neurotic disorders in others. Such a person is often called a *workaholic*.

It is exactly the same with the excessively energetic woman; in fact, it is perhaps even worse, because such an attitude in life is even more contrary to her feminine nature. By nature a woman is less inclined to be assertive, and therefore she is less strongly driven by a need to do and to achieve in a competitive way. Nevertheless, she possesses these emotions and for her, too, it is proper and even an asset to have a certain amount of push and energy. However, this does not change the fact that the assertive emotions are not typically feminine. If, then, this emotional energy begins to develop to abnormal intensity in a woman, her emotional life will be even more seriously affected than that of the man. The matter-of-factness, coolness, and emotional restraint that accompany this attitude are much more foreign to her nature. Tenderness and compassion disappear; she can no longer give of herself. Her devotion cools off and turns into purely intellectual concern. She becomes a little too independent. All these things contribute to her own unhappiness and, if she marries, to that of her husband and children. Although her talents and capabilities may quite well assure her of an enviable position in society, she is no longer authentically feminine. Sooner or later such distortion of her nature cannot fail to take its toll.

We have already said that in highly successful individuals an excessively energetic orientation will not lead to a neurotic disorder because in them the feelings and emotions serving the procreative drive and the drive for self-realization are usually not repressed. It follows that if the energy does direct itself against those drives, an energy-based repressive disorder will be sure to develop. If a child who is resolute by nature is led to consider sexual feelings—or whatever one presumes to be sexual feelings—as harmful, it may easily begin to try to repress those feelings by force. This is the beginning of a conflict which will grow into a neurotic disorder as a result of repression by the emotional energy. The actual process has already been outlined: the repressed emotion remains active, the energy continues to repress, the tension increases as the repressive force becomes stronger; the end is a neurotic disorder.

Energy-based repressive disorders have their own characteristic psychological and somatic symptoms, as a result of the fact that the emotions of courage and daring (strivings that are characterized by the assurance of success) come too much to the fore. This presumes a psychological disposition which differs completely from that of fear-based repression. While the latter brings on a timidity, a hesitation, a lack of action, or even a recoiling, the courage and daring provide a stimulus not to evade an issue, but to persevere in the certain knowledge that one is going to achieve one's goal. If this ambitious attitude is not directed at external objects, but at emotions and feelings, this driving force will also take a prominent place in the clinically observable psychological manifestations. The undesirable emotions will be radically repressed, so effectively in fact, that the victor seems to be a balanced person. While repression by fear is accompanied by a persistent and noticeable unrest and agitation, repression by energy even causes an outward appearance of efficiency. These individuals believe they are equal to the struggle and are sure of winning the battle of life. They want to be the boss and they are the boss; though difficult, they master and control themselves.

This restraint, however, is not the same as the natural subjection of the emotional life to the intellect. The latter assumes that emotion conforms to reason, that it will tend toward the sense object enlightened by reason. Such is not the case in these people; their self-restraint is nothing but a forcing back, a certain attitude imposed from outside. Their normal psychomotor reactions are inhibited and replaced by an overregulated voluntary motor activity. The unconscious spontaneous quality disappears and a consciously willed attitude takes its place. No wonder, then, that an air of constraint hangs over the personality of these people. If the repression is pursued in a consistent fashion, the whole being will reveal an unnatural inflexibility and constraint. The degree of this enforced attitude is determined by the intensity of the repression as well as the personality of the patient. In some, the repressive mechanism attains a technical perfection, while the voluntary motor system deceptively imitates the true emotions in the eyes of all except those who can see and feel beyond the surface.

In persons with an energy-based repressive disorder, no *emotional rapport* is possible concerning the emotions that have been repressed. Their responses lack the tone of natural feeling. If one lets one's own feelings go out to them, one is confronted by a wall, impenetrable and unyielding. One cannot reach his or her true inner emotional life and so remains a virtual stranger to these persons. Persons with energy-based repressive disorders are lonely individuals, but their rigid self-control has caused them to be so preoccupied with themselves that they are not even aware of their loneliness. They do not experience a need for contact with others; still less do they want sympathy or help, for they are sufficient unto themselves.

This self-control determines their attitude toward others. They readily display an air of coldness, even of hardness, toward others. All emotions, even those of others, are interpreted in a sober, dispassionate, matter-of-fact manner, and although this may be entirely reasonable, humans are not merely intellectual beings. They remain separated from other people by an unbridgeable chasm.

The lives of persons with energy-based repressive disorders are lives of restraint.[10] This is the essential feature of their disorder, but as this control is not a true restraint, the emotions they keep in check, that is to say, repress, do not disappear but persist in a latent state and are manifested involuntarily. They do this in the form of a *generalized tension* or—under certain circumstances—in the form of aggression. The general tension is revealed in their deportment, their manner of speech, and the way they react; they often betray a vehemence which is much greater than called for under the circumstances. Their aggressive attitude shows itself whenever one of their emotional conflicts is aggravated; the resulting outburst is in extreme contrast to their usual even disposition. Their words become harsh and biting, and they become intolerant in their opinions.

The other actions of repressed emotions, discussed elsewhere, also occur in this form of repressive disorder. A good example can be found in obsessive-compulsive symptoms, although they are more inclined to be interior symptoms because one's will to restrain the emotions prevents the outward manifestations as long as possible.

Energy-based repression makes great demands on the psychological powers of these individuals. They are fully aware of everything they do and

10. This control of emotion also extends to the imagination. It is a striking fact that persons with energy-based repression, in contrast to those with fear-based repression, dream little or not at all; at least they have no recollection of having had any dreams. During therapy, when the energy begins to abate, the patient begins to have dreams.

prefer it that way because they consider this the road to perfection. This constant conscious preoccupation with self demands so much psychological effort, however, that at long last they become completely *exhausted* and are unable to go on. At this stage, the defense against their repressed conflicts also breaks down and patients who strove so hard and so long for self-control now witness the collapse of the edifice they had so carefully constructed. This breakdown sometimes makes these persons go to a psychiatrist. Usually they do not take this step very readily because they are convinced that the correct way to live is by repressing and that they are too energetic not to win out in emotional difficulties. It is hard for them to realize that they are ill or to give credence to the explanation of others that they are ill. These generally very intelligent and gifted people have steered their lives intentionally in one particular direction and drawn conclusions from their mistaken attitudes with unwavering consistency. Such persons believe that the *spiritual life* demands an absolute repudiation of all feelings, and they usually carry this through in everything they do. They even eliminate such feelings as love of nature and art and consider it their duty to enjoy them no longer.

Because of their talents and strong force of will, the prognosis would be favorable for these individuals if they could be shown at an early stage how incorrect their philosophy of life really is. By the time they come to the attention of the psychiatrist, however, the prognosis is often less hopeful, because the neurotic process has progressed too far.

Persons with energy-based repressive disorders may also show certain physical symptoms which could well owe their origin to their psychological state. In the physical examination of these patients, we have been struck, for instance, by their markedly *decreased or absent muscle-stretch reflexes*.[11] This may be explained by the inhibiting action of the cerebral cortex on the reflex centers. This is only one of the ways in which the excessively strong infiltration of the intellectual life into the sensory life shows itself to a marked degree in energy-based repression. These reflexes become more active following successful treatment of the disorder.

We have observed still other physical symptoms in persons with energy-based repression which may be attributed to pressures in the emotional life. These are *low systolic and diastolic blood pressure*, and a *low, flat*

---

11. Editors' Note: The involuntary response when a tendon is tapped with a reflex hammer (as in a knee-jerk).

blood-sugar curve which returns to below-normal values. These findings, too, have been observed to return to normal after successful therapy.

Persons with fear-based repression, on the other hand, show normal reflex activity, normal blood pressure, and a normal blood-sugar curve. This difference parallels that between the structures of these disorders. Fear-based repressive disorders and their symptomatology are confined more to the sensory sphere, while the more consciously intellectual influence in energy-based repressive disorders creates a greater pressure, which will naturally make itself felt in the sensory and vegetative spheres as well.

Fear-Based Repression Camouflaged by Energy

Now that we have discussed fear-based repression and energy-based repression, we must mention a syndrome which could be called a mixture of both; namely, fear-based repression camouflaged by energy. Although it is energy that maintains the repression, it is fear that forms the driving force behind the repression and activates and keeps activating the energy. Therefore, therapy must be aimed at alleviating the fear.

This type of disorder is essentially a fear-based repressive disorder. Like fear-based repression, it originates in a deep-rooted fear that first develops in childhood. Because this fear brings about a repression of a pleasure emotion, the latter cannot develop in a normal manner. In true fear-based repression this fear is of a purely sensory nature, but this is not so in patients with this particular type of disorder.

These persons are by nature strong-willed, and a feeling of fear does not agree with their nature, not even in childhood. When their fear is aroused, it is usually caused by factors of a predominantly intellectual nature; the thought of duty and obligation, and consequently the need to live up to their own expectations. Basically, this concern is also a fear, a fear that controls all their subsequent actions and attitudes. Although the resulting repression in these people is begun by fear, it is not sustained by it as happens in true fear-based repression; it is energy that maintains the repression. These people do not allow themselves to be consciously influenced by fear. Whenever they experience fear, they rise above it. This, however, is actually a repression, because psychologically they are not yet capable of handling and integrating this fear in a rational manner.

We have here a *double repression*: First, a repression of the emotions of the pleasure appetite by fear which they do not consider acceptable, and second, a repression of the fear by energy.

First of all, they repress the pleasure emotions which they do not want to admit and which originally aroused their fear. What happens here psychologically is exactly the same as what happens in true energy-based repression, with the difference, however, that it happens in an individual with a different kind of personality. The psychological process is the same: we see the same attitudes, the same repression of emotions, the same external rigidity and unconcern, the same lack of rapport with other people, the same insensitivity in the spiritual life, and the same compulsive manifestations of the repressed emotions.

In these cases, the repressing action of the energy occurs in a *personality which is completely different* from one in which true energy-based repression occurs. In the latter, the energy dominates exclusively, but in the former, the energy is always tempered by a deep-rooted fear. Fear and courage are opposite emotions, and although in camouflaged fear-based repression the courage is conscious and the fear is unconscious, these two emotions nevertheless influence each other. The whole clinical picture, therefore, is different in the two types of disorders. In persons with true energy-based repression there is something compulsive, something strange; one always senses in them a "desire to achieve," which annoys other people. This is much less true in the case of persons with camouflaged fear-based repression, however, for their "desire to achieve" always contains a measure of fear that holds them back. Besides, their excess of energy is not a consequence of their natural disposition, as in the case with true energy-based repression; it is a neurotic symptom caused by fear, which constantly activates the energy. We are not dealing here with naturally domineering and strong-minded people; on the contrary, these persons usually possess a naturally intense and warm emotional life, but it has been repressed by fear.

Typical of this type of disorder is the repression of fear in addition to the repression of the pleasure emotion. Although fear is the cause of the repression of the pleasure emotion, these people do not want to be dominated by fear; they are too energetic and strong to want to live in fear, and therefore they repress this fear. In the process, however, the fear suffers the fate of all repressed emotions: since it is not integrated, it does not quiet down but is left in a state of tension. As such, it continues to make itself felt, though naturally unconsciously, and it imparts a measure of uncertainty to the emotional life of the individual.

This uncertainty is always concealed from the outside world because these persons consciously exclude the fear from their actions and want to carry out with complete self-control what they believe they should do. Sometimes this uncertainty may become evident in a great concern for their own welfare. Since such concern always contains a semblance of reasonableness, it is more easily admitted, but these people do experience their fearfulness within themselves. Time and again they realize that for reasons unknown to themselves they are restless, hesitant, fearful, alarmed, and indecisive. When they do make a decision, they want to change it. They lack the determination that is really theirs by nature. When they want to change and correct their fearful uncertainty, they do so in a violent manner, with the result that others are surprised that such a seemingly level-headed or reasonable person could say or do something in such a vehement manner. In the meantime, the fear which is repeatedly repressed keeps on growing until finally it becomes so intense that all their energy is insufficient to control it and they no longer dare to do certain things. Their fear also frequently manifests itself in *somatic* symptoms, such as *tics* and *tremors*.

We must now take a closer look at the nature of the repression in this type of disorder. The repression here is not an immediate reaction to the fear-producing object, as happens in true fear-based repression. When persons with true fear-based repression are afraid of sexual feelings, their fear represses those feelings at once. In fear-based repression camouflaged by energy, there is an intermediate phase, which consists of an intellectual judgment.[12] When these persons experience a fear of something, they realize it and decide that it has to be suppressed; they then go on to repress it. In these cases the repression has less of a purely sensory character than in pure fear-based repression, since the intellect takes part in the process.

This leads us to various conclusions. We have often noticed that people with this type of disorder have a much better than average intellect. This is readily explained by what we have just said. The repression in this case presupposed a usefulness judgment as a connecting link between the original fear and the actual repression. Since in true neurotic disorders the repression always begins in childhood, the sensory cognitive faculties in

---

12. Properly speaking, this is an act of the utility or usefulness judgment which is a higher sensory cognitive power because of the influence exerted by the intellect. For the sake of convenience we use the term intellect.

these patients must have been influenced by the intellect at an early age. This suggests the presence of a very keen intellect.

Furthermore, the intervention of intellectual judgment results in the fact that the intellect usually determines the expansion of the repression to other objects. In an earlier chapter, we explained that there are two possible causes of such expansion. First, there is an expansion based on *association*, when an object resembles the one that is feared. For instance, a man may have a fear of looking at seashells, because they are associated in his imagination with the female genitals. Secondly, there is an expansion based on *intellectual grounds*, when he discovers in other objects the same quality that caused him to avoid the first object, as when one has a fear of sexual matters because they are too sensuous, and therefore he begins to avoid all sensuous things. In the disorder under discussion here, the emphasis is always on the second form of expansion. This, in turn, results in a repression which is consistently expanded over a vast area. Sometimes it is even possible to observe this expansion in process as one repression leads to another.

Finally, the understanding of the nature of this repression provides an explanation of the *difference in personalities* between the sufferers of pure fear-based repression and of camouflaged fear-based repression. The former generally react immediately and spontaneously; the latter react indirectly because the emotional life is more subordinated to reason. Generally speaking, persons with camouflaged fear-based repression are talented persons with a keen and discerning intellect, with a sensitive and naturally harmonious emotional life, and with a well-directed will, as is common in all persons with obsessive-compulsive repression.

There remains to be discussed a condition which has a striking clinical resemblance to a true repressive disorder but is not identical with it. On the contrary, the differences are so marked that in our opinion one is permitted to treat it as a separate clinical entity.

This condition may develop in persons whose emotional life unfolded harmoniously together with the intellect during childhood and adolescence. Although not in the least neurotic when they reach adulthood, they may begin to repress certain emotions when exposed to situations which they feel they cannot tolerate or control in a rational manner. At such a time they will assume a certain attitude by which they *suppress*[13] feelings

---

13. The act of suppression is a conscious one. It is performed for seemingly rational motives, yet these motives, objectively considered, are not truly reasonable. An example

which properly ought to be expressed in some way or other, as without such communication the situation will continue unchanged. This naturally amounts to repression. The results are the same as in a repressive disorder, namely, persistent activity of the repressed emotions in the unconscious and ultimately abnormal clinical manifestations.

All of us are familiar with this kind of reaction in everyday life. For instance, it is commonly said of the woman who has suffered great sorrow that it would be better for her if she were to shed tears. We have all experienced how our resentment decreases as soon as we have confronted the anger-provoking situation. Inability to deal with an emotion in a rational manner always leads to tensions that continue to exert a pathological influence in the psychological life. Moreover, if this state of affairs lasts unduly long, these persons, even if they are otherwise entirely normal, begin to show real disease symptoms that fully resemble those of individuals with neurotic disorders. These are the *pseudoneurotic reactions* of which we shall give a few typical examples.

The first case is that of a thirty-eight year old nun who, after six years of cloistered life, began to complain of headache, vomiting, talking in her sleep, and sleepwalking. She had never shown these symptoms before. Examinations by a general practitioner and a consultant in internal medicine failed to reveal any abnormalities. When she came to us she was found to be in poor physical condition. Her reflexes were very brisk and there was considerable extension of the reflexogenic areas.[14] She was intelligent,

---

would be the suppression of tears because we consider it childish to cry. Suppression, therefore, must be distinguished from mature rational restraint, as well as from neurotic repression.

14. This descriptive term is used to indicate, in the case of the *quadriceps femoris* reflex (knee-jerk reflex), for example, that this reflex may be elicited not only by percussion of the tendon, below the kneecap, but also by percussion of the quadriceps muscle itself. The more proximal the percussion of this muscle is effective, the greater is the extension of the reflexogenic area said to be. This, of course, is an indication of the greater excitability of the muscle, and is a reliable indicator of the degree of tension and irritability resulting from intrapsychic conflicts. We have seen two cases in which the knee-jerk reflex could be elicited readily by tapping the area of the groin with a reflex hammer. One of these was the husband of a patient who was contemplating divorce after years of serious marital discord. The husband asked permission to see us in order to have us persuade his wife to change her mind. Seeing his distress we suggested that in the meantime he seek some relief of his own tension. He grudgingly consented to a brief neurological examination for the purpose of ruling out other possible causes of his tension. The examination was normal except for the above-mentioned extension of the reflexogenic area to the groin, mydriasis, and excessive sweating. We prescribed a tranquilizer, but he did

but of little erudition. Her emotional life appeared intact, and there was no reason to assume the presence of a neurotic process.

In the initial interview, she could not think of anything that might worry her. She was happy in her cloister and had no desire for anything else. When it was suggested in the course of the interview that hidden psychological conflicts sometimes express themselves in bodily manifestations, she did not show any observable response.

Three months later, she returned for another interview. She looked much better and stated that most of her complaints had disappeared suddenly and almost miraculously. It seemed that the suggestion given in the first interview had done its work. Reminiscing one day in the chapel, she had suddenly remembered the day, several months before the appearance of her complaints, that a friend had paid her a visit in the cloister. This friend had told her several stories of how her elderly father was supposedly having an affair with a young woman. Although she had been quite upset by these stories, she had not dared to reveal her feelings to her superior. For weeks she had tried to overcome her fear that these scandalous facts would become public knowledge and her superior then would think her to be a liar, as she had always tried to impress her with the high moral standards of her family. That day in the chapel, she had at the same time understood what had been suggested to her in general terms, namely, that her repulsion of these matters had expressed itself in vomiting. This association was proven conclusively by the fact that her vomiting stopped that same day.

The uncovering of the repressed emotion had been made easier by the fact that her visit to us had enabled her to see her relatives again after a long separation and to see for herself that the stories about her father had been untrue. Several months later she returned for another visit, feeling her old self again. The symptoms of somnambulism and talking in her sleep, which had persisted for a while after the vomiting had stopped, had now disappeared, and she could be discharged from treatment as completely recovered.

---

not have the prescription filled. Instead, he shot himself fatally in the head. The second case was that of a middle-aged woman whose husband had repeated extramarital affairs, drank to excess, and beat her up occasionally. Her nagging protests and repeated threats to leave him were in vain. Over the years her increasing tension could be relieved only by alcohol. When she finally sought professional help, her knee-jerk could be elicited readily by tapping the entire length of the quadriceps femoris muscle up to and including the groin. When marital counseling brought about a favorable reversal of the intolerable situation, her tension decreased and so did the extension of the reflexogenic area.

The second case concerned a thirty-five year old woman who came in with complaints of fatigue, irritability, and sudden changes of mood. She had been married for eleven years and her children were ten, eight, and five years of age. There was no history of serious illnesses in herself or her family. She possessed a good intellect but had received little education. She was a sensitive woman with a well-developed emotional life. Her reflexes were very brisk and the reflexogenic areas were slightly enlarged.

During the interview it was learned that she and her husband practiced withdrawal and felt very guilty about it. She ascribed her nervous condition to the fact that she lived over a carpenter's shop and was bothered all day long by the noise of an electric saw. Although she had lived there ever since she was married, lately she felt that she could not stand the noise any longer. Obviously, she wanted us to advise her husband to move to another home.

We diagnosed her condition as a pseudoneurotic reaction caused most likely by her practice of withdrawal and its resultant psychological tensions. Therapy, therefore, was directed at giving her an explanation of the psychologically harmful effects of this sexual practice. She was also referred to her family physician for instruction in methods of natural family planning, using basal body temperature graphs, cervical self-examination, and so on. Under treatment her condition improved gradually, and after ten months all her symptoms had completely disappeared. Interestingly, she had been asked to move to a new home but preferred to stay where she was, in spite of the persisting noise of the saw.

A third woman, twenty-nine years of age, married two years, with a child of five months, complained of fatigue, irritability, lack of sexual pleasure for several months, and falling out of hair, which the dermatologist thought to be of a psychogenic nature. She had been reared by understanding parents and her childhood, spent in a somewhat protected environment, had been happy. Intelligent, she possessed a well-developed emotional life. Until a few months prior to her first interview, her marital life had been happy.

At the end of her first hour, she hesitatingly confided that her mother-in-law, who visited her daily, had made her realize that she had been raised in a very inadequate manner and was a very poor wife and mother. Since then, she had tried to emulate her energetic mother-in-law in everything she did but, she was convinced, without any success.

The physical and neurological examinations revealed a tachycardia, a blood pressure of 130 systolic and 90 diastolic, paleostriatal tremors of the hands, and considerably diminished reflexes without extension to the reflexogenic areas. A diagnosis was made of the pseudoneurotic reaction with energy as the repressing factor. Therapy consisted of discussing with both the husband and the patient the unhealthy attitude of trying to adopt a personality structure so foreign to her own. She was advised to be her natural self and, if possible, to move away from the home of the mother-in-law, especially as the husband of the patient had been unduly influenced by her too. She was seen again after approximately a year and a half, during which period her mother-in-law had suddenly died. Soon afterwards her complaints began to leave her and after that she felt like her old self again.

All these cases have this in common—the patients were persons with normal, healthy emotional lives who had been driven to repression by an external circumstance and had developed pathological symptoms as a result. In the first case, it was the shame of the conduct of one of the members of the family; in the second one, the withdrawal; and in the third, the influence of the energetic mother-in-law. The symptoms disappeared once the conflict had been resolved. None of the three persons was neurotic, but each had developed an acute pseudoneurotic reaction which brought on the typical clinical syndrome.

These pseudoneurotic reactions, like neurotic disorders, may assume different forms. The first case, that of the nun, is a *hysterical pseudoneurotic reaction*. The repressed feelings, the disgust with the alleged immoral situation at home which she wanted to keep secret at any cost, manifested itself in vomiting, and as happens in all such hysterical reactions, the symptom disappeared when she became aware of the act of repression. It cannot be stressed enough, however, that this woman was not in the least a person with a hysterical neurosis; on the contrary, she was completely normal.

The other two cases represent *obsessive-compulsive pseudoneurotic reactions*. In the second case, the repression was the result of fear—fear of pregnancy, which led to withdrawal, and fear of the moral wrong of this act. In the third case, it was excessive energy which led to repression in a woman whose natural disposition was not at all inclined to be so energetic.

Although these three illustrations concern adults, this does not mean that pseudoneurotic reactions do not occur in children. A normal child, too, may repress a certain feeling at a given moment and be subject to neurotic complaints. This of itself does not amount to a neurotic disorder, however. Of course, it could lead to a neurotic disorder in later life if the repression is repeated and the conflict is not resolved immediately. One can safely state that pseudoneurotic reactions *occur frequently in children*. Since the emotional life of the child does not lend itself readily to guidance by reason, it must be guided by that of the parents, and this, of course, easily opens the door to conflicts. Rümke had this in mind when he said: "Every child has a neurotic symptom at some time, but it usually disappears by itself in an understanding *milieu*." Only if such a symptom becomes fixed is it necessary to resort to psychotherapy.

Pseudoneurotic reactions in adults, it must be remarked, are not generally described as a clinical entity. We would much prefer to do so, however, especially if the repressive process has resulted in lasting pathological symptoms. In such cases we are dealing with a real clinical syndrome and not with a transient and spontaneously disappearing symptom. On the other hand, one can hardly speak of a neurotic disorder in these cases, because these people present an entirely different clinical picture. Persons with neurotic disorders have a truly pathological personality structure; the illness has become part of their psychological makeup and determines their entire behavior as well as the manner in which they discuss their illness.

All this is different in people with pseudoneurotic reactions. When they go to a psychiatrist, *they present their complaints in the same way as physically ill persons do*: "Doctor, I don't know what is the matter with me lately; I have such trouble with my stomach and my family physician can't find anything wrong. I can't sleep and I used to sleep like a baby. I feel so strange and I am so restless and irritable with the least little thing." These people dissociate themselves much more from their complaints than those with neurotic disorders do; they look at their symptoms objectively, whereas the self-image of persons with neurotic disorders are distorted by their illness. Once one has seen both types, it is easy to recognize the difference.[15]

We believe that it is also important to make this distinction from a therapeutic standpoint. For example, deep analysis has no place in the treatment of pseudoneurotic reactions. Treatment is not a matter of solving deep-seated conflicts, but rather of straightening out the circumstances that have brought on the pseudoneurotic reaction. Once this has been accomplished, the symptoms of the pseudoneurotic reaction disappear by themselves, although this usually will take some time, often a few months or so. Consequently, while in those with neurotic disorders a change in

15. Incidentally, this discussion also explains why we prefer to term this reaction a pseudoneurotic reaction rather than a situational neurosis. The fact that the reaction does not represent a true neurotic disorder is more important than its being caused by a stressful situation.

external circumstances will have no more than a favorable or unfavorable influence on the course of the disease, it is of decisive importance for the cure of a pseudoneurotic reaction.

Pseudoneurotic reactions are thus illnesses of emotionally healthy individuals; anybody may acquire them. In the thirty years or so that we have studied this reaction, we have been impressed by the fact that it occurs more often in women than in men. This is naturally to be expected as the woman's emotional life is less influenced by reason and is more susceptible to manifestations resulting from repression. The fact that pseudoneurotic actions occur frequently in children is explained in the same manner, for the feelings of a child are not yet controlled by the intellect. Furthermore, we found that people who develop these reactions usually are simple individuals with little inclination to introspection and with primitive, uncomplicated emotional reactions. This, too, points to a lesser degree of penetration of the emotional life by the intellect.

It is self-evident that knowledge of this type of reaction is important for the general practitioner or primary care physician. Whereas the *treatment* of neurotic disorders must be left to the psychiatrist or psychotherapist, it is a different matter as far as pseudoneurotic reactions are concerned. Primary care physicians are usually the first to see the development of neurotic symptoms in people whom they have known as normal. If this happens, it is certainly their task to search tactfully for difficulties and conflicts that the patient does not bring up spontaneously. These are often related to the patient's marital life, especially to the use of withdrawal or to an insufficiently enlightened and poorly motivated practice of periodic sexual abstinence. The frequency of occurrence of abnormal psychological symptoms as the result of abnormal sexual relations is only too well known to every practicing psychiatrist or psychotherapist. If primary care physicians proceed with the utmost discretion, they will have no difficulty in effectively helping such patients with their personal problems and thus relieving them of their neurotic symptoms. Family physicians, with their personal knowledge of all the members of a family, often including several generations, and in their unique position of trusted confidant, can make a tremendous contribution to the successful treatment of these people. If they are unable to find the cause of the pseudoneurotic reaction themselves, they can refer the patient to a psychiatrist or psychotherapist, but even then such physicians will be able to complete the therapeutic program already started.

CHAPTER IV

THERAPY OF REPRESSIVE
DISORDERS

Psychotherapy unrelated to either religion or metaphysics tends to produce an
"anxiously fostered middle-class tranquility, poisoned by its triteness."

E. Przywara, *Das Geheimnis Kierkegaards*

IT IS ONLY LOGICAL to expect that a new theory of the nature of a disease
should be accompanied by a new approach to its treatment. If the treatment
proves to be effective, it may be confidently concluded that the theory of
the root cause of the illness on which this therapy is based must be sound.

This book would not have been written if the results of our therapy
had not fully satisfied us that our theories about the nature of neurotic
disorders are fundamentally sound and provide well-defined therapeutic
precepts for each of the various types of disorders.

The case histories in Chapter V show how our therapeutic method can
restore many persons with neurotic disorders to full psychic [psychologi-
cal, spiritual and emotional] health; here we shall present a detailed discussion of our particular method of treatment.

Therapy of Hysterical Neurosis

In hysterical neurosis, it is of primary importance to bring the repressed emotion into consciousness. This is necessary because the emotion has been placed beyond the guiding influence of the intellect and thus beyond control of the will. As recovery cannot be called complete unless the emotional life is subject to rational guidance, it is to be expected that this will become possible only if the patient is completely aware of the presence and activity of *all* his or her emotions.

The mere discovery on the part of patients with this disorder that they might well harbor such a hidden emotion is not enough by itself. Only if they actually become aware of this emotion, and only if they literally sense this emotion to be active within them, will it be possible for them, with the help of the therapist, to find the proper means of responding to and dealing with the emotion. As soon as this happens, the hysterical symptom will no longer serve any useful function and thus will disappear.

Therefore, two things are required for the successful treatment of a person with a hysterical neurosis: first, the repressed emotion must be brought into consciousness, and second, the patient must be taught how to deal with the emotion in a rational manner.

In order to bring the repressed emotion into consciousness, the therapist uses all the customary means of *psychoanalytic therapy*. It would be superfluous to discuss these methods here. At the same time, it is necessary to eliminate the factors that caused the repression and that resist the analytic techniques by which the patient is made aware of the emotion. These resistances vary as to their nature; they may be general, as when they represent mistaken notions of morality, or specific, as in the case of particular desires or fears that cause the inner conflicts. Whatever their nature, the psychoanalyst has the task of applying the necessary corrective measures. This may be done by eliminating an external cause, by removing ignorance, by substituting correct insights for erroneous ones, and by helping the patient to see things in their true light and to appreciate their true value. In this way, the psychoanalyst simultaneously lessens the resisting forces and sets the stage for the rational guidance which the patient needs as soon as he or she becomes aware of the emotion.

The resolution of a hysterical symptom does not mean, of course, that the general personality structure has been changed, and therefore there may be a recurrence of similar hysterical reactions. To eliminate the possibility of a recurrence would require a radical change in the personality structure, a more complete victory over excessive fear or energy, and this can be achieved only through a more radical therapeutic approach. However, patients with hysterical neuroses do not usually lend themselves to such fundamental personality modifications because they are usually deficient in intelligence and introspective power, or, if this is not the case, because their personality structures are somewhat psychopathic, i.e., there exists a constitutional defect in the relationship between emotional and intellectual lives. In either case, such qualities are contraindications to the radical therapeutic modification of the personality structure necessary to prevent further hysterical manifestations.

Therapy of Obsessive-Compulsive Repression

The therapeutic approach in obsessive-compulsive repression differs materially from the treatment described for hysterical neurosis. Instead of concentrating primarily on making the repressed emotion conscious, the therapy of the obsessive-compulsive repression is aimed first of all at dealing with the repressing emotions of fear or energy.

In these cases, too, the repressed emotions have become autonomous as a result of the repressive process, and the consequent release from control by reason and will may manifest itself in various obsessive-compulsive symptoms. Yet, these symptoms lack the complete unawareness and absolute autonomy which are typical of hysterical symptoms. Patients with obsessive-compulsive repression are intellectually so aware of the life they lead, so busily occupied with their own emotional experiences, and so intensely concerned with either controlling their instinctive urges or avoiding dangers, that the total unawareness which is characteristic of hysterical neurosis is an impossibility. The essential feature of this illness is the forceful restraint of the pleasure emotion by the usefulness judgment, which for this purpose perverts the natural function of the emotions of the assertive drive.

From a therapeutic viewpoint, therefore, it does not make sense to deliberately bring more repressed material into the patient's consciousness. If one were to do this without simultaneously alleviating the fear or the energy, one would merely intensify the repression and make the illness worse. In these cases, the therapy must be directed first of all to reducing the repressing emotions to a lesser intensity, namely, diminishing the fear or curtailing the excessive energy. In this way, the repression will lose its force and the repressed emotions will gradually emerge by themselves into consciousness, where they can ultimately have the satisfaction, so to speak, of becoming amenable to rational direction and guidance. However, it is not to be presumed that the first acts of the newly released emotions are controlled human actions.[1]

We shall now discuss separately the therapy of fear-based repression, energy-based repression, and camouflaged fear-based repression.

Therapy of Fear-Based Repression

The first and most important thing to be done in fear-based repressive disorders is to combat the fear that dominates and characterizes this illness so completely. Only when this fear diminishes can a cure be effected. Thus, initially it is necessary to decide how to lessen the fear.

The primary requisite, we believe, is the patient's *trust* in the therapist. Fear is primarily counteracted by trust. Fear sees a threatening evil; trust removes this threat. Fear causes uncertainty and agitation; trust gives determination and stability. Fear causes one to retreat; trust gives one courage to proceed. The more the trust grows, the less will be the fear.

Persons with fear-based repressive disorders, therefore, must develop trust. Being dominated by fear, however, they do not trust themselves as normal persons do; they know only fear. Consequently, they must find this trust in another person. Trust in the psychotherapist provides these patients with a quiet haven in their emotional life; here at last they sense a certain stability, a certain degree of safety. This growing feeling of safety counteracts the fear, which then begins to loosen its paralyzing grip. Thus a foundation is laid on which a normal psychological life will be able to develop, slowly and gradually of course, but building upon this foundation of trust in the therapist these persons will eventually gain trust in themselves.

This bond of trust between the patient and the psychotherapist must also be an emotional bond; that is to say, the patient's trust must not only be a rational reasoned trust, but an *emotionally felt trust or feeling of confidence*. As long as this feeling has not been aroused, the fear is not counteracted in the emotional life. Purely rational considerations do not touch the feelings of a person who is so dominated by emotions as is a person with a neurotic disorder; of themselves, such considerations are of no avail. A strictly impersonal relationship between the therapist and the patient, as is indicated

1. Cf. Chapter VIII.

in the analysis of the patient with a hysterical neurosis, has no place in the therapy of a person with a fear-based repressive disorder. It must be an ever growing emotional bond that gives the patient an increasing feeling of certainty and security.

What is called *transference* in psychoanalysis has a totally different meaning in the therapy of fear-based repression, and it must be handled in a manner different from that used with hysterical neurosis. Transference in hysterical neurosis is a relationship in which the patient's feelings for its repressed object have found an analogous object in the person of the psychoanalyst. This, of course, is a relationship that eventually has to be resolved, because it is not a manifestation of a wholesome emotional life; this is one of the major tasks of the psychoanalyst in treating hysterical neurosis.

In fear-based repression, on the other hand, the bond with the therapist is a very healthy feeling because it enables the patient to develop the rest of his or her emotional life. The therapist must encourage this feeling to grow spontaneously. Once the therapy nears its successful end, the bond between the therapist and the patient will loosen by itself, because by that time the fear will have decreased so much that the patient has attained self-confidence and the courage to act according to personal convictions and beliefs.[2]

This necessary feeling of confidence presupposes the presence of two conditions in the patient: first, trust that the therapist's understanding of emotional disorders and their related moral aspects is correct; and second, confidence in the therapist as a person.

As regards the first condition, the patient needs to have trust not only in the therapist's understanding of emotional disorders in general, but also in the therapist's understanding of the patient's own particular illness. The patient must be certain that the therapist's insights—psychological and moral—are correct and the advice given may safely be followed. This is the reason, for instance, that a non-Christian therapist is not always the most suitable person to treat a Christian with fear-based repression, for such a patient will often lack an inner conviction that the therapist will provide proper guidance. What is more, when the patient is a Catholic whose use-fulness judgment has been misinformed in early life by Catholic educators,

---

2. This may be explained in Thomistic terminology by saying that transference in persons with a hysterical neurosis is a pathological manifestation of a repressed concupiscible emotion, while in persons with fear-based repressive disorders it represents a normal expression of an assertive emotion.

it is absolutely necessary for the patient to be treated by a Catholic psychotherapist who has successfully integrated—in his or her therapy as well as
in his or her own personal life—the teachings of the Magisterium of the
Church with the principles of philosophical anthropology and psychopa-
thology as set forth in this book. For a patient with fear-based repression,
at least, the Catholic psychotherapist whose therapeutic approach is influenced and molded by a theology in conflict with magisterial teaching has
nothing of real value to offer and should be avoided.

By the same token, patients who have been in psychoanalysis cannot
be treated successfully by a non-Freudian therapist, as they usually have
been so imbued with psychoanalytic ideas and interpretations that they
will not accept the opinions of the non-Freudian therapist. In general, the
psychotherapist must avoid advancing opinions and theories that are unacceptable to the patient; otherwise, the patient will find it difficult, if not
impossible, to develop the degree of trust necessary for complete recovery.

Furthermore, it is of even greater importance that these patients feel
that they themselves and their feelings and actions are understood by the
therapist, not only in the sense that the therapist can explain them scientifically, but also that the therapist is sympathetic in the understanding of these
feelings and actions. "To feel understood" is an intuitive, not a reasoned
knowledge. One might say that it is either present or not, that it can grow
or be destroyed, but it cannot be denied that it is an absolutely necessary
quality if these patients are to feel safe and to develop trust and confidence.
The art of psychotherapy depends to a great extent on the ability of the
therapist to cultivate this sympathetic understanding.

Finally, patients need to have confidence in their therapist's attitude
toward them as individuals, in their esteem and affection for them as human beings. We dare say that the most beneficent aspect of the therapy of
fear-based repression is *sincere affection* on the part of the therapist, not an
affection of the will alone but even of the emotions—all, of course, within
the bounds of the therapist-patient relationship in which the therapist seeks
only the good of the patient.

A basic requirement for successful therapy is recognition of the patient as a human being who desired the good and did the best to achieve it.
By showing the patient this recognition, which must be sincerely felt, the
therapist strengthens the patient's sense of dignity and sometimes provides
the patient with the most fundamental knowledge of himself or herself. The
therapist must be able to see the good in all patients, although it is different

in each one; this ability requires a talent which is as much a gift as that of the artist to recognize beauty in everything he or she beholds. It has been our personal experience that therapy is deprived of its greatest force if the therapist's desire to do good for each patient does not also resound in the therapist's feelings. This affection for the patient must remain consistent throughout the therapy. The patient must come to realize that no matter what he or she says or does, the therapist's affection remains the same; that even if the patient irritates and annoys the therapist, the therapist will not become resentful. In short, the patient must feel entirely safe in this relationship with the therapist so that nothing in it will activate his or her feelings of fear or interfere with growing feelings of trust and confidence in the therapist.

Another aspect of the therapy of fear-based repression is the therapist's need to become acquainted with the nature and form of the patient's fears. *Dream analysis* is very helpful here, because both the repressed and the repressing emotions manifest themselves in dreams. The fact that the repressing emotions do this, too, is of the utmost importance in treating a patient with fear-based repression. Whereas in the therapy of hysterical neurosis it is important that the repressed emotions make themselves known, either directly or as symbols in dreams, this is less important in fear-based repression, in which we are primarily concerned with the form of the fears and the extent to which they dominate the psychic life of the patient.

In the dreams of persons with fear-based repression, the intensity of the fear is particularly revealed in its relationship to the repressed pleasurable object. For instance, we had a patient who at the beginning of therapy dreamed of an evil that happened to her; in the next phase of therapy the evil merely threatened but did not actually happen; later on, instead of dreaming of an evil, she dreamed of a good but failed to obtain it (a tree full of luscious apples which moved out of her reach when she tried to pick them); finally, however, in her dreams, she came to possess the good things she desired.

Such dreams are not only of diagnostic value; they can also be a therapeutic aid because the patients get a better understanding of their fears from the explanation of their dreams. It must be emphasized, however, that the *interpretation of dreams should be limited* to an explanation of the *forms* of the emotions observed in the dreams themselves. Moreover, this progression in dreams serves to reveal to patients the extent of their improvement in therapy, and this gives them more confidence and courage to continue with the treatment.

Frequently, the dream shows us the degree of influence exerted by the intellect in the action of the repressing emotion. This is also of great diagnostic value. For example, we had a patient—a person with an energy-based repressive disorder—who in his dream saw water run up a mountain, and while dreaming he was able to find an explanation for this unusual phenomenon. Persons of superior intelligence with fear-based repressive disorders often dream of all kinds of arguments to prove that evil should befall them.

The important thing in the dream analysis of persons with fear-based repressive disorders, therefore, is not so much the object of the fear, but the form of the fear. In the beginning therapy we usually have these patients write down their dreams, and we let them continue to do this for approximately three months, depending on whether they are able to recall them sufficiently. After this period we stop dream analysis altogether, except for an occasional analysis to determine the degree of progress. As we have already explained, these persons usually dream a great deal, in contrast to persons with energy-based repressive disorders who dream but little or not at all.

Next in importance to the therapist are the *objects of the patient's fears*. These can be many and varied. Patients may have fears of conscience, fears of contact with other people, fears of authority figures, fears of their tasks and duties in life, fears of the future, of failure, of disappointments, of disease and insanity, of accidents, and of certain concrete objects (phobias). In short, fears may be directed at anything that can possibly represent a danger or a threat to the human person. The nature of these fears may give us an idea of the patient's personality, as well as an indication of the direction the therapy should take.

In the beginning of therapy, the therapist's main task is often to deal with overwhelming acute fears. For this, tranquilizers or sedatives may be used when it is necessary to combat the insomnia which commonly afflicts persons with fear-based repressive disorders. The therapist must also do everything possible to reassure the patient. Naturally, the therapist cannot allow himself or herself to be satisfied with these superficial methods, but must attempt to discover the causes of the patient's fears and combat them directly.

Two kinds of causes may be responsible for fears in neurotic disorders due to repression: either a mistaken understanding of moral obligations, or certain concrete facts that initially aroused these fears. To the first category belong false notions of morality (the nature of God, the relationship between the human person and God, sexuality, religious duties, etc.). The second category comprises such concrete factors as fear-producing conditions in which the patient was brought up (a father who was too strict or a cruel, fault-finding stepmother), or certain childhood experiences which, combined with generally mistaken notions, unduly stimulated the fear. (For example, if a child has been told repeatedly that anything sexual is very bad, it becomes afraid when natural biological phenomena occur, and it begins to live in ever greater fear as long as its understanding of such matters is not corrected or is even strengthened by continued exaggerated teachings.)

It is the task of the therapist to discover and eliminate these causes in the course of therapy. As far as mistaken notions are concerned, the therapist must assume the role of a teacher and clarify the issues to the satisfaction of each patient. In doing so, the therapist must consider each patient's degree of intelligence, for the greater this is, the greater the need to understand fundamental and basic issues. What counts here is whether the patient can be convinced of the incorrectness of his or her own ideas. Explanations which the patient does not understand have no effect. Obviously, this presents a serious difficulty in the treatment of a person with limited intelligence who has a fear-based repressive disorder; since one cannot give them sufficient insight into the problems involved, the cause of the fear continues to exist. All that the therapist can do is diminish the effects of the fear by cultivating the patient's confidence in him or her so that the patient will not be overwhelmed by these fears. A complete recovery in these patients is well nigh impossible.

It is mandatory to recognize, express, and resolve the concrete factors which led to the development of the fear or contributed to its growth. As long as these factors remain anchored in the emotional life, they continue to exert their influence by creating unrest and fear, even if the understanding of them has changed. They must be given expression with full participation of the emotions, for only in that manner—called *catharsis*—can the tension that they caused and still cause be broken. A strictly business-like account to the therapist is not enough, because the associated emotional tension is not discharged. Frequently, patients cannot bring themselves to express these conflicts except very gradually, for they have locked the conflicts within themselves and have built up resistances that first must be torn down. As a rule, these conflicts have not become entirely unconscious; in fact, sometimes these patients are constantly aware of them, although this does not lessen the resistance in any way.

In this connection, we must pose a very important question, namely, whether psychoanalytic methods are indicated and justified in trying to make repressed emotions conscious in persons with fear-based repressive disorders. The answer to this question has to be in the negative; in fact, it is our opinion that *psychoanalysis is actually contraindicated.* Psychoanalysis aims directly at making repressed emotions conscious. In persons with a hysterical neurosis this is an absolute requisite for recovery, for as long as the emotion remains unconscious, it will continue to exert its pathogenic activity. The situation is different in persons with fear-based repressive disorders, in whom the repressed emotions have not entirely disappeared from consciousness and can continue to exert their influence autonomously and independently of the fear.

Although this of itself constitutes reason enough to avoid psycho-analysis, there is the additional danger of activating the fear more strongly by deliberately making the repressed emotions more conscious. The more one is conscious of an emotion one fears, the greater the fear it creates. If fear has caused a person to repress sexual urges, even the most remote associations of that urge are sufficient to stimulate opposition and repression. Therefore, if one *deliberately* tries to uncover the objects of the repression, one may be sure that the fear will become worse. Such a procedure is therapeutically justified only if one is absolutely certain that the patient will be capable of handling the greater fear that is sure to make itself felt. Otherwise, one may be arousing forces without knowing whether they can be quelled and controlled. However, no therapist who sets out intentionally to uncover these repressed objects possesses this certainty; nobody can know beforehand what emotional value a person attaches to a certain object. It may easily be much greater and stronger than the therapist anticipates.

This explains why we advise against a systematic analysis of persons with fear-based repressive disorders. Their conflicts and hurts must be allowed to emerge gradually and spontaneously. This occurs automatically in the course of therapy, provided one is successful in diminishing their fears. As the fear becomes less, its repressing action also diminishes, together with the resistance, with the result that the repressed emotions are allowed to emerge more into consciousness. From then on it is only a matter of these patients having sufficient confidence in their therapist before they will express them—if necessary, with a little help from the therapist if they so desire. Under these circumstances, patients will be able to deal with the emerging conflicts and emotions adequately, as the fear of them has already been diminished.

The therapist must always *refrain from urging* patients to express emotions when they do not feel like doing so. Persons with fear-based repressive disorders interpret such prompting as an aggressive gesture and react by withdrawing. The revelation of their conflicts and emotions must come spontaneously, because patients themselves feel the need to talk about them and have found the courage to do so. Under such circumstances the catharsis will be complete. Here everything depends on the confidence that has gradually developed in these patients; this confidence ultimately unlocks their hearts as well as their mouths. The therapist must demonstrate great patience in this respect, for it may be years before these patients will reveal their innermost feelings, although they may already have shown considerable improvement. By taking this course, there is never any danger that these patients will be harmed. Moreover, by not violating the respect that they must have for the most intimate aspects of every human being, including the emotionally ill human being, therapists truly justify the trust their patients have put in them.

The therapist must also realize that patients with neurotic disorders are uncomfortable with all their emotions; persons with fear-based repression because they fear the consequences of their emotions, persons with energy-based repression because they are scornful of what they consider inferior aspects of their humanity. Such patients often do not realize themselves how ill at ease they are with their emotions. A severely handicapped woman with obsessive-compulsive repression, whose phobias and compulsions made life impossible for herself, her husband, and her children, defined her difficulty in the following manner: "Doctor, I have no self-confidence at all; I have to *think* everything out in the most minute details!" Pointing out the paradox of her statement, we explained that she was actually saying: "Although I have no confidence whatsoever in my feelings, I have the fullest confidence in my reasoning processes, and I rely on them to the exclusion of my feelings." Essentially, that is what persons with repressive disorders do; they mistrust their feelings and rely solely on thinking. From there it is but one step to the stimulation of their imagination, which works overtime, and usually to their detriment, in the anticipation of all the terrible things that might possibly befall them.

Another patient, also with a severe obsessive-compulsive repressive disorder, was equally unaware of the aforementioned paradox, especially as he claimed to be capable of normal emotional reactions (which were actually willed emotional manifestations as he did not wish to appear fearful). In one of our books he had read that a thorough understanding of the nature of neurotic disorders is of great benefit to patients in therapy. He had interpreted this to mean that he should, that is, was obliged to, understand his disorder fully, and to that end he felt compelled to read the book over and over again, until he became so enraged by this perverted action of his practical reason that he tore the book to shreds. When we complimented him on having done that, he replied, "I realized already before I came to you that I should ignore all `I musts' or `I must nots' and 'I shoulds' or 'I should nots,' and just do as I please, but I never really dared to do that." We told him that he was absolutely correct, and that his attitude was the underlying principle and aim of our therapy—learning to trust one's feelings, "to leap before one looks," in the confident realization that the more the feelings emerge, the more they will become amenable to guidance by the higher faculties, instead of being opposed and suppressed by fear or energy. From then on, the patient improved steadily; his emerging emotions became increasingly integrated with his common sense, and he was able to live spontaneously and happily.

Another task of the therapist is to support patients in whatever way he or she can. For example, the therapist must convince patients of the good qualities they possess. As many persons with fear-based repression are also troubled by feelings of being evil, they need to be assured by the therapist that they are good, not evil. Patients must not only discover this from what the therapist tells them, they must also perceive it in their therapist's attitude and feelings toward them. As the realization that they are good grows within them, the fear begins to abate and they gain new courage to continue on the road to recovery.

Little by little, the therapist must encourage patients to act less from motives of fear. For example, when patients are constantly held back by fear of committing a morally wrong act, the therapist must explain to them that there cannot be any question of committing a morally wrong act or sin unless they know what they are doing and freely will to do it. Moral laws provide the norms for controlled human actions, but persons with fear-based repressive disorders are not capable of this, at least not in matters influenced by their fear, for in these matters the normal subordination of the emotional life to reason is lacking. Every motive that stimulates a patient's fear must be eliminated and replaced by motives supplied by the therapist that do not stimulate the fear. In some persons who cannot be moved by any motives, the therapist may have to rely on his or her authority to provide the motive to act less and less out of fear.

If the therapist succeeds in this task, the repression will automatically diminish, with the result that various repressed emotions will begin to emerge and manifest themselves. This is a favorable sign and proves that the repression is losing its strength. It then becomes the major task of the therapist to guide and help these patients by providing a reasonable solution for emerging conflicts and feelings. However, when there is no chance of guiding these feelings in a reasonable manner, due to the fact that they have developed an abnormal intensity as a result of repression over a long period, *the therapist must permit them to be expressed.* To do otherwise, to forbid their expression, is tantamount to forcing these patients to repress their feelings again, which only makes their condition worse.

Frequently, when a repression in which religious concepts played a role begins to recede, these patients will express violent antireligious sentiments. When a patient has repressed sexual feelings, they may surge up strongly in the course of therapy.[3] If a patient has repressed feelings of hate and anger toward unsympathetic members of his or her family, these may now break through and lead to a complete severing of these relationships. It is up to the therapist to handle these situations and to see that the released emotions do not progress beyond reasonable and just limits. Although these emotions of hate and anger must indeed be released as far as the patient's recovery is concerned, this does not mean that they must be relived again or expressed directly to others. At this stage of therapy, the therapist must proceed with the utmost circumspection and show great prudence in the advice given, for this provides the patient with a reasonable motive for his or her actions and makes it unnecessary to repress further.

In particular, the therapist must refrain from directly telling these patients to express their repressed emotions or from indirectly doing or saying anything that might bring on this expression. When the therapist realizes that certain emotions have been repressed, he or she may be quite

3. For more on the subject of morality and the expression of emerging sexual feelings *see* p. 111.

easily tempted to lead these patients to do things that are related to these emotions. From a therapeutic viewpoint, however, this is incorrect, for as long as these emotions are not expressed spontaneously, patients are not yet prepared to deal with them, and the fear must still be assumed to be too strong. If, as a result of the therapist's influence, these patients are made to feel that they must express what was repressed, they have no choice but to repress their fear with other emotions, and thus they do precisely what they should not do. Freud realized this quite well when he warned against any aggressive approach in psychoanalysis.

The advice that one must *never force the expression of repressed emotions* in persons with fear-based repressive disorders is merely a special application of the general principle not to force their fear. Although they must learn not to be guided by fear in their actions, they should do this only to such a point as is indicated by the actual circumstances and by their own condition at any given stage in the treatment. Practically all patients know, without being told, how far they can go. If at times they feel that they are no match for their fear, they *must suffer it passively rather than try to overcome it at any cost*. If a patient who is afraid to cross streets can reasonably avoid doing so, he should not force himself to cross the street on those occasions when the fear is too strong. He must do so only when he feels up to it. To do it any differently means repressing.

Repressed emotions must emerge gradually. The process of recovery is one of continued interaction between the decrease of repression on the one hand, and the emergence of repressed emotions and the solving of conflicts on the other. As the fear diminishes, the emotional life becomes more free, and this in turn lessens the fear. Gradually, the emotions regain their proper values and become amenable to rational guidance; the emotionally determined, and thus *entirely subjective, values which persons with neurotic disorders attach to things* gradually take their place in the objective scale of rationally determined human values. With this, they are liberated from their compulsions and become persons capable of true human acts.

It hardly seems necessary to remark that this therapy, which respects the natural relationships within the emotional life and permits its healthy elements to grow gradually and spontaneously, cannot be completed in a few days or weeks. Its duration depends entirely on the depth of the repression, and thus on the innate disposition and the age of these patients. The more favorable the innate disposition, or, in other words, the greater the natural tendency of the emotional life to be guided by reason, the more favorable the prognosis. The younger patients are at the time they start treatment, the greater the ease with which their recovery can be effected. Moreover, the course of therapy may be influenced to a considerable extent by external circumstances, for if these are detrimental, they may well retard the patient's progress.

Patients must have regular contact with their therapist, although the actual frequency of visits depends on individual circumstances. In general, therapy may begin with weekly visits of one hour; more frequent visits are seldom necessary or indicated, for patients needs ample time to absorb and reflect upon their impressions after each interview. Their further progress will indicate when the visits can be spaced farther apart and when they can be discontinued altogether.

Therapy of Energy-Based Repression

In energy-based repressive disorders the objects of repression are potentially the same as those in fear-based repressive disorders. If they happen to be the human person's most fundamental drives—the sexual drive and the drive for self-realization[4]—the repressive process will have the most serious consequences in terms of neurotic symptomatology. However, here the similarity ends, for the repression takes place in persons with a psychological makeup which is entirely different from that of persons with fear-based repression. They are courageous people, full of confidence in their own strength; in fact, their greatest mistake lies in the fact that they overestimate their strength and believe that they can achieve the impossible, namely, the successful repression of the emotional life. Yet it is in this impossible undertaking that they suffer a crushing defeat.

In these people, excessive emotional energy and activity dominates the entire psychological life and particularly the rest of the emotional life. They never allow themselves the free expression of their feelings; the will controls and determines every emotion to such an extent that every spontaneous emotional manifestation is lacking in them. The most natural human emotions become more foreign to them with the ever increasing atrophy of their emotional life; they do everything in a deliberate manner.

---

4. With all their energetic striving for achievement, persons with energy-based repressive disorders nevertheless repress their innate drive for self-realization which also demands the expression of their natural emotions.

The two chief characteristics of this type of repressive disorder—the hypertrophy of the emotions of the assertive drive and the atrophy of the emotions of the pleasure appetite—determine the task of the psychotherapist. On the one hand the therapist must try to diminish and dissolve the excessive energy, while on the other he or she will attempt to restore the repressed emotions of the pleasure appetite to their proper place and function. Either achievement presents a difficult challenge, for persons with energy-based repression carry a deep conviction that their own way of life is the correct one. While persons with fear-based repressive disorders cannot help but realize that there is something wrong in their emotional life, persons with energy-based repression have no such thoughts; in fact, they firmly believe the opposite to be true. When actually faced with the fact that they are bothered by neurotic symptoms, they consider this merely the result of insufficient will power and will make every effort to repress even more deeply. This is the reason why persons with energy-based repressive disorders generally lack insight into their illness, and why it must be considered an important step in the right direction when the therapist succeeds in changing their minds on these matters.

Rest is one of the first things that the therapist should prescribe for persons with energy-based repression, especially when their excessive activity has led to psychological and physical exhaustion of such proportions that they have finally been prompted to seek psychotherapeutic help. It is here that the therapist immediately runs into opposition from these persons, who seldom are willing to accept advice to take a rest. Being idle is foreign and distasteful to their philosophy of life. They will endure such an enforced rest period only so long as their health prevents them from being active, but as soon as they feel their former strength returning, they want to get going again.

It becomes even more difficult when the excessive energy chiefly involves the inner life of these patients, for in the case of psychological overactivity a period of physical rest is of no benefit whatever, and the therapist must try to arrange for more effective *relaxation*. Here, too, however, these patients will cooperate only as long as they have no psychological reserves and really have no other choice in the matter. The therapist, therefore, will have to exert a reasonable degree of pressure in order to protect these patients against their own mistaken attitudes.

Rest alone, however, is not enough. It may arrest the progress of the neurotic illness and may at times cause some of its symptoms to disappear, so that patients will be somewhat better prepared to function again at their former level, but it does not affect the cause of the disorder. A causal therapy in these patients must attack the very mainspring of their pathological activity. To do so, it is best to distinguish between what we may call a *volitionally* determined energy-based repressive disorder and a more *intellectually* determined one.

In the volitionally determined energy-based repressive disorder, the cause of the excessive energy is the *determination of the will* to reach a certain goal in life. The will becomes so strong that it begins to dominate these persons, making them eliminate and disregard their emotional life to the point that the emotions are repressed when this is deemed necessary in order to reach their goal. Although such an attitude unerringly distorts the true nature of the human person, it seldom leads to a genuine neurotic disorder in the strict sense of the word, because in such cases those emotions whose repression is particularly prone to produce a neurotic disorder, namely, the sexual drive and the drive for self-realization, are usually not involved. Moreover, whatever feelings are repressed in these cases are usually repressed not in childhood, but at a later age. Yet there are cases—like those individuals described by Alfred Adler as being driven by their "will-to-power"—in which persons are obsessed even in their younger years by a powerful desire to achieve something great. It is easy to see how a true neurotic disorder can result in these cases if this burning desire has led to the repression of the sexual drive. Naturally, the therapist must be able to recognize the presence of this particular driving force, which, in view of the clinical picture presented by these persons, is seldom a difficult task. It may be much more difficult to make patients see themselves as they really are, to make them understand why they drive themselves so unrelentingly. Yet, this is an absolute necessity if these patients are to change their attitudes at least to the extent that it will be effective in reducing their untiring striving for the desired goal.

Although in most cases these patients are not entirely unaware of what is driving them on, they will rarely be inclined to admit it, and certainly not as something wrong or unhealthy. In this respect, they differ fundamentally from persons with fear-based repressive disorders, for their strivings are determined predominantly by rational motives. Whatever they do is done because they consider it right and proper, and they are much less subject to emotional reactions as compared with those patients who are driven by fear. Their desire for superior achievements, their eagerness to make something of their lives, or their longing to be all-powerful, are the things they feel and believe give meaning to their lives. To give this up, to change their outlook, requires a complete modification of their personality. Frequently, nothing short of a serious psychological and emotional collapse will open their eyes to the truth and make them realize that their philosophy of life, which brought on this disaster, could not possibly be the right attitude for any human being.

At any rate, the therapist must try to provide patients who have a volitionally determined energy-based repressive disorder with a correct understanding of these matters, even though this may be a difficult and time-consuming task. If the therapist succeeds in this, however, the patient's recovery will be assured in principle. If the therapist does not succeed in giving the necessary insight, the chances of recovery are nil, and all that can be hoped for is that these patients will benefit from symptomatic therapy.

Finally, in the rare case in which the patient is absolutely unaware of what originally moved him or her to become so excessively energetic, a systematic analysis might be the means of bringing about the desired recovery. This, however, is the exception, for in ordinary cases a systematic analysis is definitely not indicated.

The more intellectually determined energy-based repressive disorder develops when the excessive energy is a reaction to a *mistaken understanding of moral and ascetical obligations*. When persons believe that they owe it to their intellectual and spiritual life to suppress their emotions, and when these persons have an innate disposition to be energetic, they will use all their willpower to oppose the workings of their emotions and repress them. Likewise, if they believe it necessary to reject only one particular aspect of their emotional life, such as the sexual drive, they will do so in the same manner; however, in this case, the repression does not remain restricted to the sexual drive but will gradually spread to other areas of the emotional life.

Yet another false belief leads to the development of an energy-based repressive disorder: the mistaken idea of what persons can accomplish spiritually by virtue of their own natural powers. As human nature is imperfect, human beings cannot achieve perfection merely by their natural powers alone. They are obliged to do what they reasonably can, but since it is God who in the end restores human nature, the only proper attitude for a person is to surrender to God's operation in his or her soul. When persons conduct their lives as if everything depends solely on their human powers, they may easily come to overestimate them; from here, it is but a step to train and exercise them to such an inordinate degree that they hypertrophy and bring on an energy-based repressive disorder.

When such a person seeks psychotherapy, the first task of the therapist is to *correct these mistaken notions*. Naturally, this will often be difficult, not only because the patient's whole life has been determined by these notions, and years of application have made them an integral part of their personality, but also because the psychotherapist must enter a field in which he or she is not an expert, at least not officially. The therapist must touch upon matters of moral theology, philosophy, and religion, in which some patients have greater knowledge than the therapist. Thus it may be necessary to consult a recognized expert in this field, for as long as mistaken beliefs are not corrected, the cause of the illness remains.

The therapist must not only combat the excessive activity and energy, he or she must also aim at the *restoration of the repressed emotions*. These are frequently so deeply repressed in persons with energy-based repressive disorders that there remains hardly a trace of the most normal human feelings, especially of the feeling of love. These patients have become hardened and callous, and, what is worse, they often regard these qualities not as a sign of imperfection, but as highly desirable. Since at times they do not have the slightest notion of what might be wrong with them, the therapist is faced with the long and arduous task of correcting this situation. The therapist must start out from the small amount of feeling that may remain and try to persuade these patients not to oppose these feelings but to permit them to grow. In this way, it may be possible for the innate humane emotions to develop gradually, provided the energy is made to recede simultaneously. Here, too, we see a constant interaction between the repressing emotion and the repressed natural feelings; for the more the activity of the repressing emotion of energy is tempered, the more the hidden natural emotions can emerge; and vice versa, the greater the emergence of normal "humane" emotions, the less the restraining influence of the pathological energy.

What is important in fear-based repression is even more so in energy-based repression; namely, that this must be a *gradual and spontaneous process* in which the therapist *does not intentionally activate these emotions*. To do otherwise would be absolutely wrong, for it results in unnatural, deliberate will-acts, rather than in naturally emerging emotions. This is a real danger in persons with energy-based repressive disorders. As soon as they have realized that the absence of a certain feeling represents an imperfection and that they cannot recover without it, they will employ all their sensory energies to restore it to its rightful place. They want to feel love, they want so intensely to be happy, that they may face the issue and actually retard the normal growth of this feeling. These persons must *aim at passivity* in their psychological life; for them this is the most difficult thing there is, but it is the only way to recovery.

The same holds true in regard to the repressed emotions that may emerge in persons with energy-based repression, in much the same fashion as we observed in those with fear-based repression. They should not try to push them back, as that would lead without fail to repression. As long as they are not capable of guiding these emotions in a rational manner, their hypertrophied energy will be only too eager to take over control. Likewise, these patients should not try to arouse the emotions they know have been repressed, for if they do this, they anticipate the recovery process and inten- sify their pathological energy.

It is the therapist who must provide the guiding hand at all times. To be able to do so, the therapist must possess each patient's full trust. Although not different from persons with fear-based repression, the trust that persons with energy-based repression have in the therapist is not emo- tional; it is determined by an intellectual, calculating attitude. These per- sons consider the therapist a suitable means for effecting their emotional recovery; they do not establish a warm personal rapport with the therapist. There is nothing resembling transference as we observe it in persons with fear-based repression, at least not in the early stages of treatment, and fre- quently not even at a later stage. If at some time this personal rapport is established with a patient, it must be interpreted as a sign of progress be- cause it means that the patient's feelings have been moved; yet it never is of the same decisive significance as in the person with fear-based repression. Persons with energy-based repression are too accustomed to set their own course in life to be able to feel this dependence on their therapist as a neces- sity. Most likely this is also due to the greater influence of their intellect on their emotional life.

Finally, it seems appropriate to ask here whether a systematic analy- sis is ever indicated in persons with an energy-based repressive disorder. Although we have already considered this possibility for the volitionally determined energy-based repressive disorder, we must repeat the ques- tion for energy-based repression in general. Again we must reply in the negative, because such an analysis tends to intensify patients' excessive preoccupation with themselves. These patients have always been intent on maintaining deliberate control over their emotions and have succeeded in mastering all their spontaneous manifestations. An analytic approach would only encourage this deliberate control, because they would then use every ounce of energy in analyzing and interpreting repressed material, thus aggravating the very process from which the therapist wants to free them. Therefore, the only proper method of therapy with these patients is to allow their emotions to grow spontaneously, without interference or assistance from their own consciously employed energies.

Therapy of Camouflaged Fear-Based Repression

In this syndrome, a combination of fear-based and energy-based repression, the fundamental reason for the repression is fear, although the repression itself is effected by energy. It occurs in people who are forceful by nature, but whose youthful emotions inspired a certain amount of fear, which led them to repress these emotions by their own willpower. The therapy, therefore, must be aimed at the fundamental fear and at the energy activated by this fear.

It must be recalled, however, that in this type of neurotic disorder the repression is always preceded by a judgment of the intellect; the repressive process is set in motion not because the basic fear itself represses, but because it leads to a judgment that calls for repression. Consequently, the first thing the therapist must do is the same as in cases of intellectually determined energy-based repression; namely, *the therapist must correct the patient's erroneous judgments*. These patients must be made to see that it is wrong to repress feelings that made them fearful; they must come to understand that the only proper thing to do is to guide their emotions by reason. Only this understanding can halt further progress of the repressive process and make it possible for them to let their repressed emotions emerge. As this is a *conditio sine qua non* for their recovery, and as these patients are usually extremely intelligent, every effort must be made to give them an intellectually satisfying insight into these matters. Once this has been accomplished in a manner similar to that explained for persons with energy-based repressive disorders, it will be possible for the therapist to help them diminish and eventually halt the repression. As long as these patients have not gained the necessary understanding, however, their basic fear will continue to activate their energy.

This fundamental fear, therefore, is the focal point of the therapeutic process, notwithstanding the necessity of tempering the energy. As these patients do not have a natural and innate disposition to achieve great things, their excessively developed energy is not a natural outgrowth of temperament. They are endowed with fundamentally well-balanced personalities in which, however, *the energy has been stimulated unduly by acquired fears*; these, of course, will always continue to activate their energy unless corrected. In this respect, the therapist must follow the approach outlined for fear-based repression. Here, too, patients must have a feeling of confidence in their therapist, even though this feeling will have a more intellectual coloring than it does in persons with true fear-based repression. Yet the need for trust is equally great in both, for in both the fear must be counterbalanced by a feeling of confidence; both need to be assured by a feeling of stability and safety.

Furthermore, the therapist must give patients the necessary reassurance in respect to all the fears they may have about their past, the emotions which are emerging here and now in spite of the repression, and all repressed emotions which may and will do so in the future. What we said in this connection in our discussion of the treatment of fear-based repression also applies *a fortiori* in these patients.

The appearance of repressed fears in this type of neurotic disorder is a most striking occurrence. Endowed with a strong nature, these patients never wanted fear to enter their psychological life; rather, they had a strong will to eliminate it, and in order to do so, they repressed it by means of their emotional energy, because as yet they were incapable of controlling it rationally. It was unavoidable that this fear should remain deeply rooted in them and continue to exert its influence unconsciously. In the unconscious, the fear spread in all directions, manifesting itself, in spite of all their efforts, in all kinds of symptoms, however indirect or disguised. They never allowed themselves to be dominated by this fear, and although they tried to conquer it again and again, they were never able to succeed entirely.

It follows that if the repressing activity of the emotional energy begins to weaken as a result of psychotherapeutic treatment, this repressed fear will gradually emerge, even to the point of attacks of intense fear. It will be up to the therapist to help patients during these attacks; patients must be allowed to express their fear freely; the therapist must never oppose this or aggravate the repression by telling patients to get hold of themselves. Allowing patients to express these emerging fears, no matter how emotionally charged these episodes may be, represents a beneficial catharsis for them. For a while, it may seem that their condition is getting worse, but this is only apparent, and after a while patients experience deep calm as a result of these emotional discharges. When these patients are no longer repressing, the fear can be discharged, and as a result it loses its stimulating effect on the energy. As this in turn permits the emergence of the repressed emotions, it becomes evident that the reintegrating process can take its course.

Mortification Therapy of Sexual Obsessions and Compulsions*

We want to include in this book a special discussion of the moral aspects of our psychotherapy in those persons with obsessive-compulsive repression who have repressed their *sexual* feelings since early life. In our previous writings we have deliberately avoided giving details of this delicate process because it lends itself to misunderstanding and possible abuse.

For example, moral theologians who do not understand the fundamental difference between neurotic repression and rational guidance of emotions, might conclude that our therapeutic advice fails to meet the criteria of moral laws. Others might accuse us of letting the end justify the means, if they were to believe that we directly prescribe, rather than merely tolerate, the inevitable transient behavioral consequences of our therapeutic advice. Others again might jump to the conclusion that our therapeutic advice—*always given to an individual with an obsessive-compulsive repressive disorder and never to all such neurotic persons in general*—constitutes license for all persons with neurotic disorders to commit objectively immoral acts. This risk would be even greater if they failed to grasp the difference between "may" and "must" in the context of the clinical and philosophical arguments presented in this discussion.

The risk of possible abuse of this presentation is inherent in the currently popular trend to be one's own therapist by applying self-help techniques contained in books or passed around by word of mouth. As far as our particular therapy is concerned, no one should proceed on his or her own, neither in the matter of diagnosing one's own illness, nor in applying our therapeutic directives. Of even greater danger, especially in Charismatic Renewal and Pentecostal circles, is the popular practice of "inner healing" by minimally qualified persons. They may possess the necessary faith and goodwill toward their brothers and sisters in Christ who have neurotic disorders, but too many are either similarly affected without realizing it, or lack the professional knowledge necessary to effectively help severely afflicted patients short of a rarely occurring instantaneous cure. If these patients are also suffering from Emotional Deprivation Disorder, these minimally qualified persons would be *unable to sustain these patients* through the difficult and trying periods that occur during virtually all psychotherapeutic processes, once the initial beneficial effects of fraternal concern and prayers have worn off.

We repeatedly see patients with this combination of two neurotic disorders, or with only Emotional Deprivation Disorder, who have made considerable progress toward maturity through the prayers, kindness, attention and time spent with them by Christian "therapists," only to have been abandoned during the difficult time of psychosexual integration by these inadequately qualified persons. This seems to happen not only as a result of a lack of professional qualification, but also because these persons engaged in "inner healing" were themselves troubled by significant immaturity in this area of their personality development. *This abandonment, often with the implicit or explicit accusation that the persons prayed for were at fault, can have disastrous consequences for these patients.* Their sense of self-worth and confidence, gradually acquired in the early stages of caring and praying, can be destroyed and replaced by severe depression, feelings of guilt and hopelessness about ever being whole.

Unfortunately, this could also happen to a person under the care of a professionally qualified person, for not all of them are necessarily psychosexually mature and integrated, much less cognizant of the moral aspects of psychosexual development. The fact that one is under the care of a professionally qualified psychiatrist or psychotherapist is no guarantee that the moral requirements for a successful therapy of obsessive-compulsive repression and/or Emotional Deprivation Disorder will be respected.

To minimize the possibility of such unfortunate occurrences we suggest that prayerful non-professionals make every effort to pray for inner healing of persons with serious psychological disorders in cooperation with a Christian psychotherapist, preferably, but not necessarily, one who is accustomed to praying with his or her patients. When this is done, patients with a major emotional illness have a much better chance to be healed because the healing effects of the therapy are enriched by the superior healing power of God's love, transmitted by the nonprofessional's compassionate prayers.

No matter how considerable these aforementioned risks, we consider ourselves obliged to provide our colleagues with the details of our therapy. By not doing so we would deprive the morally responsible psychiatrist or psychotherapist of an approach that has proven to be of inestimable value for persons with obsessive-compulsive repressive disorders. Another reason for this presentation is our desire for moral theologians to be fully informed of the psychopathological aspects of our therapy. In recent years, some Catholic moral theologians have considered it necessary to propose new pastoral guidelines, presumably in their concern for the large numbers of emotionally and spiritually afflicted Catholics. By means of this chapter we want to make it clear beyond a shadow of a doubt that *there is absolutely no need, either for the prevention or the treatment of neurotic disorders, to lower or abandon moral values* as has been done in the aforementioned pastoral guidelines.[5] On the contrary, these guidelines are certain to precipitate new forms of emotional and spiritual disorders, as we shall discuss in the last chapter of this book.

What is sorely needed in the treatment of obsessive-compulsive repressive disorders is the moral and spiritual guidance of well-informed moral theologians for both patients and psychotherapists. The prevention and eventual eradication of this emotional illness—for so many generations the chief source of unparalleled intense psychological and spiritual suffering—will be guaranteed through the combined efforts of knowledgeable psychotherapists and moral theologians. What follows is written primarily for them, and thus for the benefit of present and future generations of Christians.

When a person with an obsessive-compulsive repressive disorder knows that the psychotherapist's clinical advice in these delicate moral matters is understood by and has the full approval of the patient's spiritual director, the patient is able to shed any doubts which otherwise would have impeded, if not made impossible, the healing process. When the spiritual advisor has this understanding, all he or she needs to know is the exact diagnosis of the patient's condition. The spiritual advisor must know whether or not the patient has obsessive-compulsive repression, what particular type, and whether it is associated with Emotional Deprivation Disorder. With the patient's permission, this can be discovered by contacting the

---

5. *Human Sexuality—New Directions in American Thought*, A Study Commissioned by the Catholic Theological Society of America, Paulist Press, New York, 1977. *See* Appendix C for Dr. Baars' review of this book.

psychotherapist, making sure that nothing else concerning the patient will be discussed. This is a matter-of-course, not only because of the need to respect confidentiality and privileged communication, but also because the scrupulous patient is very sensitive, if not actually suspicious, of the possibility that the psychotherapist and spiritual advisor have agreed to their particular approach more on the basis of their compassion with the patient's plight, than on the absolute correctness—psychological and moral—of the principles on which the clinical advice is based. Only the latter will give the patient the moral certainty that the psychotherapist's directives can be safely followed.

The foregoing makes it clear that the moral theologian must have absolute certainty that the psychotherapist has a complete understanding of the moral aspects of the treatment process, aimed at the mortification of the emotions responsible for the repression of the patient's sexual feelings. When a moral theologian is consulted by a person who doubts the morality of his or her psychotherapist's therapeutic advice, the theologian should consider it an important duty to investigate the therapist's competence in these psycho-moral matters. The theologian can do this without divulging confidential and privileged information simply by asking the psychotherapist for an opportunity to discuss his or her clinical approach to persons suffering from obsessive-compulsive repression. Any conscientious psychotherapist will welcome such a request and make the necessary time available to discuss with the theologian all pertinent facets of the therapy of obsessive-compulsive repression. By proceeding in this way any misunderstandings, and worse, can be prevented.[6]

Having outlined these calculated risks and how to circumvent them, we can proceed with the presentation of our therapy in the expectation that no psychiatrist or psychotherapist, or for that matter any reader of this book, will use this information without fully grasping its psychological and moral implications.

Because persons with obsessive-compulsive repressive disorders cannot live a normal life as a result of the many and varied consequences of the chronic repression of their sexual feelings by fear or energy, or both, it is necessary for them to learn to undo this pathological process. We shall discuss this learning process for persons whose irrational fear or excessive

6. See for example, *Feeling and Healing Your Emotions*, by Conrad W. Baars, M.D. (rev. ed., Suzanne M. Baars & Bonnie N. Shayne, eds., Bridge-Logos, Gainesville, FL, 1979, 2003).

energy were excessively and prematurely stimulated by mistaken teachings on the part of their educators in their early life. Mistaken, either because their content had been lacking in clarity or should have been qualified, or because of the pedagogically premature presentation of correct content. (We do not discuss those patients in whom the fear or energy had their origin in traumatic sexual experiences early in life.)

In the individuals with obsessive-compulsive repression under consideration—always persons of superior intelligence with a naturally healthy emotional disposition, and possessed of sincere desire and strong will to do what is right—early observations and exposures to certain teachings and attitudes concerning sex always led to an overpowering usefulness judgment of "you must not," "you shall," or any similar form of "oughtism." It is especially the negative form in which the moral law is frequently expressed—"you must not," "thou shalt not,"—which later leads these youngsters to obsessive-compulsive repression because they believe that the moral law is a protest against and a condemnation of their sexual feelings. Deeply convinced of the correctness of their own interpretation of moral law, and identifying their interpretation with the objective meaning of moral law, these individuals draw the conclusion that their human feelings—especially the sexual feelings and so-called "negative emotions"[7]—are dangerous and must be mortified and gotten rid of.

These mistaken interpretations are most likely to be formed when educators—parents, teachers, relatives, and/or religious instructors—convey to these young persons, directly or indirectly, that sex is actually potentially harmful, if not an occasion of sin.

The histories of nearly all individuals with obsessive-compulsive repression, who have repressed everything sexual from an early age, is replete with stories of having been punished or threatened with going to hell when they were caught in "sex" play with other children; of never having received proper instruction on sexual matters because parents never talked about such things and showed disapproval or uneasiness when asked about these things by the child; of educators having put relatively heavy stress on the 6th and 9th commandments[8] compared with their presentation of the

---

7. Editors' Note: The authors are of the strong opinion that all emotions, whether unpleasant or not, are positive, inasmuch as they are part and parcel of psychological wholeness. Referring to emotions as negative can unintentionally reinforce their repression.

8. Editors' Note: The Sixth Commandment: "You shall not commit adultery." The Ninth Commandment: "You shall not covet your neighbor's wife."

other commandments; of having been made fearful of sex by their educators' own irrational fear of sexual matters, even when this was not verbally communicated; or of a particular educator's energetic pursuit of overcoming his or her own sexual feelings, thoughts and fantasies which in turn left its mark on the emotional life of the child.

When persons with this kind of background present themselves in whatever stage of their neurotic illness to the psychiatrist or psychotherapist, two basic things are necessary.

1. They must be taught that sex is a sense good to which the natural response should always be an arousal by the pleasure appetite (according to the principle that every emotional response has its origin in the object, not in the subject who experiences the emotion. For instance, if I love a rose, it is not because *I* arouse this emotion or will it, but because the qualities of the rose—shape, color, fragrance—stimulate my feeling of liking.) These patients must be given to understand that this sequence of events was never possible for them, because, from the beginning, sex had been presented to them as something harmful. This had left them no choice but to respond with an arousal of an emotion of their assertive drive, fear or energy. Even though it is true that sex is good, in persons with neurotic disorders, this intellectual knowledge is not accompanied by a *"feeling knowledge"* that sex is good.[9]

2. To enable patients to develop this *feeling knowledge,* the therapist must also help them to rid themselves of the cause of their repressing fear or energy, i.e., their usefulness judgment that sex is harmful. Since the usefulness judgment was formed and sustained by the admonition, "you *must not* feel pleasure in sexual things" (to mention only one of many such admonitions), the patient must learn and dare to substitute "I *may* feel pleasure in sexual things." Or, to give this advice a simple and practical form for all possible eventualities—feelings, fantasies, thoughts, memories, etc.—we tell them that the substitution of "you may" for "you must not" in sexual matters will eventually *set them free.*

They must learn to do this consistently in all matters pertaining to sex and associated feelings, if they too have been repressed, without exception. For if there were exceptions or limitations to this rule, these persons, and particularly scrupulous persons, would immediately begin to focus all their

9. The expressions "connatural knowledge" and "affective knowledge" are found in philosophy as well as in phenomenological philosophy. *See,* for instance *Summa Theologica,* I-II, 1. 45, a. 2.

attention on these limitations and exceptions, and thus keep their fears and anxieties alive.

One may object that the fear of sinning in sexual matters, i.e., the fear of committing a certain act, does not have to stimulate the fear of sexual feelings or fantasies. This, of course, is true for healthy, mature, and fully integrated persons, but the same cannot be said for persons with obsessive-compulsive repressive disorders. For it was the very fear that they might commit sinful acts in early life that led them to first suppress all such acts, and then to repress any feelings that might tempt them to commit such acts.

It is for this reason that the psychotherapist must help these patients to be consistent in the *mortification* of their fear or energy. They will do this by explaining that the acts which might follow their gradually emerging, gradually less intensely repressed, sexual feelings, e.g., masturbation, are in their case not the acts of a free person, and therefore not acts for which they are morally responsible. This follows from the observation that in persons with repressive disorders the repressing emotion has grown to such an intensity and strength that it has poised itself as a *wedge*, so to speak, between the sexual feelings and the will. In other words, the repressing emotion has taken it upon itself to assume the role of the will in dealing with sexual feelings.

It is precisely this abnormal situation of an emotion having eliminated the will that must be corrected by these patients. Because this is not an easy task, patients need all the help they can get; first, that of the therapist who will consistently support them with great patience and compassion, as well as with a flawless explanation, often repeated, of the moral and psychological aspects of their condition and its treatment. Second, if at all possible, that of an equally well informed spiritual director who will ease the burden for these patients, e.g., not allowing them to include in their confessions those acts and thoughts in which they lack freedom of the will.

Not infrequently, patients will object to their psychotherapist's assertion that their will is not free in sexual matters—while being free in other areas—and claim that they are able to will not to masturbate if they "really set their mind to it." We fully agree with this claim, but explain to these patients that what seems to be an act of their will is actually a repressive act. Their mistaken belief that sex and everything sexual is harmful, if not actually sinful, cannot but stimulate the repressive emotion, because reason and will are precluded from dealing with sexual matters. The thought of

gratifying their sexual desire through masturbation momentarily intensifies their emotion of fear or energy, with the result that the sexual act does
not take place at that moment.

Another indication that patients with obsessive-compulsive repressive
disorders are not free in sexual matters, is the increase in fear and restlessness that follows when they forego the gratification of the sex urge. In non-
neurotic persons, the freely renounced act of masturbation is followed by
calm and peace, and, in time, an ever greater ease in guiding and directing
their sexual desires in such a way that they lead a truly moral life. This is
in stark contrast to persons with obsessive-compulsive repression whose
repressing emotions gain in intensity over the years, and sooner or later
lead to obsessive preoccupation with sexual thoughts and fantasies, and
compulsive performance of acts they have always willed not to commit.
Because their disordered neurotic condition is foreign to human nature,
time is always against them. Sooner or later, their outwardly successful repressive mechanism will break down with all its frightening and disabling
consequences.

It is a common observation that persons with obsessive-compulsive
repression have an intense need, even in therapy, to continue relying on the
repressing emotion for the sake of leading a moral life. Persons with fear-
based repression are intensely afraid of mortifying their fear, because they
have always been led to believe—usually by authoritative sources—that
fear of sin is virtually the only way to lead a blameless moral life. Persons
with energy-based repression have always been attracted by the idea that
they can "earn" heaven by their own unrelenting efforts to do what is right
and virtuous, i.e., in their case, to relentlessly repress all sexual feelings. To
change this attitude is not at all an easy or appealing task, for either type of
disorder.

Because of this resistance of persons with obsessive-compulsive repressive disorders to become free persons—persons who rely on God to
protect them and are eager to surrender to Him in faith and trust—we offer
special help in the process of mortifying, of literally killing, the pathological
fear and energy. This help aims at making this process as easy and spontaneous as possible, so that these patients do not have to determine the
particular moral details of each and every occasion that they are aware of
a sexual desire, e.g., whether they have dwelled on a sexual fantasy longer
than they should; whether they allow themselves to experience the sexual
feeling longer than they should, and so on *ad infinitum*. This help is an

extension of our basic advice to substitute "you may" for "you must." We shall explain it in detail.

Our first directive is: "You may *everything*." Patients may fill in whatever verb would apply in a given circumstance. For example, whenever necessary they will remind themselves that "I may feel a sexual desire," "I may do everything," "I may think whatever I want," "I may look at whatever I want," etc.

We should explain here that the initial purely sexual repression has usually been extended to related feelings and concerns, e.g., sense experiences, sense pleasure, literature, movies, moral duty, etc. This implies that our first instruction also has to be applied to matters not immediately of a sexual nature. To give an example, scrupulous persons in addition to their primary fear of sex are often also fearful of a transgression of positive laws of the Church, e.g., the obligation to attend Mass on Sunday, to refrain from servile work on Sunday, and so on. Because their fear of a wrathful God must be transformed into a healthy reverence and love of God, they will repeatedly have to tell themselves, for example, "I may stay at home today, Sunday, and work all day in the yard;" or, "I may receive Holy Communion today because I desire it (even though I masturbated yesterday)."

Our second directive is: "For *you* there are *no rules, laws, or commandments*." This is a necessary instruction because it is precisely the person's *interpretation* of moral rules, laws and commandments, that have been the source of, and continue to stimulate, the repressing emotions in response to certain emotions and feelings which in themselves are good and natural. If a commandment is not interpreted by patients in the way it should be understood, namely as the help and support God intends it to be for them, then that interpretation is of no practical use in helping them to live a freely willed moral life. Instead they live a life full of anxiety and other neurotic symptoms because of that commandment.

By our instructing these patients that they are to ignore rules, laws and commandments, we free them of interpreting them in the wrong way. Persons with obsessive-compulsive repression are incapable of proper interpretation. This is an unavoidable consequence of their longtime inflexible understanding of, and rigid adherence to, these rules, laws and commandments, which know no alternative.

Persons who have repressed their sexual feelings and all related sexual thoughts and fantasies, usually come to believe that by following our instructions, they live in *freedom from* morality in the province of sexuality.

When they share this concern with their therapist they will learn, however, that they are on the way to *freedom for* morality. When their adherence to our directives gradually becomes easier, they feel as if a heavy stone has been rolled away from the spot where their sexual feelings have been buried alive. When at long last they are able to experience these feelings as they truly are, i.e., pleasurable, their nature, distorted in early life, is in the process of being restored.

In therapy, the person with obsessive-compulsive repression has to walk the same developmental path as the child does. The child's emotional life has to grow without unnatural obstructions if the child is to learn to conduct a truly moral life. Feelings and emotions are necessary to develop a connatural knowledge of the goodness of moral laws. The patient has to discover for himself or herself the feeling knowledge *and* the intellectual knowledge that moral laws are both good and necessary, since they are but the expression of human nature. This is a gradual process that takes less time than it does in children, because patients are already grown in many other areas of their personality; for instance, the same superior intellect that got them started on the path of neurotic repression will now also enable them to reverse the repressive process in a relatively short period of time. Of course, patients are always eager to attain their goal of moral freedom as soon as possible and will often try to shorten the interval between the last stage of the repression and the beginning of the natural guidance of their feelings and emotions by their intellect. However, each time these persons allow themselves to act in hasty anticipation of their ultimate goal, they discover that they are regressing to their previous state of repressing because of the reappearance of some of their neurotic symptoms. With the help of the psychotherapist, they again learn from these temporary setbacks and develop ever greater insight and the courage to proceed *gradually* in faith and confidence that their own developing nature is the best pace setter.

At this point, it is well to remind patients, and the reader, of the essential meaning of *the human person's free will*. This will deepen their grasp of the correctness of our teaching contained in the first two directives. It will also accentuate the nature of the goal they are pursuing with our therapy, the very goal they have never been able to attain in many years of neurotic efforts. This goal is for us to help each patient to become a person who is free to opt for or against God in the realization that they are fully dependent for their happiness on a loving, merciful and forgiving God.

When God created men and women in order that they would have the opportunity to share in His happiness, He willed them to have a say in the matter rather than impose His will for their happiness on them. For this reason He gave them a free will. He then indicated to them what would make them happy or unhappy. For the rest, He left it up to them to choose one way or the other. In other words, He told them, "You may do what you desire and will; I will see to it that you obtain what you have freely chosen. I will not get angry when you choose to do what I told you would make you unhappy, nor will I force upon you what is good for you, when you have chosen what is evil. I will not force heaven on you, when you have freely chosen hell. I so respect your free will that I will never interfere with it."

This, in our opinion, is the essential meaning of God's wish for human beings. However, it is self-evident that these things cannot be stated as such for all people at all times. To be of practical value, they must be formulated as commandments, laws or rules that can be understood by even the simplest person. Even a positive law, like, for example, "You must obey the speed limit" could be formulated, "You may obey or disobey the speed limit; if you obey it you will be happy to get to your destination without interference; if you disobey it you will be made to pay a fine."

The essence of a healthy upbringing is an attitude on the parts of educators which is in fundamental agreement with that of God. This means that they respect the need for children to become free human beings and abstain from anything that would interfere with that freedom, such as the undue stimulation of potentially repressing emotions. They can only do this if they have a reasonable trust in the basic goodness of every human being, i.e., that humans have continued to be oriented toward the good in spite of the imperfection of their nature caused by original sin. This trust implies that children will also learn from their faults and mistakes, because they interfere with finding what they really want—that which is truly good and fulfills their nature. The educator who lacks this trust in the fundamental orientation toward the good, and, in a certain way, believes that the evil is more attractive than the good, has no choice but to employ *training methods* that will force children to attain the good by means of fear or energetic pursuit.

We like to suggest to these educators that they think of laws and Commandments as road signs that show travelers what direction to take in order to reach their destination by the shortest and safest route. Such a sign does not say to travelers, "you *must* take this or that road," but rather, "you *may* go in this or that direction, but you are free to ignore this sign, and travel in the opposite direction. I have confidence that when you discover that you are not getting closer to your destination, or that you are lost, you will be more inclined in the future to mind road signs that want to help you to reach your destination by the safest and most reliable route."

This is not to say that the "must" and "ought" form of the moral law is merely of importance as instruction, and does not belong to the essence of the law itself. On the contrary, "must" and "ought" belong to the very essence of moral law and moral value. What our remarks on this subject have intended to convey is that this "ought" and "must" do not express an obligation from outside our heart and mind.

Thomas Aquinas said that the moral law is a law of the spirit, of the mind, and is therefore intelligible, capable of being understood as reasonable and connatural to our being. In order to be understood and loved, however, as well as obeyed with joy, there has to be an integration of mind and heart, an inner unity of the emotional and intellectual lives. The person who has not attained that integration is focused more on the "ought" form of the law, in contrast to the mature, integrated individual who is attracted more to the goodness of the law (according to the old Aristotelian principle: "a thing is received according to the mode (way of being) of the receiver").[10]

Because it is precisely this kind of integration that is the goal of our therapy for persons with obsessive-compulsive repression, it also prepares them for a better, more profound understanding of the Beatitudes, the declarations of supreme blessedness pronounced by Christ in His Sermon on the Mount. These Beatitudes, e.g., "Blessed are the poor in spirit, for the reign of God is theirs; blessed are they who hunger and thirst for holiness . . . ," are formulated exactly as mature, integrated persons would put them into words; not in the "ought" form but in the way they themselves would experience the law: "Supremely happy is he who. . . ."

We must return to the subject matter under discussion, namely our special aid for persons with obsessive-compulsive repression to successfully mortify their overdeveloped fear or energy. Our third directive is, *"The pleasure you experience as the result of abiding by the other directives is the most perfect thing for you."* This particular part is usually very startling to

10. Quidquid recipitur secundum modum recipientis recipitur—Thomas Aquinas, *Commentary on Aristotle's ON THE SOUL*, Book II, Lesson 24, No. 552, and *Summa Theologica*, I, 84, 1.

the patient, as it undoubtedly is to many a reader. Its explanation and justification are as follows.

We must remember that patients with obsessive-compulsive repressive disorders have used their repressing emotions to repress, directly and by association, all the emotions of the pleasure appetite.[11] The complete reversal of the natural and healthy relationship between the primacy of the pleasure appetite and the ancillary function of the assertive drive, has increasingly deprived these patients of the capacity to be joyful. Success in leading the moral life gives them a satisfaction that they may believe to be happiness; however, unless a person's satisfaction derived from willing and doing good is accompanied by the feeling of joy, his or her happiness as a human being is incomplete. Even persons of good will need the full complement of their pleasure emotions in order to experience the happiness for which they are created. More than anybody else they deserve a well-developed pleasure appetite. Without it, they cannot experience the joy of living affectively.

Although we have written on this topic in our other publications, we want to briefly discuss this most important topic for the benefit of those readers whose first introduction to our ideas is this book. We define *affectivity* as "the habitual disposition of the heart to be moved by the good of the other (and other things and beings) and to act on his or her behalf." Affectivity consists of the fully or adequately developed emotions of the pleasure appetite in their close interaction with the intuitive intellect. Persons living *affectively* find their greatest happiness in what is good for others, more so than what is good for themselves. For them the good, the happiness of the other is the fundamental source of their own fulfillment and greatest happiness as an authentic human being.

This capacity or disposition, however, is the very thing that has been made impossible, or at least strongly diminished, in persons with obsessive-compulsive repressive disorders. Healing for them will exist in the reduction and ultimate elimination of their overdeveloped emotions of the assertive drive insofar as they interfere with the emotions of the pleasure appetite, and in the belated flowering of their atrophied, underdeveloped feelings of love, desire, joy, affection, tenderness, compassion, and kindness.

It is understandable that the reduction of *effectivity*, i.e., "the habitual disposition of the mind to see and grasp the other (and other things and

---

11. According to the principle that one cannot pick and choose to repress one emotion without involving other emotions in the repressing process.

beings) for his own utilitarian purposes," and the emergence of one's affectivity, has to be a gradual process. Everything in nature grows and matures gradually, and this law holds true in our therapy. During this more or less time-consuming process, patients with obsessive-compulsive repression can help themselves in the development of this sorely needed affectivity in two ways.

First they whittle away at the repressive force of their overgrown fear or energy with the aid of the above-mentioned three directives, and allow themselves breathing room for the emerging emotions of the pleasure appetite. This part of the growth process is facilitated by our directives to the patient, "If what you do and experience as the result of abiding by the first two directives is pleasing to you, then you are assured that doing so is the most perfect thing for you."

Second, they create opportunities for the growth of their pleasure emotions. This may be done by living at a slower pace, by eating more slowly and savoring their food, by exposing themselves to whatever is good and beautiful in nature and handcrafted works of art, by taking time to learn new truths, for example, in non-utilitarian, i.e., diploma-oriented ways, for truth is also a source of joy. This second way often presents considerable difficulty for patients with obsessive-compulsive repression, however, because they take life most seriously in those areas in which the repression of the pleasurable and enjoyable, and the pursuit of what is difficult and arduous have a prominent place.

Therefore, they need constant intellectual and emotional support from the therapist's intellectual understanding of their difficult situation, and from the therapist's compassionate and affectionate participation in their sufferings as well as their joys whenever they succeed in new applications of our basic directive, "You may everything; for you there are no rules, laws or commandments; and whatever is pleasing and gives you joy is the most perfect thing."

This basic outline of our particular advice to persons with obsessive-compulsive repression requires some *additional comments and warnings*.

1. Sooner or later the patient will ask the psychotherapist whether our advice applies to sexual activities involving another person. Our answer to this question is, of course, in the negative. No person, whether in good psychological health or with a neurotic disorder, is allowed to involve another person in an act which is objectively morally wrong. This reply seldom produces difficulties for persons with obsessive-compulsive repression,

because in order to abide by this advice it is not necessary for them to re-press their sexual desires toward another person. All that is necessary is a well-developed sense of justice, something most, if not all, of these persons already possess.

2. *At no time during therapy is the psychotherapist to instruct the patient to masturbate or do anything else that is morally wrong.* No person can do this without being guilty of a moral wrong. Moreover, such advice or instruction would also be *psychologically irresponsible and counter-productive* because patients would then start to will these acts. Persons with fear-based repression will do this by repressing their fear, persons with energy-based repression by intensifying their energy. In both instances, these acts would not contribute to the goal of therapy at all, namely to permanently eliminate the repressing activity of the emotions of fear and energy.

The objectively immoral acts which patients may happen to perform during therapy are to be *tolerated* because the patient could only abstain from them by repression. That this is morally permissible has been made clear by Pope Pius XII in his allocution to the delegates attending the Fifth International Congress of Psychotherapy and Clinical Psychology, held at Rome in 1953.

> From this a conclusion follows for psychotherapy. In the presence of material sin it cannot remain neutral. It can, for the moment, tolerate what remains inevitable. But it must know that God cannot justify such an action. With still less reason can psychotherapy counsel a patient to commit material sin on the ground that it will be without subjective guilt. Such a counsel would also be erroneous if this action were regarded as necessary for psychic easing of the patient and thus as being part of the treatment. One may never counsel a conscious action which would be a deformation and not an image of the divine perfection. (*Osservatore Romano*, 16 April 1953).

3. The foregoing can be expressed in still another way. In the therapy of patients with obsessive-compulsive repression, *passivity* on the part of the therapist is of much greater importance than activity, such as making patients do things, training them to assert themselves, insisting that they feel this or that emotion or feeling, etc. Their repressed feelings, no matter what they are, sexual or non-sexual, are *never to be aroused intentionally.* The therapist never knows if patients will be able to cope with emerging feelings or when they will be able to do so. Only when an emotion rises to

the conscious level in a natural and spontaneous manner will patients be able to deal with it.

The same is true for passivity on the part of patients themselves, particularly when they have an energy-based repressive disorder. They must be passive in the sense that they must wait for the repressed emotions and feelings to make themselves felt, instead of trying to arouse them deliberately by making themselves do things for which they have no desire yet. However, they may be active in halting or reducing neurotic activities that make it impossible for the repressed emotions to emerge. For example, they may force themselves to take regular rest periods if their drive for achievement or perfection has never allowed them to do so; or they may try and eat more slowly so they can savor their food; or they may take a leisurely bath instead of a hurried shower, to name only a few examples of what persons with obsessive-compulsive repression can do to facilitate the emergence of long-repressed feelings and emotions.

4. For this therapy to be successful and lead to complete healing, the therapist must have a well-developed understanding of the psychological and spiritual matters involved. He or she must have full knowledge of what is morally wrong and morally right. Since the most effective teaching of a truth is the teacher living the truth, it follows that the *therapist must live what he or she teaches the patient*. Persons with obsessive-compulsive repression are quick in realizing whether the therapist is authentic in this therapy, morally as well as affectively. If he or she is less than authentic in both areas patients will not develop the trust they require to learn to surrender to God through their therapist.

5. What we have already said about the futility of self-therapy can benefit from a qualification. Very intelligent persons with obsessive-compulsive repression who cannot see a psychotherapist regularly, could successfully proceed on their own, once the nature of their illness and the appropriate therapy have been fully explained to them by the therapist, who has also advised them of the exact nature of their diagnosis. One of our case histories in Chapter V exemplifies the truth of this observation.[12] However, under no circumstances should persons try to diagnose themselves. They would not know, for example, the difference between obsessive-compulsive repression and Obsessive-Compulsive Personality Disorder. They should seek the advice of a competent therapist to know whether they can benefit from our therapy.

12. *See* p. 143.

6. Sometimes we are asked if our therapy is limited to Catholics. Our answer is negative. It is also applicable to other Christians and members of other non-Christian faiths, if their obsessive-compulsive repression was also the result of similar distortions in teaching the tenets of their faith in early life. It has happened more than once that one of our non-Catholic patients with obsessive-compulsive repression has converted to Catholicism simply because he or she realized that our psychological principles are in total conformity with the basic tenets of the Catholic faith. There cannot be any fundamental conflict between sound moral theology and sound philosophical anthropology.

As psychiatrists and psychotherapists, we must never forget that we are not treating a psychological disorder, but a human being whose suffering is both of a psychological and physical nature. Both the psychic and physical suffering of many persons with neurotic disorders is such that in addition to the primary psychological approach described in the preceding pages, the conscientious and judicious use of physical and pharmacological treatment is indicated. When using ancillary treatment methods, psychiatrists must preserve the proper balance between primary and secondary treatment methods and guard against the danger of using secondary treatments, particularly pharmacological treatment, to the exclusion, or near exclusion, of primary psychotherapy. This danger is greatest when the case load of the psychiatrist is heaviest and time available for psychotherapy is limited. The remedy for this situation can never be more effective psychotropic drugs alone, for drugs by themselves are never sufficient to heal disturbances caused by psychological factors. The profession needs more effective psychotherapies, both short and long term, which in turn requires a better understanding of the neurotic process and of the difference between repressive disorders and Emotional Deprivation Disorder.

We do not intend to discuss the pros and cons of the many different medications available—sedatives for insomnia, tranquilizers for tension and anxiety, anti-depressants for depression, stimulants for inertia, analgesics for headache and backache, and so on. There is no shortage of information on the proper use of these various medications.

Insomnia is a common complaint among patients with neurotic disorders, even though most persons with energy-based repression and Emotional Deprivation Disorder have no trouble at all in this regard. The former sleep soundly all through the night and rarely remember dreaming. The latter sometimes give the impression that they use sleep as an escape, as many of them sleep much longer than the average person, twelve or more hours at a stretch. Persons with anxiety disorders, and those with Emotional Deprivation Disorder whose condition is complicated by a superimposed anxiety disorder, frequently experience difficulty in falling asleep. Often their sleep is fitful because of frightening dreams. These persons usually require, at least temporarily, some sedative to provide a good night's sleep and adequate rest.

Throughout their treatment, however, we remain alert to the psychological aspects of insomnia and direct our efforts toward the gradual resolution of its underlying causes. In many persons with neurotic disorders the main cause for insomnia is the effort to bring about sleep, instead of allowing sleep to overcome oneself gradually and surrendering to it passively. This particular attitude toward the process is usually an integral part of their fear of not being in control of every situation, of not daring to be unprepared for spontaneous and natural happenings or encounters. This attitude, which also accounts for their fear of general anesthesia, results from their total lack of confidence in their own feelings, and their reliance on and preference for a deliberate intellectualized or rationalized approach.

For example, many victims of the anxiety/insomnia cycle have become aware of a causal relationship between a poor night's sleep and being tired, moody, and irritable the following day. This mood is precisely what they fear most, since they believe it endangers their need to be loved and accepted at any price. If, after having discovered this cause-and-effect relationship, a reasoning process were necessary—which it is not—to arrive at a solution to the problem, it would run somewhat like this: "I want to be loved, so I must never hurt people's feelings and always be nice to them; it is easiest to be nice and please others when I am fully rested and full of energy (to repress the feelings of irritation and anger); consequently, it is imperative that I get a good night's sleep; every night I must sleep well so I will wake up fully rested; when I retire I must get to sleep soon, if I am to get a sufficient number of hours of sleep; I MUST SLEEP!"

Whatever other reason there may be for this anxiety/insomnia cycle—a childhood pledge never to hurt other people as they themselves were hurt by the uncontrolled emotions of their parents, a fear of sinning through "unjustifiable anger," a fear of breaking the vow of chastity, and so on—individuals with neurotic disorders "try to get to sleep" by virtue of their own effort and willpower. Before long they are caught in a vicious circle, for when their efforts do not bring forth the desired result, their tension and anxiety mount and they resort to certain routine activities before retiring, such as abstaining from coffee, taking a nightcap, using sleeping pills, and so on. These patients are best helped through the gradual development of insight, the use of relaxing exercises with or without hypnosis, and a judicious temporary use of soporifics until they have learned a more wholesome philosophy of living and a realistic acceptance of themselves and the world.

Anxiety and *tension* are, of course, the most common complaints of nearly all patients with neurotic disorders and need to be relieved as much and as soon as possible, if only to make the patient more comfortable in and amenable to psychotherapy. The initial approach by the therapist, and the confidence he or she inspires by empathy and understanding the nature of the patient's illness, are the chief therapeutic measures, but in many instances these have to be supplemented by daytime sedatives or tranquilizers.

Depression is another complaint expressed by many persons with neurotic disorders. This is hardly surprising, for their unfortunate tense and anxious state deprives them of the enjoyment of most of the goods life has to offer. Unless their depression is severe, incapacitating, and possibly life-threatening, we prefer to treat it only as a secondary symptom which will disappear when we succeed in eliminating their anxiety and tension by helping them, for example, to assert themselves and squarely face the obstacles in their lives with the use of the emotions they have learned to repress so effectively.

Of all neurotic symptoms, depression perhaps most readily responds to a sympathetic and understanding attitude on the part of the therapist and to the realistic hope this therapy offers for the relief and healing of neurotic disorders. This holds true particularly for persons with Emotional Deprivation Disorder when they first discover, with amazement, hope, and gratitude, the true nature and cause of their illness. Feelings of depression, despair, and hopelessness lose much of their intensity and impact as soon as patients sense that their condition is understood by another human being and can be healed.

A considerable number of individuals with neurotic disorders complain of being tired a great deal of the time, of finding it difficult to carry on because of chronic *fatigue*, and some are forced by exhaustion to quit their work altogether. The latter, especially if of sturdy build, cause the psychiatrist or psychotherapist to suspect the presence of an organic cause for their fatigue, such as acute or chronic infectious diseases, anemic states, metabolic or endocrine disorders, and toxins. However, each time these causes have been ruled out through exhaustive clinical and laboratory studies, the therapist is reminded again of the fact that psychogenic causes *per se* are capable of producing the most severe fatigue states. Over the years the process of repressing requires ever greater amounts of energy, while persons with Emotional Deprivation Disorder find it increasingly harder to cope with the demands and expectations of the adult world in which they must live by sheer willpower.

Since individuals with neurotic disorders experience little if any joy because of the undeveloped state of the emotions of the pleasure appetite, and since relaxing is something virtually unknown to them, it is not surprising that they feel exhausted and dead tired, even after waking up from a long night's sleep. This way of life is so difficult, demanding, and frustrating that the awareness of being inadequate and the feeling of being unable to carry on seldom leave them. These feelings constitute the essence of what these patients mean by fatigue, just as others might say they are tired when for some reason or other a mental or physical task at hand seems too much for them.

Fatigue diminishes gradually during therapy when patients become more hopeful that they can recover from their neurotic disorder, when they learn more adequate ways of coping with their problems and conflicts, when they dare to follow their emotions, and when the continued affirmation and support of the therapist enables them to begin finding love, joy, respect, confidence, peace, and calm. The latter experiences are especially enhanced by a comparison between ancient Greek culture, which was based on leisure, and our own society's utilitarian, work-oriented lifestyle.

We often prescribe a suitable cycle of activity and rest, and we instruct patients in the performance of daily relaxing exercises and the use of warm and cold baths to produce relaxation and general muscle toning. These baths may be taken several times daily, particularly following their preferred form of physical exercise, which may be jogging, swimming, bicycling, tennis, golf, and so on.

Many patients suffering from neurotic disorders derive considerable benefit from massages and movement therapy provided by experienced, psychologically oriented physiotherapists. A specialized form of this is *psychotactile therapy*. Based on anthropological phenomenology, it is a natural development of the manual contact in massage and provides a tonus regulation which goes beyond the ordinary concept of muscular relaxation. It requires a certain active participation of response on the part of patients themselves, and the resulting affirmation, once commenced in the encounter with the patient-oriented hand of the physiotherapist, continues to make itself felt later—independently of the therapist. It is indicated for persons with fear-based repression and those with Emotional Deprivation Disorder, but contraindicated for persons with psychotic disorders and persons with sexual deviations.[13]

Finally, we want to mention that special *self-help CDs* are available for English-speaking individuals who want to accelerate the process of freeing their long-repressed emotions.[14]

There is yet another subject to be discussed in regard to the therapy of neurotic disorders (particularly repressive disorders, whether occurring by themselves or superimposed on Emotional Deprivation Disorder); namely, certain factors that enable us to decide *whether therapy is indicated in a given patient.* These factors, to be sure, are intimately related to the nature of neurosis, which consists in an acquired disturbed relationship between the human person's emotional life and the intellect and will.

In normal persons, the emotional life is subordinated to reason, with the result that the many varied appetites and inclinations constitute a harmonious whole. In persons with neurotic disorders, however, this harmony has been disrupted because of repression or deprivation, and as a result the emotional life functions to a certain extent independently of reason. Therapy aims at restoring the natural order by enabling the intellectual powers to assume their full normal direction and guide the emotional life. However, this therapeutic task is undertaken on the assumption that the emotional life's innate disposition is such that it can be subordinated to reason in a natural manner; in other words, that it is fundamentally sound enough to develop and grow in a healthy manner once the factors that brought on the neurotic disorder have been eliminated.

This, of course, represents the essential indication for therapy, but how can one determine whether a patient's emotional life has the innate capacity to be guided by reason? Here the psychiatrist or psychotherapist will naturally rely first of all on the impression he or she gets from the patient's anamnesis and personality makeup. A good therapist spontaneously senses

13. This fascinating form of therapy has been developed by its originator, F. Veldman, Director of the Academy for Haptonomy and Kinesionomy, Nymegen/ Overasselt, Netherlands. One of his books is entitled *Lichte Lasten (Burdens that are Light)*, Spruyt, Van Mantgem & De Does, N.V./Leiden, 1970.

14. For a list of self-help CDs, books and monographs, visit www.BaarsInstitute.com.

what kind of fiber the patient is made of, while the experience accumulated in years of practice will give added certainty and perspicacity to his or her judgment. Nevertheless, certain *objective* signs may confirm or, if necessary, correct such subjective feelings and judgments about the patient.

One source of objective information is *psychological testing*. Although valuable in itself, testing has a disadvantage, especially in persons of superior intelligence: it creates a certain feeling of distrust in regard to the psychotherapist. Such people sometimes consider the test as a means whereby the therapist attempts, against their will, to obtain knowledge of their innermost thoughts. This, of course, would seriously interfere with the psychotherapeutic process because the first requisite is the development of a feeling of confidence in the therapist. There is also another objection to an excessive reliance on the use of psychological tests: it may influence the therapist's personal understanding of the patient, for he or she will see the patient mainly through the test results and not sufficiently in the light of the clinical intuition which can be of such great importance for therapy. For this reason we prefer to reserve the use of tests for cases in which there is serious doubt whether a diagnosis is correct.

Fortunately, other objective data may help in determining whether a patient is a suitable candidate for therapy. These objective signs are obtained from study of the patient's physical condition, for the human person is a psychophysical unit, and it must be assumed that psychological conditions possess certain somatic aspects. Although present methods of investigation do not allow us to determine the precise somatic changes in every possible psychological state, it is possible to do so in regard to the particular psychological disposition that interests us here. This conclusion is the result of thorough physical and neurological examination of thousands of patients with neurotic disorders seen in our practice. We have found that there are two main signs which give an indication of the interior state of the patient's emotional life in relation to rational guidance: the size and reaction of the patient's pupils, and the activity of his or her reflexes, particularly the muscle-stretch reflexes.[15] On the other hand, we have been unable to attach prognostic significance to such vaso-vegetative signs as dermographia, hyperhidrosis, dry mouth and tongue, and similar signs.[16]

15. The term "muscle-stretch" reflex is used in preference to "tendon," "periosteal," or "deep muscle" reflex because it is more meaningful from a physiological standpoint. It indicates that the reflex is evoked by stimulation of sensory fibers or "spindles" within the muscle as a result of stretching.

16. There are, however, certain signs of importance to the differential diagnosis of

The *pupils* must be observed during the interview whenever the patient is not emotionally upset, for it is a well-known fact that the pupils become larger when a person is acutely fearful. It is the ordinary, prevailing size of the pupils that most interests us here. In our experience, small and average-sized pupils are an indication that the emotional life is favorably disposed to rational guidance. Pupils that are too large, on the other hand, carry an unfavorable connotation; the same proved to be true for a few patients with anisocoria and hippus.[17]

An even more important prognostic sign is the activity of the *muscle-stretch reflexes*. When these reflexes are normal, not too high and not too low, and the reflexogenic areas[18] are not enlarged, we may conclude that the emotional life is favorably disposed to rational guidance, and it is generally justified to commence therapy. If, on the other hand, the muscle-stretch reflexes are increased too much or show clonus, together with an extension of the reflexogenic areas, one should proceed with caution. Low reflexes do not of themselves constitute a contraindication for therapy, but indicate the existence of an energy-based repressive disorder. If a psychiatric examination suggests the presence of an energy-based repressive disorder, this diagnosis may be confirmed by the finding that the muscle-stretch reflexes are very low or absent.

When we started our psychiatric practice, the factors described above were completely unknown to us. However, when we began to keep a record of all neurological findings, both normal and pathological, it gradually dawned on us that there seemed to be a certain relationship between a person's innate psychological disposition and reflex activity. Investigating this further in the years that followed, we arrived at the aforementioned conclusions. At the same time we asked whether these findings could be

---

fear-based repression and energy-based repression. For example, persons with energy-based repression have hypotension and a glucose tolerance curve that usually shows a plateau, rather than a peak, between its low starting and end values. Furthermore, these persons show no sleep disturbances in the sense of difficulty in going to sleep, restless and fitful sleep, or early morning awakening. Persons with energy-based repression fall asleep promptly, and their sleep is deep and often dreamless, remaining so all night long, with the result that they are hard to awaken in the morning. It would be worthwhile to investigate possible further differences between these two types of disorders by means of electroencephalographic recordings and protein metabolism studies, investigations which we were unable to do systematically in all patients.

17. Anisocoria is an inequality in the diameter of the pupils. Hippus is a rhythmic narrowing and widening of the pupil, indicative of unmodifiable tension in the brainstem.

18. *See* also Chapter III, p. 80, and footnote 11 on p. 86.

explained neurologically. We are of the opinion that this is indeed the case, and that the human person's *reflex activity is influenced by the conscious will* by way of the corticospinal tract.

When this influence is essentially normal, the reflexes show normal activity, indicating that the emotional life has a natural disposition to be subordinated to the intellectual life. If, on the other hand, the reflexes are too active, it is likely that the cortex will exert a subnormal inhibitory action, with the result that sensory stimuli will bring about motor reactions without sufficient cortical control. This may be interpreted as an inadequate disposition of the physical organism to respond to the action of the intellectual life. If the muscle-stretch reflexes are too low or completely absent, the influence of the intellectual life, and thus also its inhibitory action, is too great. In persons with this characteristic the rational will is too strongly developed and interferes with the normal activity of the emotional life. This is typical of *energy-based repression.*

In *fear-based repression*, however, repression is much less of an intellectual nature; rather, it is emotionally determined, and this explains why we do not see markedly decreased or absent reflexes in these patients. While their reflexes may be higher or lower within the normal range, we become concerned only if they are much too high and the reflexogenic areas are enlarged.

This is particularly true when such very high reflexes are found in patients with a better-than-average intellect. In intelligent people, the possibility that the intellect influences the emotional life is, of course, greater. If, therefore, very high reflexes are found in persons of superior intelligence, it is an indication that their emotional life is unfavorably disposed to rational guidance and influence. In fact, in our experience there is a great likelihood that such people possess a psychopathic constitution. In people of only average intelligence it is not necessary to entertain such a suspicion.

The inhibitory influence of the will on the muscle-stretch reflexes is confirmed by the well-known fact that these reflexes often increase on *reinforcement*. It may be assumed that in the effort to reinforce the reflex—be it done by Jendrassik's maneuver, by making a tight fist, or by reading from a book held upside-down—the attention is diverted so that there are fewer cortical inhibitory impulses reaching the muscle being tested. Whatever the precise physiological explanation of the phenomenon of reinforcement, however, it provides us with important diagnostic and prognostic information in cases of energy-based repression. If the markedly decreased or absent reflexes of patients with energy-based repressive disorders are increased on reinforcement, this means that the influence of the conscious will has not yet been so strong that their low or absent reflex activity has become an inalterably fixated physiological manifestation. By the same token, it must be assumed that if reinforcement produces no change in reflex activity, this fixation has actually taken place, and that the recovery process will be more prolonged. Our experience in actual practice has confirmed this.

In *summary* we present the following conclusions:

1) Normal muscle-stretch reflexes are a favorable indication for therapy.

2) Markedly increased reflexes with extension of reflexogenic areas are an indication of a less favorable disposition of the emotional life for control by reason and will. Such findings make less likely the possibility of recovery from a neurotic disorder.

3) Very low or absent reflexes *per se* are not an unfavorable sign regarding the emotional life's disposition to rational control. Consequently, they do not militate against recovery with proper therapeutic procedures; however, recovery requires more time in patients whose reflexes do not show increased activity on reinforcement.[19]

Finally, it may be stated that the patient's age has relatively little bearing on the outcome of our treatment methods. We have effected recoveries in favorably disposed persons aged fifty years or more. It is to be expected, of course, that recovery of older patients will be more difficult and will take more time because the neurotic processes have taken deeper root.

---

19. At our request, a pediatrician has investigated the reflexes of children up to the age of ten. Her findings are in complete agreement with our findings in adults. Muscle-stretch reflexes in children with normal constitutions were high, although within normal limits. In children with psychopathic constitutions, on the other hand, reflexes were very high and showed extension of the reflexogenic areas. This difference in reflex activity was a reliable criterion for determining whether the behavior of children with behavioral disturbances was due to a psychopathic personality constitution or resulted from such external circumstances as spoiling, unfavorable home conditions, and so on.

Only once, in a five year old, did the pediatrician observe a change in reflex activity on reinforcement. This tends to confirm our remarks concerning the inhibitory influence of the will on reflex activity, for such an intellectually determined influence cannot, of course, be expected in children at that age.

Note: The authors consider themselves privileged to have received the following critical evaluation of our mortification therapy of neurotic individuals with sexual obsessions and compulsions. The Rev. Jordan Aumann, O.P., widely respected moral theologian, has been thoroughly acquainted with our professional work since the late 1950's. His moral appraisal of our therapy should remove any lingering doubts of those scrupulous individuals who find it so extremely difficult to let go of their irrational neurotic fears.

"The authors' mortification therapy, as described in this sub-chapter, is in full accord with the teaching of the Magisterium of the Church on faith and morals, and particularly the Church's teaching on sexual morality. Obsessive-compulsive neurotics are not capable of exercising free will and self-control in the area of repression. Consequently, the objectively immoral actions which may occur during the process of mortification of the repressing emotions—or, for that matter, whenever the repressive process breaks down prior to the patient's admission to psychiatric therapy—are not subjectively sinful. These acts must be tolerated—never advocated—by both patient and psychiatrist. Otherwise there is no hope of releasing the repressed emotion.

"It is important, however, to insist that this therapeutic method and advice may never be applied in the counseling or spiritual direction of psychotics, psychopathic personalities or healthy persons. This therapy is restricted to the treatment of neurotic repression, and *exclusively* to the mortification of the repressing emotions in cases of obsessive-compulsive neurotics."

Jordan Aumann, O.P., S.T.D.

CHAPTER V

CASE HISTORIES

*This, too, then seems to reside in the dictum that we desire happiness naturally
and by necessity: that we cannot make ourselves happy.*

Josef Pieper, *Happiness and Contemplation*

HYSTERICAL NEUROSIS—ONE CASE

A Semi-Paralyzed Nun

A twenty-eight year old nun came to us complaining that she had been
unable to walk for several days. This condition had suddenly developed
one morning when, upon arising, she could not move around except with
a shuffling gait. The neurological findings were typical of a psychogenic
paralysis of the legs. All muscle-stretch reflexes were increased, and the
reflexogenic areas were markedly extended. There were no pathological
reflexes.

The patient was the third in a family of six children. There was no
history of mental or emotional illness in the family. She had always enjoyed
excellent physical health. Her relationship with her parents was good and
emotionally fully satisfying. As the family had always been poor, her formal
education had been limited to grammar school. She helped support the
family by working as a maid until she entered the cloister at the age of

eighteen. Although her innate intelligence was good, she possessed strikingly little erudition. Her ten years in the cloister had been spent in doing kitchen chores.

She impressed us as being a sensible and level-headed person. She stated that she was quite happy in the cloister and always steadfast in her dedication to the rules of the order. Her superior was said to consider her an asset to the community. Clinically, there were no signs of either pronounced fear or excessive energy.

The patient was advised to return for weekly interviews, which for the next two months were spent on dream analysis. She presented a great number of dreams, all of which clearly suggested the precise nature of her conflicts. In these dreams she revealed, much to her amazement, an unequivocal dislike for the religious life.

After two months of dream analysis, we proceeded to a frank discussion of her deepest motives for entering religious life. It was then learned that as a young girl she had never been given any sex education. When, in her early teens, she had given in a few times to masturbatory desires, she had become extremely concerned with the moral implications. Heavily burdened with intense feelings of guilt toward God, she had resolved to make restitution for her sinful life. To do this, she gradually developed the idea of joining a religious order, and after a few years she took the decisive step.

In these discussions, it gradually became evident that for years she had fought against a dislike for the religious life but without ever having been conscious of it. After four months of weekly interviews, she was able to acknowledge this, and as a consequence, she immediately developed a dislike for the prayers and rituals of religious life. Initially she did not want to give in to this feeling of dislike, but after some time her resistance decreased. At the same time she realized more and more that a vow made under the particular circumstances which existed when she joined the order did not constitute a rationally justified choice of vocation. The determining factor in her choice of vocation had not been a supernatural motive but an unreasonable feeling of fear.

It was clear that the only solution to the problem in this case was to give up the religious life. When the patient had accepted this and decided to do so, the paralysis disappeared. Upon her return to the world, she was able to make her own way and had no difficulty in adjusting. About three years later she fell in love, but when this did not result in marriage, she had a slight relapse of the abasia. She returned for a discussion of her experiences and was able to accept her disappointment in love, upon which the abasia disappeared at once. It has been eight years since she left the cloister; her adjustment has been excellent ever since, and her spiritual life, too, has developed satisfactorily in every way. Our diagnosis of this case was hysterical neurosis.

FEAR-BASED REPRESSION—ONE CASE

Scrupulosity and Compulsive Hand-Washing

"I can't stop washing and cleaning!" With these words, spoken in tears and desperation, the twenty-eight year old mother of two girls began her first interview. Her hands and arms, red and raw past her elbows, were silent witnesses to her plight. For more than three years she had spent her last pennies to keep herself supplied with soap, of which she used two bars a day.

Although her troubles had been developing for approximately six years, she had never sought help, not even from her family physician, for she had been raised with the idea that a strong person can control his emotions by himself. Not even her work at a mental health clinic some time before had made her waver in this determination. Only when life became intolerable for the entire family was she willing to accept the advice of a priest to see us.

Shortly after she was married, she had become scrupulous on the subjects of sex and eating meat on Friday. On Thursdays she cleaned her hands repeatedly so that no particle of meat would cling to them come Friday and cause her to sin—or to be an occasion of sin for her husband—by inadvertently eating meat on Friday. Frequent confessions did not assuage her fears. Instead they grew in number and intensity. Her phobias of dirt and germs made her keep her children in the house year-round until they became obviously anemic. They were not allowed to have pets. She washed coins before they were permitted to put them in their piggy banks. She closed all the windows of the house on the day the garbage collector came around with his big truck. She washed and rewashed, cleaned and re-cleaned the dishes, linens, clothing, and furniture for hours each day, until there was no time for anything else, least of all rest and recreation.

Her latest phobia was an intense fear that after she had been to Mass and Communion she might bring a particle of the Host to her home, and as a result, each time she attended Mass she was compelled to change her clothing and launder the articles she had worn to church. When a priest visited her at home, she had to clean the entire house afterwards for fear that he had brought along some particles of the Host. For days afterwards she would constantly vacuum the chair in which he had been sitting and the floor on which he had walked.

Although her difficulties had not become evident until after her marriage to a kind and patient husband, as in all neurotic disorders, they had started to develop subclinically in her childhood. Four days after she was born, her mother had insisted on taking her to church to be baptized, in spite of a raging snow storm and the advice of the pastor that it was perfectly all right to postpone the twenty-mile trip until the weather had cleared. The middle of five children, she was raised in a small town by a fussy, prudish, sickly, complaining, and hard-working mother who never had time for fun, and never kissed the children or her own husband. She once overheard her mother say, "If I had to do it all over again I'd be a nun!" Her father was a kindly man who never lost his temper and avoided all arguments with his wife. When angry he would be silent for days on end.

The living room in her parental home was never used, for it was considered too beautiful to be lived in. Pets were not allowed inside or outside the house, for her mother's garden was too beautiful to be disturbed. Her mother took great pride in having the whitest wash in town and even bleached her towels. The children were continually warned not to spill water on the hardwood floors, and stepping on bread crumbs was forbidden because, in her mother's opinion, that was a sin!

Shortly after the first interview, a crisis developed in the already strained atmosphere of her household when her husband, after coming home from Mass and receiving Communion, suddenly coughed in his hands. In panic the patient started to clean everything he touched and simply could not stop. In order to alleviate this tense situation and give both the patient and her family a rest, we had her admitted to the hospital. Her physical condition proved to be good in general, except for a slight anemia and excessive sweating of the hands and feet. Her pupils were slightly enlarged, and her patellar reflexes were hyperactive bilaterally with extension of the reflexogenic areas; on reinforcement they increased markedly.

Her period in the hospital was used to acquaint her with the nature of her illness and the means by which her fear-based repressive disorder could be cured. All these things were entirely new to her, but she listened attentively, grasped them quickly, and without argumentation or hesitation began to apply our advice and suggestions concerning the necessary mortification of her irrational fears. Thus she increasingly dared to ignore all previously learned commands, "musts," and "shall-nots," and paid more attention to her own likes and desires. Of above average intelligence, she learned every day from our discussions and her own experimentations, and after one week she was ready to leave the hospital. From then on she showed steady improvement, experiencing only two temporary relapses of panic in religious matters: once when her husband brought home a blessed palm on Palm Sunday, and again when a priest visited her at home. These crises and the associated relapses of excessive cleaning and washing were dealt with in our office, and she was again advised not to think or reason things out, but rather to follow her first impulse and do as she liked.

Because the patient was convinced that our understanding of her disorder was correct, and because our advice was always in full agreement with objective morality and based upon a sound understanding of the nature of the human person, she was able to learn to "leap before she looked."

Four months after the start of therapy, she began to let her children play in the garden and swimming pool without being bothered by her previous fear of germs. During the first months of therapy she continued to attend Sunday Mass for fear of sinning if she did not, but she succeeded in tempering this fear also, and became willing to wait until her feelings would draw her to God and Church.

During the visits which followed, she recalled how she had to go to confession as a child every four weeks, but was permitted to receive Holy Communion only on the day immediately following confession, not during the remaining four-week period. Whenever she made a mistake or quarreled with some of the children, her mother would warn her, "Now you can't go to Communion, you committed a sin."

From her mother and the way religion had been presented to her—or had been interpreted by her—this patient had arrived at the conclusion that work was everything in life, that everything had to be earned, even, and precisely, Heaven, too.

Fun and leisure always had been frowned upon, and neither one had ever been indulged in by her parents. Eighteen months after starting therapy, the patient spent the "best summer of her life;" she swam, sun-bathed, read books for fun, and went on a vacation trip with husband and children. She developed an interest in politics and enjoyed life fully. The skin of her hands and arms regained their natural appearance, for she steadily gave up unnecessary washings. The anger at her mother which had surfaced in the first year of therapy began to recede to make room for a feeling of pity. Her love for her husband, whose patient support played an important part in her recovery, deepened, and the most intimate expressions of their love became a great source of joy to her.

It should be noted that this patient recovered without drugs, except for some sedatives administered during her brief stay at the hospital. During the first year of therapy she was seen a total of ten times in our office, the next year only six times, and the following two years only once every six months. Thus, without the probing approach of psychoanalytic therapy, and without drug therapy of any consequence, this woman with severe obsessive-compulsive repression made a gradual recovery—not just a symptomatic improvement—as a result of her deep trust and confidence in the therapist, a simple yet profound grasp of basic psychological and theological issues, and a courageous and steadfast adherence to therapeutic advice.

A follow-up inquiry more than five years after the start of therapy confirmed the permanence of her recovery. There had been no relapses, even when she was exposed to some intermediate stressful situations. Her relationship to God and His Church continued to improve and grew into a mature, freely determined attitude of love and respect in which fear no longer played a role.

ENERGY-BASED REPRESSION—THREE CASES

1. Compulsive Street Cleaning

Although to all outward appearances this twenty-four year old man presented a picture of physical and psychological well-being, he came to us because his obsessive-compulsive symptoms had begun to seriously interfere with his work as a teacher. He no longer dared to show himself in the street, for he often felt compelled to pick up, in full sight of everybody, such things as pebbles and orange or banana peels for fear that people might fall over them and be injured. He also complained that for the past several years he had been bothered by overpowering sexual tensions and masturbated frequently.

He was the third boy in a family of five children; his father was also a teacher. As far back as he could remember, his parents had always stressed the importance of doing one's duties and the need to study hard in school in order to amount to something later in life.

The results of physical and neurological examinations were within normal limits. His pupils were of average size and showed little or no change during the interview. Muscle-stretch reflexes were elicited with difficulty, but their activity increased slightly on reinforcement.

We made arrangements for him to see us once every two weeks and immediately began with an analysis of his dreams.[1] He soon expressed surprise at the fact that he always acted in an aggressive manner in his dreams, for in his daily life he was constantly intent on being amiable and never showed anger or indignation. In the fourth interview, he described several dreams in which he harbored hostile feelings toward others. In the same hour he told us the following story: Until the age of fifteen he had been a very ill-tempered and impulsive child. One day his mother had a serious talk with him, and expressed her concern that unless he curbed his angry outbursts, he would get in serious trouble later on in life. This talk had left a deep impression on him, and he had made the firm resolution to suppress his anger, no matter how difficult that would be, and never to express it again. Now, in retrospect, the patient himself was amazed that he had been able to adhere to his promise so well, for he could not recall a single incident following this talk with his mother that he had permitted himself to become openly angry or ill-tempered.

We used the next interview hour for a detailed discussion of our assertive feelings. We explained how it is normal for persons to experience angry feelings and also to react at times with angry words and behavior whenever they are threatened by evil or when somebody actually harms them. Such reactions are typical of all beings possessed with a sensory life. Every animal has what may be called its own zone-of-attack: when this is invaded by a potential danger, it attacks; but the animal is not concerned about things outside this zone-of-attack. Although the zone-of-attack that people have is not so sharply delimited, on account of their universal orientation, their

---

1. Although persons with energy-based repression seldom or never dream, this man's illness was of such relatively recent onset that his dream life had not yet been affected sufficiently by his expenditure of energy.

innate assertive drive nevertheless reacts as soon as they discern a threat or feel that in some manner or other they have not been given the consideration and respect they deserve. The fact that the feeling of anger, which serves the innate assertive drive, must be guided in a rational manner, does not mean that the feeling, as such, is not proper and should be suppressed at all times. If persons do this to the extent that they do not even want to admit the very first movement of anger, they violate the natural order by an unnatural repression of their emotions, with all the well-known grave consequences associated with this.

Although our patient seemed to understand this, he remarked that in his opinion it could never be reasonable or Christian to wish harm to another person, and that therefore it must always be wrong to harbor feelings of anger and resentment toward others. We reminded him of the necessity to love God above all and our neighbors like ourselves. This, we explained, meant that the natural order requires that we love ourselves first, and only then our neighbor. Seen in this light, it is reasonable to grant priority to concern for our own good above our neighbor's, and it follows that it does not have to be un-Christian or unreasonable to feel angry and even show it. The patient was most surprised at hearing this explanation, for in his opinion, one had to love God above all, the neighbor next, and oneself not at all. As soon as he fully understood why his opinion was wrong, he immediately realized that it could be reasonable to have angry feelings and likewise to express them.

Once we were this far, we proceeded to apply these ideas to his own way of life. We discussed the likelihood that he had begun to repress his natural assertive emotions after his mother's admonishing remarks had made such a deep impression on him, and that this had left him with a repressed, and consequently abnormally strong, tendency to assertion. This tendency, as well as the immediately associated unconscious repressing factor, was intensified in situations that might involve a danger to others. In view of the fact that his ideas about one's obligations to love one's neighbors had caused him to condemn absolutely any assertive act, the repression had had an opportunity to spread to the actual prevention of any such act.[2] This manifested itself in his previously described compulsive acts which, on a conscious level, however, had been interpreted as being prompted by a concern for the welfare of others.

2. This is a typical example of the intellectually determined expansion of the object as discussed on pages 53 and 79.

When it was evident that the patient understood these things, we suggested that he make it a point not to repress his assertive feelings again and allow himself to feel angry inside, permitting some kind of expression when he was reasonably comfortable with his angry feeling and the circumstances called for such a reaction. We also advised him to extend the interval between his visits and not to return for about six weeks. In the next interview hour he informed us that in the weeks gone by he had found the courage to give rein to emerging feelings of irritability and anger. His family had not known what to make of this change in temperament and his mother had reproached him for being ill-tempered again, while everybody agreed that the psychiatrist's influence was decidedly detrimental to his best interests. In spite of this critical attitude, the patient did not change his ways but continued to do as recommended. After several months, his compulsive behavior disappeared and also his abnormal sexual tensions. This latter development suggested the likelihood that the excessive emotional tensions resulting from the repression of anger had sought to be discharged along a different channel, namely in the sexual sphere.

One year after he had first come to us, his recovery could be called complete. He expressed his assertive feelings in reasonable and appropriate ways without exaggerated emotional display. His obsessive-compulsive symptoms had not recurred. Two years after therapy had been discontinued, he came back for a chat and told us about his forthcoming marriage. He was doing well in every respect and was happy with life. We used that occasion to recheck his muscle-stretch reflexes and found that their activity had increased to a near normal level.

Our diagnosis was energy-based repression, albeit of a relatively mild degree because the repression had only started when the patient was fifteen years of age. This, as well as the fact that he had come into therapy at an early age, explains why he recovered so rapidly.

2. Sexual Impotence in a Perfectionist Businessman

A thirty year old man came to us with the complaint that in his five years of marriage he had been unable to have satisfactory sexual relations with his wife. Although he had normal nocturnal emissions, he suffered from sexual impotence.

He was found to have a blood pressure of 110/80. The muscle-stretch reflexes were either completely or partially absent, but could be elicited with reinforcement. These findings, as well as the fact that his sleep was always deep and dreamless, suggested the presence of an energy-based repressive disorder. This was confirmed by his psychiatric history.

The patient was successfully engaged in his profession and enjoyed his work in every respect. He was active in social life and president of many organizations. He always took the initiative in conversations and had no difficulty in making decisions. He had little emotional rapport with others. Even with his parents, his contact was only businesslike and intellectual, yet it was pleasant, for he had great admiration for his father and did not fear him.

Neither was there any trace of fear in his relationship to God. He adhered strictly to the duties and obligations of his faith, simply because he believed that this was what he ought to do. There was not the slightest indication that he was fearful of sin or hell. In fact, he did not show the slightest fear in regard to anything. On the other hand, he was an extreme perfectionist, and everything had to be in perfect order—his work, his home, his own conduct. His garden, for example was the neatest imaginable; not the slightest detail had been overlooked. After dark he was in the habit of inspecting the lawn with a flashlight to see if there were any pebbles in the grass, and if so he removed each one carefully.

He had little in common with his wife; there was little spiritual and even less physical contact between them. All attempts at the latter had resulted in failure. This upset the patient considerably, not so much because he considered his impotence as a psychological inadequacy, but because he had to have children since without them his family and the family name would die out. The only reason, therefore, that had led him to go to a psychiatrist had been the practical one of how he could have children. He himself thought that the fault lay with his wife, who had foul breath and dressed in poor taste, according to his standards. He did not think that there was anything wrong with himself: he enjoyed his work, he slept well, and he always had energy to spare. Consequently, he requested us to be so kind as to treat his wife.

The latter, on the other hand, was found to be an entirely normal person, kind and sincere in her love of her husband, even though he had done little to develop his love. Her only complaint was that her husband was such a bore, for even though he was an excellent provider, he never hugged or caressed her or surprised her with little gifts or compliments. She had become depressed by the repeated failures of their sexual relations; it sometimes caused her to be irritable and impatient and although she tried hard not to show these feelings, she blamed herself. Finally, out of boredom she had resumed her music studies and started to give lessons.

There could be no doubt concerning the diagnosis: energy-based repression with resulting sexual impotence. This, of course, raised the important question whether it would be possible to give the patient some measure of insight into his illness and provide him with a correct view of his inner life. A few more interviews with both the patient and his wife brought about a measure of insight; at least he began to accept the possibility that the fault might not be only with his wife but with his own personality development. Once this had been accomplished, he was given an understanding of the human person's psychic life and especially of the relation between intellectual will and emotional energy, and the latter's ability to completely suppress pleasure emotions. As he was a highly intelligent man, we gave him a book of ours which explains neurosis in terms of philosophical anthropology, the contents of which he understood completely. The result was that he decided to enter therapy.

Bit by bit he began to give his history, and he himself pointed out what was wrong with the way he had been brought up. His parents considered emotions to be uncouth and uncivilized, and any expression of feeling as immoral. Their insistence on complete voluntary control over all feelings marked his attitude even as a child. This attitude was strengthened at a boarding school in which priests had strongly emphasized the need to suppress one's feelings in order to be able to lead a life of purity. This was precisely what he wanted, and he strictly adhered to this advice, all the more so because it agreed so well with the ideas on this subject that he had acquired at home. It became second nature for him to live and depend entirely on his will power. His feelings took little or no part in his conduct and everything was viewed in a matter-of-fact manner. This attitude had also prevailed in his decision to marry. During his student days, he told us shamefacedly and after much hesitation, that he had been enamored for a while with a very worldly girl. Before long, however, he had broken off with her precisely because she was so worldly and also because she was beneath his own social level. His decision to marry his present wife had been determined by the fact that she was of equal social standing, while her family background suggested that she possessed healthy hereditary factors. Moreover, he esteemed her as a person and liked her at the same time. He lacked any natural urge to have sexual relations with his wife; his attempts to do so were always prompted solely by his concern that he ought to have a child.

The more he began to understand the nature of his behavior and attitude, the more his feelings began to manifest themselves. Soon it became evident that he had never allowed himself to have feelings of an erotic nature and had never made love to anyone. During therapy, desire for all this became quite strong in his imagination, but on account of his prominent position in society, it was out of the question to express it in any manner. Yet the mere fact that he no longer prevented this desire from entering his imagination gave him a new feeling of freedom. The same young woman with whom he had been enamored as a student began to play a role in his fantasy life. His feelings for her which, of course, had been completely repressed, then became particularly strong. Only after he had spoken of them with us and also with his wife did they eventually become quiescent. All this was often hard on his wife, but fortunately she fully understood the situation and possessed enough love and devotion to meet all developments calmly. As a result they grew closer together.

Gradually, after we had explained to him that he should pay no attention, as far as this was possible, to the idea that he had to have a child, he also became more natural and more at ease in his contact with his wife. As he realized the importance of this advice, he did his best not to be guided by this idea in his relations with his wife. Prior to treatment, this idea had been so all-important that his attempts at sexual intercourse were made only during his wife's fertile period. As therapy progressed, he began to change this and tried to follow our advice of not trying to force himself to bring the sexual act to completion. The very fact that he no longer had to be concerned about this, enabled him in due time to experience the proper value of sexual stimulation so that he derived pleasure from making love to his wife. In the beginning this did little or nothing to arouse his sex urge, but he was assured that this was not important for the time being. The only thing that mattered for the present was that he should be led by the natural sex urge without striving to achieve anything definite. He made steady but slow progress, and his wife, too, was able to confirm this.

About one year later it was necessary for him to go to Sweden on business. While there, he allowed himself much more freedom because he felt less restricted by conventional rules than in his hometown. He frequently danced and flirted with girls, which did him a world of good. Following this episode, sexual relations with his wife improved markedly, and gradually he began to be sexually aroused. Whenever he tried to have intercourse in the belief that he would be successful, however, it became a failure. We repeatedly told him that even when he was sexually aroused he should not try to will intercourse, but should wait until he felt the desire for it without the intervention of his conscious will. After about two and a half years, he was able to have normal sexual intercourse; not regularly at first, but only once in a while. Finally, however, his marriage became normal in every respect. Three children were born at short intervals while he grew in his love for his wife. It should be noted that his wife's foul breath, on which he had blamed his impotence in the beginning, has persisted. The specialist in internal medicine to whom she went for advice had been unable to detect its cause.

The spiritual life of this patient also underwent extensive changes. Prior to treatment he was, as we have already stated, very strict in the performance of his religious duties, undoubtedly as a result of energetically self-imposed rules of conduct. When this energy began to let up more and more in the course of therapy, the consequences were likewise noticeable in his spiritual life. He began to resist the compulsion of his self-imposed rules, and for a while he neglected his duties completely. After some time this, too, straightened itself out, and he began to receive the sacraments regularly of his own free choice and not as a result of neurotic compulsion.

In the beginning of therapy this patient was seen every two weeks, until he possessed a thorough understanding of what was wrong in his emotional life and was able to carry out the directions which he had been given. After six months we let things take their own course and the patient came for interviews only occasionally.

This was a typical case of energy-based repression: repression of emotions and sexual feelings by energy. Therapy consisted first of providing an insight into the abnormal development of the patient's psychic life, and then leading him along the road to recovery by getting him to give up all striving and allow the emotional life, deeply buried as it was, to develop normally.

3. Sexual Impotence and Puritanism

A twenty-six year old engineer came to us because of sexual impotence in his one year of married life. Nocturnal emissions occurred sporadically, approximately once every six weeks.

The patient had been brought up in a puritanical milieu as the youngest in a family with many children. Excessive training of the conscious will had typified the intellectual atmosphere. Life at home had been good and his childhood pleasant. He never experienced difficulties with learning in school, but after leaving college he noticed that his memory was not as good as before.

His psychosexual history revealed the conviction that all sexual feelings experienced outside of marriage were sinful. All his life he had controlled his sexual feelings with great will-power and he thought it ironical that after a chaste period of engagement he had to suffer sexual impotence. Otherwise, his way of life had always been characterized by a utilitarian attitude, doing things only because he thought they were useful. The only finding worth noting in the neurological examination was the almost absent muscle-stretch reflexes.

We explained to him that he was suffering from distortion within his emotional life insofar as he always directed the pleasant to the useful instead of the useful to the pleasant. The fact that his utility appetite determined all his actions had prevented the necessary development of his pleasure appetite. This, we advised him, was the cause of his impotence. The only successful treatment would consist of responding to all emotions and desires as soon as they arose, without the interference of any utilitarian motives.

In a two-hour discussion, we succeeded in providing this man, who possessed an adequate knowledge of philosophical anthropology, with a good insight into the faulty aspects of his psychic life. For further consolidation of this insight, we advised him to read our doctoral thesis, *The Neurosis in the Light of Rational Psychology*. Since his home was abroad, he could not return for another interview, but he agreed to our request to keep us informed of his progress, and if necessary, to arrange an appointment on his next scheduled visit to the Netherlands.

Eighteen months later we received an announcement of the birth of a daughter, accompanied by a letter stating that he had followed our advice, with the result that gradually he had begun to mature in his psychosexual life. Moreover, his altered philosophy of life had resulted in a much greater enjoyment of life in general for both his wife and himself.

On a final note, the patient remarked that his recovery could in no way be ascribed to the influence of the psychiatrist because he had seen us only on one occasion, and thus that this case clearly demonstrated the correctness of our understanding of neurotic disorders.

CAMOUFLAGED FEAR-BASED REPRESSION—TWO CASES

1. Rage Reactions and Phobias in a Middle-aged Homemaker

Two case histories of camouflaged fear-based repression follow. A forty-eight year old married woman sought psychiatric help shortly after an attempt to commit suicide. She suffered paralyzing phobias: she did not dare to enter shops, was afraid to ride her bicycle or cross the street, no longer dared to attend meetings at which she had to preside or to accompany her husband to the theater or concerts; she was afraid of her father, mother, brother, and sisters, and was in a panic when they came to visit her or when she was asked to go to see them. From time to time she developed attacks of fear, during which she stayed in bed in total apathy, severely depressed and without any initiative. Sometimes such states would be interrupted by outbursts of motor agitation in which her fear changed to angry aggression. During these episodes she would tear her clothes, throw and break anything near at hand, and even try to jump out of the window. She struck fear into anyone who saw her during these outbursts, and it was no wonder that her husband and children had become very afraid of her.

When we consulted the psychiatrist who had been treating her before, he informed us that, in his opinion, the woman was a hysterical psychopath beyond any effective help.

The physical and neurological examination did not reveal any abnormal findings in this well-developed woman who had prognostically favorable low reflexes without extension of the reflexogenic areas. On a few occasions in the past, she had been under the treatment of a gynecologist on account of several miscarriages. Her menstrual periods had stopped at the age of forty-four, shortly after she had been sick with influenza. She complained of low back pain and had incontinence of urine, for which the urologist had been unable to determine a cause.

The woman had been reared in a devout family as the eldest of six children. Her father was an energetic and ambitious businessman who lived for his business. Her mother possessed only limited abilities. After high school, the patient had wanted to go to college, but her father had been definitely opposed to this idea because, in his opinion, girls were meant to marry and have children. Coercion had marked the children's upbringing, especially in regard to matters pertaining to religion and purity. She had been compelled to attend Mass daily and was seldom allowed to go out with boys. She had always lived in fear of her father, obeying him blindly, although not without inner protests which she never gave in to on a conscious level. To all appearances, she had lived as a refined Catholic girl without any indications of a psychopathic constitution.

The family history was favorable: no psychoses, epilepsy, personality disorders, or alcoholism. All of her brothers had good jobs and her sisters were happily married. At the age of twenty-two, the patient had married her present husband, whom she claimed to love dearly. Her marriage had been happy until a few years before, when she developed her attacks of fear and anxiety. Of her four children, one had been ordained a priest shortly before her illness, while the others were still in college. On account of her several miscarriages, her husband had proceeded to practice withdrawal, which often interfered with the regular performance of her religious duties.

She had been most active socially and devoted considerable time to charitable organizations. Because of her ease in public speaking and her administrative talents, she was frequently elected to the presidency of these organizations. Her fears, of course, had changed all this completely.

She had also reacted vehemently to the religious coercion of her childhood by not attending Mass or receiving the sacraments, and she made no attempts to hide her dislike of everything that pertained to religion. This attitude was a constant source of deep concern to her husband, but every attempt on his part to make her change her mind only made things worse.

This, briefly, was the situation when she came to us for psychiatric treatment. We were of the opinion that the diagnosis of psychopathic personality was not indicated, on account of her muscle-stretch reflexes, her childhood history, and the family history. We had no doubt, however, that we were dealing with a fear-based repressive disorder in which the fear had been repressed by the patient's energetic character, until finally the tension had become too great and things had exploded.

Treatment was started by seeing the patient twice a week for hourly sessions. In the beginning, she merely provided us with the aforementioned historical data gradually and did not speak of her inner feelings. As she was highly intelligent, part of these interview hours were used to give her some understanding of the human person's psychic life in general, according to the Aristotelian-Thomistic ideas contained in this book. She developed an excellent understanding of the subject matter, and it was not long before her introspective powers enabled her to see her own life in the light of her newly gained knowledge. She soon realized that she had always lived in fear, but had never expressed this fear outwardly, and had repressed it instead. She also became familiar with the meaning of repression and with the fact that the repressed emotion does not become inactive but is buried alive, trying to find guidance by reason. At this point, she came to the conclusion that her present fears were the result of the fact that she had never allowed herself to express these fears but had repressed them. At the same time she realized that if she wished to get well, she must no longer repress those fears.

It was a hard struggle for her to accept this fact. That she finally did win out was due most of all to the fact that from the very beginning she had complete faith in us. She sensed that she was being understood, that she was never asked to do things unless she understood the reason for them, and that we never exerted the slightest pressure. Strengthened by this faith, she dared to put herself in our hands and to follow our advice in spite of her fears; for although she fully understood that our advice was correct, it was so diametrically opposed to her own attitude that she would never have been able to follow it if she had to rely solely on her own strength. She required our constant and repeated assurance, which at times gave rise to considerable difficulties when we were not available. Fortunately, all these difficulties were overcome in time.

As soon as she gained the courage to accept the fact that she must no longer repress her fears, her attacks of fear became more frequent, and during the next year they occurred as often as once every two weeks. These attacks were hard, not only on her, but also on the people around her. Fortunately, her husband and her children had complete confidence in us and fully accepted our word that these more frequent attacks of fear did not constitute a permanent regression, but only a transient phase in the therapy. After about a year, the attacks decreased in frequency and finally disappeared altogether.

As a result of the gradual resolution of all those accumulated fears, the emotions which she had repressed also began to make themselves known. From the outset, we suspected that certain things had happened in her childhood which she had repressed and which had also influenced her fear. However, she did not talk about these things and we waited patiently until such a time that she would be ready to relate them. Finally, these things came out, but in a way which at first threatened to create the most serious complications, although it ultimately led to real release. It happened that a business friend of her husband's began to pay attention to her on his visits to their home, while she in turn fell in love with him. She became completely obsessed by thoughts of this man, so much so that she lost feelings for her own husband. For her, only the other man existed. Her attitude persisted in spite of the fact that this man did not care for her at all and often was inconsiderate of her. He evidently had not anticipated such an intense emotional response on her part and had been merely interested in a superficial flirtation. It was not long before he began to be more reserved and to rebuff her more and more. During this period, she spent all of her interviews talking about this man, obviously at a loss to explain her own feelings, because objectively she did not appreciate him at all and was not blind to the fact that he did not care for her in the least. One day, however, the solution to this problem suddenly hit her, and she realized that this man reminded her of another man who years before had been the cause of serious emotional upheaval in her.

When she was a young woman of about eighteen years, she had met the husband of a niece whom she visited from time to time in order to help out with the care of their children. The niece's marriage was an unhappy one, and on one of her visits the husband had fallen in love with her and she with him. Although they had never become sexually intimate, their love for each other grew very intense in the years that followed. This relationship had given rise to intense feelings of guilt, not only because of its immorality, but also because she was deceiving her niece. At last she decided to break up with this man and soon thereafter became engaged to her present husband. This engagement and the ensuing marriage had represented, partially at least, an escape from her relationship with her niece's husband. In order to prevent any possible future resumption of this relationship she told her husband everything that had happened. This had been a typical utilitarian deed and not the expression of a need to express and relieve her feelings with a loving and forgiving husband. Once she had done this, she had not given it a further thought, repressing all her feelings for the man so completely that what had happened no longer played a role in her conscious life; as far as she was concerned, it was a thing of the past and she did not want to be bothered by it again. Unconsciously, however, these feelings had persisted and manifested themselves again in her attachment to her husband's business friend.

As soon as she realized this, she came to tell us about it. Naturally, her story was accompanied by considerable emotional discharge, especially as she again became aware of the feelings of guilt about her conduct. Her need to talk about this in great detail and to repeatedly express her feelings about it was, of course, intense, and assumed the form of a true catharsis. At the same time, she recognized her morbid attachment for her husband's business friend for what it was, with the result that this attachment diminished spontaneously and soon stopped altogether. She retained a certain attraction for him in her imagination for a considerable length of time. The spell was broken, however, because she no longer saw him in the light of the repressed romantic feeling of her childhood, but in the light of reality in which the man retained none of his former appeal.

Following this phase in the recovery process, this patient's relationship with her husband improved steadily. Although her love for him had never really been absent, it had, of course, been strongly influenced by her repressed emotions, but now it began to grow to its fullest proportion. This was clearly demonstrated by the fact that she never experienced an orgasm with him until after the above-mentioned developments. In the end, their married life became entirely normal.

Furthermore, she began to see why she had been so fearful of social contacts. Unconsciously she felt ashamed and embarrassed with people who looked up to her because of her prominent place in a number of charitable organizations, while in reality she had been such a "bad sinful person." With the gradual disappearance of these fears, her emotional life also developed in more positive ways. She began to enjoy her housework again after having neglected it for years; her first achievement in this regard was to clean all her closets and cupboards. She also became once more an excellent homemaker and mother to her children, who during most of her illness had been away in boarding schools, as it would have been too hard on them to remain at home during those difficult years.

The patient's various physical complaints disappeared spontaneously, and she was no longer incontinent of urine. For a long time, however, she continued being bothered by insomnia, having difficulty in falling asleep, and waking up frequently during the night. Ultimately, after years of using sedatives, this also returned to normal.

Her spiritual life also became entirely satisfactory, after we introduced her to a sympathetic priest who had an excellent understanding of her illness. He did not force her in anything and let things quietly take their course. As a result, her obsessive-compulsive attitude toward her religion disappeared spontaneously and on her own initiative she again returned to the sacraments. At present she is a deeply devout woman.

The entire treatment took five years. Until the time that she told us about her relationship with her niece's husband, the interviews took place twice weekly; after that, once a week, and then once every two weeks. She appreciated our relationship immensely and even feared to get well, because there would then be no more need for regular visits. However, the termination of treatment took place spontaneously and without difficulty.

Therapy was limited to face-to-face discussions and no psychoanalytical interpretations were made at any time. Her trust and confidence in us caused her to bring everything out.

It has been five years since she recovered. She has become a pleasant and dedicated wife in every respect. According to her husband, she was never as kind and loving as she is now and their marriage never as happy. She delights in the work of her priest-son, and the happiness of her grandchildren. Although some of her children were involved in serious difficulties, she was able to meet these situations squarely and philosophically. She is a great support to her husband and is able to perform all necessary social duties.

2. Blinding Headaches and Ulcer in Young Lawyer

A thirty-three year old lawyer came to us after hearing a lecture by one of the authors which made him realize that he was suffering from a serious emotional illness. He had already resigned himself to a life of frequent ophthalmic migraines, diets for a recently discovered stomach ulcer, and a general state of tension and rigidity which was rather painfully evident in his way of walking and dressing. Of superior intelligence, well-read in philosophy and theology, ambitious to succeed, and well aware of his talents, he had largely ignored his pains and discomforts, just as he directed all his willpower to suppressing the anxiety and fear which had been with him in varying degrees of intensity for as long as he could remember. From the age of twelve he suffered from severe scrupulosity in regard to morals, his studies, and lately his profession in which he was most successful, as he devoted all his time to it and never engaged in purely pleasant and recreational pursuits. Having dated very little in college, he had remained single, and even a causal glance at girls caused him immediate irrational fears.

Before we present the patient's own comments about his background and the treatment process, we must mention some data concerning his family history. His paternal grandfather had experienced terrible headaches for many years, and hanged himself at the age of fifty. His father had a gastrectomy for an ulcer at the age of forty-nine. His mother had developed a gastric ulcer in later life. His brother, one sister, and a paternal aunt had migraine headaches. There is a possibility that one paternal uncle was psychotic.

The patient was seen once monthly during the first year of therapy, ten times the next year, and three times the third year. Soon after his last visit he sent us the following summary of his past life, his illness and experiences in therapy.

> I was the eldest of eight children. My parents were both devout Catholics who conscientiously raised us in that tradition. All of the duties prescribed by the Church were faithfully followed. The family thought of itself as closer to the Church than most others seemed to be. The dominant religious influence was imparted by my mother, who was raised in the strict Prussian tradition, and was rather reserved in showing her love for the children. My father was a quiet, passive, and emotionally reserved man without hobbies, who liked to spend his free time playing cards in a tavern with his friends. From my mother, the local parish priests, and especially the nuns who taught me through the grades and high school, I learned a fear of God and horror of sin and hell which I believe profoundly affected my emotional stability. I vividly remember my fright at being summoned at the age of nine to answer to the pastor for having received communion in good faith after inadvertently breaking my fast. Another experience which remains a painful memory occurred at the age of twelve when we prepared, over a period of several days, to make a general confession in preparation for receiving solemn communion. Incredible as it may seem now, we were instructed to make a written list of our sins if we feared we might forget them (and who could help but fear!). The confessional had a burning candle so that we would be able to read our lists!
>
> As many other children were subjected to the same treatment without apparent ill effects later in life, I am inclined to believe that a premature development of a sense of duty and responsibility was

a significant factor in making me vulnerable to such emotional stresses. As the eldest child I was expected at an early age to watch the other children and to be a good example for them. Thus I could never play with that carefreeness and abandon which is essential to healthy growth and development. Mother insisted on very early toilet training, and also on absolute cleanliness. In this connection I recall the thorough discomfort I felt when I was about five years of age at being unable to sit down anywhere outside for fear of getting my good pants dirty.

Sexual matters were the source of most guilt feelings; as a child there seemed to be no sin as great. Common and harmless sexual experiences became the source of anxiety with confession and were subject to endless repetition. By the time true sexual feelings developed they were always associated with fear and anxiety. This fear was augmented by the manner and content of the sex instruction we received from the pastor. By the middle of my seventeenth year I was involved in compulsive masturbation accompanied by intense anxiety. The confessors to whom I manifested my anxieties and scruples were unable to offer any lasting assistance. I came to rely more and more on my own strength in banishing my fears. Within three years, before I was twenty years old, by sheer force, I had destroyed my sexual desires—I no longer masturbated, persons of the opposite sex no longer seriously interested me. I became interested in the academic life and decided to become a lawyer. In my third year of college I began to suffer from migraines. The attacks at first were severe and debilitating even though infrequent. At first I was quite alarmed by these attacks, then discouraged by their persistence, and finally, simply resigned myself to accept them as a part of life.

The anxiety and fear which had been my constant companions did not leave when I entered law school. Instead they were even more evident as I applied myself to the discipline of the spiritual life and sought the pharisaical perfection of self-imposed rules and self-examination. The more ardently I struggled the more the tension increased. Reception of the sacraments became a torture. The confessor only aggravated my illness by urging more intense mortification and requiring me for instance to eat even less meat than I did already and to quit smoking. I manifested my doubts and scruples to various confessors but none was able to help. Were it not too tedious and of doubtful value itself I could recount in detail some of the agonies I experienced. By exerting extreme energy I was able to maintain an even and placid composure. Few if any were aware that I was anything but a model student and promising attorney. Only those to whom I manifested my conscience were aware of my condition. Naturally the illness did not "go away" with graduation as one confessor predicted it would. Rather, anxiety accompanied every act of preparing a brief, or counseling a client. And thus it seemed that I was destined to live for the rest of my life. I had tried every remedy with no success. My prayers for deliverance became more incessant and urgent.

Then, at the age of thirty-three, after years of suffering what at times were excruciating pains and agonies, I happened to hear one of the authors describe the symptoms of the obsessive-compulsive neurosis, which were so similar to my own that I suddenly realized I was emotionally ill. When that awareness came it was soon followed fortunately by the knowledge, gained from reading an earlier work by the chief author, that I could be cured. Thus I was spared the agony of those who know they are truly ill but wander about from doctor to doctor finding some temporary relief perhaps, but no permanent cure.

Despite my intellectual conviction that their theory was plausible and their therapy in conformity with morality, I understandably lived through moments of intense fear that I was sinning by no longer mortifying my pleasure appetite. For as soon as I was able to live and act without reference to law and obligation and to mortify the energy and fear which had dominated my life for so long, the repressed sexual emotion swept over me like a tidal wave. Despite the fear, I allowed myself to experience pleasure, stopped dieting, and dared to live a gradually more relaxing life. I began to have nightmares—mostly dreams of heights from which I fell and awoke in fear. After some months these dreams grew less frequent and finally stopped. During all this time I avoided any attempt to control my sexual emotion (other than not involving someone else). I understood that twenty years of repression could not be healed overnight. Moreover, I was convinced that the emotional life was not destructive or damaging to the self but was designed to function in harmony with reason and will, and thus would find its own level and balance if it could be freed from the tyranny and violence of an imperious utility appetite. Happily this conviction was borne out.

The first visit to the doctor was anticipated with fear. It proved to be deeply satisfying and created a deep need to return. Throughout the first year of therapy I was anxious to return and realized my complete dependence upon the therapist. I had no doubt of his ability. My confidence grew to admiration and love and I felt myself being healed by him. I believe my confidence was enhanced by his knowledge of theology and philosophy as well as by his masculinity and the knowledge that he was husband and father. His own maturity and love of life made me want to be like him. Gradually the feelings of dependence diminished and I was able to lengthen the time between visits. Now that I feel myself healed and at peace I experience a sense of independence and freedom. I am able to make decisions that are truly my own. Emotions are no longer exerting an uncomfortable pressure. Life is full, rich, and joyful. It is hard to convince others of the joy and happiness which are now so much a part of my life. Inner conflict has disappeared and I am truly alive. In some ways I feel like a man raised from the dead, saved, given a new life. I am overwhelmed with gratitude.

During therapy, the patient gradually lost his fear of God as a punishing judge, and little by little learned to understand, as well as feel, God's real goodness and love. With the gradual integration of the sexual drive into the intellectual dimension, he became more relaxed, enjoyed the good things of life without suffering stomach pains or headaches, developed and responded to his growing need for feminine non-sexual love and friendship, and four years and four months after the beginning of therapy he entered into what promised to be a happy marriage.

There seems little doubt that the relatively rapid cure of this severe obsessive-compulsive repression was due in large measure to this man's brilliant mind, which afforded him rapid and profound insights into basic philosophical, psychological, and theological concepts related to the cause of his illness.

COMBINED EMOTIONAL DEPRIVATION DISORDER AND REPRESSION—THREE CASES
1. Mother with Beard Phobia

A thirty-three year old woman, mother of three boys aged nine, seven, and five, was referred to us by her family physician. She was the youngest in a family of three girls, and prior to her marriage at the age of twenty-three to a man fifteen years her senior, she had never been sick except for measles when very young. During the first year of her marriage she began to suffer from a left-sided sciatic pain which became especially excruciating during her pregnancies. Several times she had been hospitalized for this condition, but all treatment, including fever therapy, had been to no avail. Her entire married life was influenced by this pain: she slept in a bag made from a woolen blanket, she wore two pairs of stockings in the middle of the summer, and she always carried a small bag of sand on the small of her back because she claimed that without it she was unable to lift the children from their cribs or to do her work around the house. After the birth of the youngest child, she and her husband had taken particular care to avoid further pregnancies and for that purpose they practiced withdrawal.

During her last hospitalization, approximately six months before she came to us, she happened to share a hospital room with a woman who had an excessive growth of hair on her face. A few days later the patient developed a fear that she, too, would grow such a beard. In the beginning she repressed this fear, but after she left the hospital it became so intense that she walked around all day with a pocket mirror in her hand to check her upper lip and chin. After a while she became afraid to show herself in the street. A severe depression set in; she cried easily, slept poorly, lost interest in everything, and neglected her household and family. Such was her condition when she came to see us.

The patient was of pyknic body build with normal secondary sex characteristics, and her nutritional state was fair. The only abnormality revealed by physical and neurological examinations was a strongly positive Lasègue's sign on the left side. There was, however, nothing to suggest a sciatic nerve root syndrome, nor any signs of paralysis or muscle atrophy. The muscle-stretch reflexes were brisk bilaterally while the reflexogenic areas were only slightly extended.

Clinically, the patient impressed us as being of superior intelligence in spite of limited formal education, having completed only grammar school. Nevertheless, in the years that followed, she had shown a keen interest in developing herself further. She possessed good practical judgment with a clear understanding of important issues and an ability to see them in their correct relationship. She was of good will, desiring only what was right, yet she felt powerless to realize her desires. She felt deeply, but she was very fearful and uncertain of herself. During the initial interview she cried repeatedly, complaining of depression and of being tired of living. She also suffered from marked feelings of inferiority in regard to her appearance, her origin, her education, her achievements in housework, her children, and her attitude toward her husband.

She expressed herself with ease about conscious fears and conflicts; in fact, she felt an urge to do so and could not talk enough about her fear of developing a beard. She told us that she had never experienced a sexual orgasm with her husband, and that as a result she had indulged in masturbation, about which she suffered severe pangs of conscience. She also felt extremely guilty about their practice of withdrawal.

Her spiritual life had been influenced to a great extent by her emotional disorder, for although she still attended Mass, she was unable to pray and entertained doubts about articles of faith. Not long before coming to us, she had thought of leaving the Catholic Church and embracing another religion.

Her husband was fifteen years her senior and had grown up with a strong attachment to his mother. He had married the patient chiefly for utilitarian reasons. He was a well-meaning man, faithful in his duties, but with a poorly developed emotional life. His lack of understanding and feeling for his wife undoubtedly aggravated her emotional state.

We made the diagnosis of fear-based repression in an inadequately affirmed person, and considered the prognosis to be favorable in view of her superior intelligence and introspective ability, as well as the absence of any psychopathic personality features.

At the beginning of therapy, the patient was entirely obsessed by her fear of growing a beard. She hardly talked about anything else. However, it was obvious to us that treatment aimed directly at this particular manifestation of her deeper fears would not alter the basic personality structure. We therefore told her right away that we intended to ignore her beard phobia, since it would disappear as soon as its cause—namely her general state of fear—had been alleviated. We dramatized this advice by comparing her phobia to the fever in a person with pneumonia; the fever disappears automatically once the infection has been treated successfully. She accepted this advice without reservations.

In order to help the patient on the way to recovery, it was necessary to make her understand her own condition. Basically, two factors were responsible for her symptoms: first, a deep-seated fear of all kinds of things, and second, directly related to the first factor, a strong feeling of inferiority which led to total uncertainty about her own actions. Obviously, therapy had to be directed at these two factors.

The patient knew quite well from daily experience that she was possessed by numerous fears: fear of growing a beard, fear to walk in the streets, fear to be with people, fear to displease her husband, fear that she would fail in her duties as a mother and housewife, and so on. We soon realized that she was completely unaware of the fact that all these fears were rooted in a fundamental fear of the emotions of her own pleasure appetite. As she would be unable to fight these fears successfully unless she realized this fact herself, we began by giving her an outline of our understanding of the normal human personality. We told her, for instance, about the two different kinds of emotions in the psychic life: those by which one desires pleasant and nice things and those by which one avoids dangers or does useful things. Her superior intellect proved a valuable asset in the therapeutic process, for it did not take her long to understand these things thoroughly. We pointed out to her that her fears probably were always directed at her own pleasure emotions, and that she became fearful if she experienced some desire or other. We advised her of the need to realize that the main difficulty lay in the fact that she did not dare to let her emotions take their course.

Fortunately, the patient had great confidence in the therapist from the very beginning and this, together with her quick grasp of psychological factors, enabled her to make good progress in therapy. She was able to look at her own life and behavior in the light of our discussions and became more and more convinced that what we had told her was right. In each of her weekly sessions she reported certain new insights which had helped her to make further progress. To make it possible for her to counteract her fears, we advised her systematically to follow her first impulses and not be deterred in this by subsequent thoughts which undoubtedly would be inspired by fear. Therefore, her motto was to be: "Leap before you look!" When she put this into practice, she discovered that she always did the right thing and did not do anything wrong or strange. Her own experiences proved to her that she was on the right track and gave her the confidence necessary to continue. Her natural emotions made themselves felt more and more as the repressing fear receded. Little by little, she allowed herself to have feelings of affection, of desire, and, in time, of joy and happiness, feelings which had earlier been completely absent. To give an example, instead of spending all her free time in knitting, for fear that otherwise she would be wasting her time and not doing something useful, she now was able to spend her time doing just what she liked. The gradual development of her sexual feelings was helped by the changed attitude of her husband, as we shall discuss in a moment. The feeling of dissatisfaction in her marital life disappeared and made room for a normal relaxation in their sexual relations.

Fear, however, was not the only outstanding symptom of her illness, for equally important was a closely related inferiority complex. The patient thought she was different from others, that her feelings were peculiar and that she was an unfit wife and mother who never did anything right. The knowledge we had of her past, as well as our objective impressions of her, however, completely belied this, for she possessed an excellent intellect and judgment and felt deeply for others. As a result of circumstances, however, she had never developed self-confidence in regard to anything. The basic fault had been in her mother's attitude toward her. Although deeply concerned for her children's welfare, her mother had never shown any love for them; she had spoken only about duty and criticized them when they failed in performing it. Moreover, the family had frequently made fun of the patient because of a slight but insignificant physical deformity. Neither the period of engagement nor her marriage had been of any help to her in gaining self-confidence. Her husband was matter-of-fact and not inclined to a romantic relationship. Soon after the honeymoon, he had told her that other women made love much better than she did, and this remark, of course, had deepened her lack of self-confidence in this respect.

Since these feelings of inferiority had to be banished, we proceeded to bring out her good qualities and to tell her in what manner we thought she was likable and sympathetic. She was truly amazed when she realized that she had not been aware of her own assets, especially when she became more and more convinced that we spoke the truth. This we always did, since only a truthful attitude can form the foundation for a healthy emotional life. A change for the better in the attitude of her husband did much to increase her confidence in herself. This well-meaning man, who did not understand his wife in the least, was brought to a better understanding of the problem. In our first interview with him, he praised his wife highly, although apparently he had never expressed this good opinion directly to her. The patient was quite surprised when we told her how her husband really felt about her. Although he loved her dearly, he had never told her so himself; the only attestation of his love had been an occasional "You know that I love you, I don't have to tell you that." We explained to him that a woman needs concrete expressions of her husband's love, and the more the better; for example, by hearing endearing words, by feeling his kisses or a tender caress, by seeing his loving smile or receiving a little gift, and so on. Fortunately, he understood these things and completely changed his attitude toward her, with the result that her sense of personal worth was restored not only by us, but also by her husband.

A minor incident illustrates the increasing trust she developed in her husband. One of the rooms in her home had been newly wallpapered, but a small edge had been left unfinished. The patient worried about this, the more so when her sister—who was equally neurotic and equally intent on fault-finding—severely criticized the relatively small imperfection. She tensely awaited the arrival of her husband, hoping that he would solve the dilemma of what to do about it, and fearful at the same time that he would be unable to do so. As soon as her husband entered the room, he noticed the imperfect workmanship and remarked: "That suits me fine. It is just in the spot where I wanted to hang a book rack." Immediately her unrest disappeared as if by magic, and her faith in her husband was further strengthened.

As a result of our way of counteracting her fears and her ideas of being inferior, she made quick progress. After five or six weeks, her beard phobia had already decreased considerably, although we had never discussed the subject. At the end of the sixth interview, she herself remarked that she had not even used the word "beard" in her conversation that day. About three months later, the beard phobia disappeared completely. She had been afraid to have more children and therefore had practiced withdrawal with her husband; but after about five months of therapy, she told us that she again wanted to have a child and had resumed normal sexual relations. During the subsequent pregnancy there was no trace of depression or of the sciatic pains that had plagued her during earlier pregnancies. The birth of the child brought her great happiness.

She steadily became more ambitious in her housework, not because of worry that she would do a poor job, but because she enjoyed the work. The atmosphere in the home changed dramatically, for instead of worrisome concern, there was now quiet cheerfulness. Her compulsion to clean things over and over disappeared; she did things more quickly and more efficiently so that she had time to spare for other activities. She became interested in her appearance and began to dress better and more tastefully. She also changed in her attitude towards the children. Formerly, her own concern in their regard had been whether they were—to say it in her own words—clean, dry, and fed. Now she played with them and loved and caressed them, and for the first time in their married life both she and her husband really enjoyed the children. The children had been seriously affected by her earlier abnormal condition: the two older ones had become neurotic, one suffering from nocturnal and diurnal enuresis, and the other being exceedingly shy and withdrawn. Fortunately, as a result of their mother's change for the better, a natural emotional rapport was established so that the children's neurotic symptoms disappeared in about one year. The patient's relationship to other people also underwent a complete change. She began to realize that she was not inferior to them and that her emotions were as healthy, if not in some respects deeper and truer, than those of others.

Her neuralgia, so bothersome before, no longer troubled her, not even during her pregnancy. Both its objective signs and its subjective symptoms vanished. Her prophylactic measures against this neuralgia, which previously had taken most of her time and concentration, were gradually omitted on her own initiative, until at last she no longer resorted to any of them. She made the spontaneous observation that her nervous tension must have been the cause of her neuralgia. Her marital life became truly happy. Her love for her husband kept growing by the day and so did his love for her. She is happy in her family and plans to have more children. Her spiritual life, too, straightened itself out. At one time she had thought of changing her religion because for years she had been irritated by the fact that nothing was ever said from the pulpit about a husband's duties regarding his wife. This, a neighboring woman had told her, was the most popular subject in the sermons of the missionary church she belonged to. Later on, during the process of recovery, the patient spontaneously realized how absurd her plan had been and remarked that her intellectual horizon could not have been very wide at the time she entertained the idea of conversion to her neighbor's religion. Her doubts about her own religion and her difficulties in praying likewise disappeared. The doubts had originated entirely in her emotional life because her fear of God had prevented her from recognizing Him as good and gentle and had caused her to see Him only as the cause of a frustrating interference with everything that is good. When her fears receded, all this straightened itself out without difficulty.

Obviously, the process of recovery was gradual. For example, her relationship with her husband, which at first was very unsatisfactory due to her fearful inhibition and self-preoccupation, improved little by little. At first she was still so hypersensitive that she withdrew from him at the smallest difficulty or least disappointment, or she would become overwhelmed by fears as soon as her husband fell short in showing her his love. These reactions, however, gradually became less intense, and toward the end of therapy, although still aware of similar feelings when minor incidents occurred between her and her husband, she was able to be objective about them. Later on, even these feelings disappeared altogether.

When the emotions of her pleasure appetite came to the fore, we were impressed by the fact that they did so in the order indicated by rational psychology: pleasure—desire—joy. First she experienced a feeling of pleasure when in the presence of a certain good; later on, when the fear diminished, she got a desire for that good; and finally she dared to enjoy it and be happy. The enjoyment, too, grew in steps. At first, her depression was interrupted by brief periods of happiness; then those moments began to last longer. Gradually, a more lasting state of happiness won out and became more or less habitual with her, except for ever briefer moments of depression until these, too, almost entirely disappeared. The fact that from the very beginning she possessed the utmost confidence in the therapist played, of course, a major role in her recovery. She accepted without reservations what she was told and felt entirely secure when she followed our advice. She once told us that she had developed the habit of talking to her therapist during her daily activities. "I ask myself what the doctor would say, and then I go ahead with my work without worry." By following our advice, she discovered for herself that it was based on sound principles. This deepened her insight until the knowledge of these principles became her own. This enabled her to gradually rely less on the psychiatrist and more on her own judgment; her need to submit everything for approval to the therapist steadily became less, until she came in only occasionally for a chat.

As a result of her confidence in the psychiatrist, all the conflicts that had caused her neurotic disorder gradually emerged, and she herself brought them up for discussion without ever being prompted. The therapist never probed for these conflicts, but waited patiently for her to discuss them voluntarily. This she did one by one, and whenever she did, she was obviously prepared to face them and to accept the psychiatrist's help in solving them.

She proved to have numerous conflicts. Her fear of sex stemmed from childhood experiences and memories of the days when she slept with her parents in the alcove bedroom and witnessed them having sexual relations. Her feelings of inferiority, as explained before, had their cause in the cold and impersonal attitude of her mother and her husband, and also in the ridicule encountered as a result of her physical handicap. The beard phobia appeared to be related to the fact that in childhood she had known an aunt who had to shave every day; apparently this had left her with a latent fear that became manifest during her state of agitated depression.

This represents the extent of our therapy. We only combated the fear and the related feelings of inferiority, so that the emotions of the pleasure appetite, which had been totally repressed, could be released. We never analyzed or interpreted isolated symptoms, nor did we ever prescribe rules of conduct or moral standards other than the most general ones. We merely assisted her basically healthy personality, endowed with a good will, to throw off the compulsion of an abnormal fear and resume its interrupted development.

2. Exhausted Nun With a Doll

One day, a thirty-eight year old nun came to see us in the company of her superior. The latter's request to see us first was granted with the permission of the sister. The superior informed us that the sister had always been a very fine nun who excelled in the performance of her duties. For years she had been in charge of a hospital in a foreign mission where she was the confidante of physicians, priests and patients. The superior, since she had been mistress of novices there at the time, had known her ever since she entered the cloister at the age of eighteen. The patient had always been a happy and cheerful person who never caused any difficulties in the religious community and led an exemplary spiritual life. For the past year she had complained of increasing fatigue for which several medical specialists had not been able to detect a cause. Even the performance of her duties in the religious community had become too much for her, and they had been at a loss until it was suggested that she see a psychiatrist. This they finally decided to do, although the sister had been indignant at the thought of having to consult a psychiatrist.

Because of this feeling, she was given only a physical and neurological examination on her first visit, and no attempt was made to take a psychiatric history from her. Her general physical condition was satisfactory. The pupils were of average size and steady; there was a tremor of the hands, and the palms of her hand and the soles of her feet showed marked hyperhidrosis. The activity of her muscle-stretch reflexes was low, without extension of the reflexogenic areas; while reinforcement resulted in pronounced increased activity of these reflexes. Her blood pressure was 130/80. She was advised that on account of her excessive fatigue she would have to rest in bed for fourteen hours out of every twenty-four, and take daily walks by herself for about two hours each day, preferably in the country. She was put on a high protein and carbohydrate, low-fat diet, with large doses of vitamin B-complex. She was asked to come back again in six weeks.

There was no noticeable change in her condition, either objectively or subjectively, on her second visit. As formerly, she was not asked to give any information about herself other than what pertained to her physical condition and her complaints of fatigue, and after ten minutes she left the office with advice to return in another six weeks.

It so happened that a few weeks later her superior came to see us about another nun, and took the opportunity to tell us about the difficulties which she had encountered with our patient. In contrast to her usual reserved attitude of keeping a certain distance between herself and others, the patient had confided in the superior that she had become aware of an irresistible longing for motherly tenderness. The superior possessed enough sympathetic understanding to interpret this longing in the proper sense, and since she was a very stable and wise religious woman, we advised her to treat the sister as she thought best. When the superior also informed us that the patient had expressed a desire to discuss her difficulties with us as soon as possible, an appointment was made for the next afternoon.

The sister, who impressed us as a most intelligent and basically calm and stable woman, began the interview by telling us that she had changed her mind about psychiatrists, because in the previous interviews she had not been pressed for information that she had not been ready to give at the time; also, she said, she felt confidence in us after having read some of our publications. Recently, as a result of manifesting her feelings in her association with the superior, she had acquired a different view of herself. She always had been of the opinion that no matter what happened she would be in control of her emotions, but this had become impossible in her association with her superior. When we asked her whether she would mind some questions concerning her earlier life, she told us that she had been the youngest in a family of nine children. The other eight were all boys. Her mother had not wanted a girl and she herself, the patient remarked spontaneously, had always behaved like a boy as far back as she could remember. She only played boys' games, the more dangerous the better, like crawling on roofs, walking on the parapets of bridges, and climbing high trees. She had not been afraid of anything. She had never really had any girl friends and associated mainly with boys. As a result of reading our books she had become familiar to some extent with philosophical anthropology and recognized that in everything she did she was guided by utilitarian motives.

She never approved of doing something because it was pleasant, and therefore she never did it for that reason. She had felt extremely humiliated when her affection for her superior had taken the upper hand.

The interviews that followed—at weekly intervals—saw a rather sudden change in her condition. The physical fatigue diminished somewhat, and where formerly she had never dreamed, she was now tormented every night by dreams in which she did all kinds of dangerous things just as she had in her childhood. Although these acts had never frightened her in the least in childhood, dreaming of them now caused such intense fear that she could not stay in bed. In this way she relived many periods of her childhood, and although at first she was fearful in the daytime when thinking about her early experiences, this gradually diminished until at last they caused no fear whatever. However, when she happened to find a book with photographs of her place of birth, the memory of various dangerous games she had played there became extremely vivid and caused her to have several attacks of fear.

In one of the interviews, she related that she had never received any motherly love because her mother had brought her up without any display of affection. Her relationship to her father had been equally lacking in emotion. Her relations with her brothers had always been most companionable and still were. Although all other personal relationships in her life had been pleasant, she realized that deep inside she had never really cared for anybody until she had opened her heart to her superior. With her, she felt like a child; she had an emotionally satisfying rapport because the superior was able to meet her on her own level of emotional development. Her relations with others, because they were entirely volitional, were devoid of emotional response. The superior, who had excellent insight into the situation, continued to treat her tenderly, like a small child, and this did her a world of good.

For a while, the patient used the interviews solely for a discussion of the psychological aspects of her case and spent many hours studying this subject. But one day, about six months after beginning therapy, she came to tell us shamefacedly that she had become aware of a strange desire. Until now she had spent many a pleasant hour of her leisure time making little dolls of clay, and in order to encourage this, we had arranged for her to attend an arts and crafts course. Although she achieved little in this course, the very manipulating of the clay pleased her; she derived the same pleasure from finger painting that children do when they get used to the feel of the substances used in play. During this particular interview she confided that she wanted to play with a real doll. We explained that this was a healthy desire, entirely in accord with our understanding of how one learns to trust others through his or her experiences as a child, first with matter itself (playing in the sandbox) and later with symbols representing "others" (the teddy bear, the rabbit, and finally the doll, which, though representing the human "other," is an "other" completely subject to the child). In the light of these ideas, the patient was able to accept without conflict her desire to play with a doll, and she did so for three months, hugging it, feeding it, and making clothes for it just as any small girl would do. On several occasions she brought the doll along to her interviews. This phase passed in three or four months, and from then on she never mentioned the doll again. During this stage of therapy, she saw us only once every two weeks. Her relationship with the superior continued unchanged because she experienced a feeling of safety only with her. When a year or so later the superior was transferred elsewhere, the patient was at first greatly upset, but soon came to feel that she would be able to stand it, provided she was allowed to visit her occasionally. This was arranged to her great satisfaction and it proved unnecessary to increase her therapy hours.

In the meantime, her frightening dreams had stopped, and the subjective feelings of fatigue had practically disappeared. Only a conscious fear of adults persisted. She herself remarked that she had no fear of small children; in fact, she was aware of an emotional rapport with them that she had not possessed before. However, the children had to be small, not more than three or four years old; older children caused her to be afraid.

As she had developed an intense desire to take care of babies, we suggested that she find work in a hospital taking care of infants. After having done this for a while, she told us that her emotional life had developed considerably in her contact with the babies. However, she still was afraid of the other nurses, and although the volitional aspect of their relationship was the same as before, it now had become distinctly distasteful to her.

Meanwhile, her mother died. Her death, however, failed to affect the patient emotionally, though she considered it a release from the volitional signs of affection they had shown for each other. These had caused great repugnance and sadness in her, especially since she had established a much more sincere and warm relationship with her religious superior. It had even been impossible for her to call her own mother "Mother," and she had begun to call her "Grandma" instead.

Six months later she began to work in another hospital and was able to work with adults without fear. Her interviews were reduced to only once a month. Her uneasiness with her colleagues was the last symptom to disappear. Most recently she reported that her work in a leading position in a hospital has been most satisfactory both to herself and to others.

The evolution in her spiritual life deserves special mention. When she first came to us she had an intense dislike of the religious life and was seriously considering leaving it. She no longer participated actively in the life of the cloister, nor did she receive the sacraments. However, when she began to make some progress in therapy, she gradually and spontaneously began to pray again and to receive the sacraments, until at last she again performed all her duties, but with this difference: she no longer did them in a purely volitional way and her emotions were also activated. At first she was only a passive participant in the pleasure derived from things accidentally related to the religious life, for example, singing in church, decorating the chapel, listening to organ music and observing the ceremonies. All these things seemed strange to her, as if she were experiencing them for the first time. In her attitude toward God she first felt like a baby, then like a small child, a girl, and at last an adult. At that stage, she renewed her religious vows because her original vows had lost their meaning to her.

Her psychosexual life showed a similar gradual and fully integrated development. At present she is a mature and happy woman who has found great enjoyment in her work, to the benefit of everybody involved.

Our diagnosis was first of all Emotional Deprivation Disorder: as a result of a lack of emotional rapport with her mother, the patient's own ability to love others had not been developed. Because of her intelligence and balanced disposition, this emotional deficiency matured fully in only two years time. The extremely fortunate circumstance of the patient's relationship with her superior undoubtedly also played an important role. Superimposed on this Emotional Deprivation Disorder was energy-based repressive disorder which was resolved by our therapy.

3. Teddy Bears and Insulin Subcoma Therapy

A twenty-eight year old highly creative nun sought our aid. As an art teacher, this patient had intense feelings of inadequacy and mounting irritability with her pupils, recurrent suicidal thoughts, depression, boredom, and constant fatigue. These were accompanied by feelings of bitterness about twelve years of nothing but hard and dutiful work in her religious order and years of severe insomnia and fitful sleep from which she would frequently be aroused by her own sobbing and screaming. These and other things prompted the patient to seek psychiatric treatment.

Sister X, a companion with some psychological schooling, had tried for many years to help the patient to adjust to life as a religious and a teacher by encouraging her: 1) to use her willpower to do what was expected of her; 2) to suppress her feelings ("emotional control is thought control!"); and 3) not to complain about her epigastric pains, her frequent and severe headaches, her recurrent sore throats, and her amenorrhea of five years' duration. Only shortly before the patient came to us, she had been receiving medication for ulcer symptoms, sore throat, and irritable bowel syndrome. Over the years, she had proven such an apt pupil of Sister X that no one in her community suspected how she really felt inside and how much she suffered from the strictly structured regulations imposed on her nature. "I feel like I have two selves, Doctor; I live behind a mask." Although she tried hard to maintain her poise during her first visit, she soon broke down into tears, and said, "I don't want to like you, Doctor, or to be dependent upon you like I was on Sister X. I have tried so hard for ten years to prove to her that I was a good sister and an adequate teacher; I know Sister X thinks well of me, but I don't feel this way myself. I want to forget her so I don't have to constantly wonder if she loves me for what I am."

The severe scrupulosity of the patient's childhood and adolescent years regarding the matter of purity, persisted in her present compulsion to be a perfect religious, and to prove to God that she loved Him in everything she did. Her intense self-criticism centered on her unmortified and uncontrolled eating habits, her weakening prayer life, and her fears of being a burden to her congregation by her sickness and need of psychiatric therapy. Underlying her intense drive to please God and others by leading a perfect life were her deep fears of everybody and everything, as well as her bottomless sense of insecurity, and her frustrated need to be loved for herself. "If I am to get well, Doctor, somebody is going to have to do a 'miraculous' and 'out-of-this-world' amount of loving me. It is going to have to be freely given love *because* I am lovable . . . But I am not lovable and I'll never get well. The hardest thing for me to believe is that God and people can really love me. I think it will always be impossible. I am sure that I can never be genuinely and deeply convinced of that fact." The depth of her sense of worthlessness, in spite of her proven creative accomplishments in the artistic field, her excellence as a teacher, her superior willpower in doing what is right regardless of her subjective feelings and moods, is best expressed in her own words: "Doctor, I feel like Miss Nothing walking on the edge of nothing, holding a withered bunch of nothing. I feel so empty that it is one constant pain, only it hurts worse than any physical pain. I could fall over the edge into the nothing and disappear immediately and forever."

In her dreams the patient was often hunted and pursued to be killed, or severely maltreated and maligned, or captured and tortured by Communists, her parents, sister companions, and other people with whom she felt angry. In spite of her deep depressions, she drove herself to work so hard for so many hours that she could no longer fall asleep and was often too exhausted to eat properly. In her better moments, she was still receptive to the joys of hiking, ice skating, painting, making things for others, dancing, laughter and good conversation, and the genuine goodness, sincerity, and enthusiasm of the people around her. It was not difficult to sense her underlying openness and responsiveness to all the good things of God's creation—her kindness and desire to be of service to other people, her superior intelligence and her need to get to the bottom of things, her creativeness, and her need to share these things with others.

Later in therapy, when hospitalized, the patient told us with unusually early recall, that since the age of two and one-half she had been highly creative, always drawing and coloring, planning and making things, and reading much. As the oldest of six children, she was terribly lonely, and lived a severely secluded and sheltered life in relative poverty. Her very earliest memories were feelings of anxiety, fears of dark rooms, dreary days, sickness, jealousy toward her sister, and extreme scruples and guilt feelings even at the age of three or four. She also recalled severe colds, rheumatic pains, fights with brothers and sisters, and long, hateful, enforced naps to keep the kids out of the way of a too-busy mother. The most pleasant memories of her childhood years were centered around the house where she spent time among the flowers, ran through flowered meadows or worked in the garden with her father—in her own words, "the grandest man I know, an eternal worrier even over the smallest matters, yet so kind and charitable to his family and all needy people, in spite of, or perhaps because of, his tremendous personal sufferings." She vividly recalled, and often relived during her days in the hospital, the many ways in which her mother rejected, belittled, punished, and found fault with her. Some of these memories follow in the patient's own words.

Once when I was two and one-half, I had to go around and shake hands with all the relatives attending the baptism of my little brother. I was terribly fearful and horrified at the thought of being held or caressed by anyone. An older uncle did manage to grab me as I dashed toward the door; I felt so foolish, fearful, and unworthy with his hand on my head. Even with my father I felt the same way. When he wanted me to sit on his lap, I would sit on the very edge of his knees, and escape as promptly as possible, ducking quickly as he tried to pat my head.

Around the age of three, I often wandered around the house all morning, tortured by feelings of guilt that I might have cheated my mother or sister in some way. When my father came home, I would ask him whether this or that small incident might have been dishonest or uncharitable, but no matter how well he explained things and tried to put my mind at ease, my fears and worries about these things were never really dispelled.

During these same early years, I often overheard my mother telling my father about all the naughty things I had done that day—enumerating all my character faults. Each night this happened I cried myself to sleep. I do not recall, however, my father ever talking to me or punishing me for the things of which my mother had accused me.

Whenever the children did something naughty, my mother would blame me for it and urged my father to punish me. No matter what I said or did, my mother would rather believe the other children. I can still feel the burning, aching, hurting frustration of it all. When I was about ten, I stayed away from my brothers and sisters as much as possible; it was safer that way. When I got punished for something my brother had done, I would try my best to realize that I really must have been at fault. I forced myself to control the terrible hurt and resentment I felt toward my brother, and later told my parents I was guilty and had done wrong.

I was also fearful of being rejected by the kids at school who often called me names. I usually felt that I was about as bad and awful and good-for-nothing as a person could be. At the age of twelve, I was so extremely self-conscious and scrupulous that I felt I was actually going insane. I remember being so afraid of committing sin against chastity that I could not bring myself to make a step across the floor. I would stand teetering in the middle of the floor, trying to make a step, and withdrawing my foot because I was too frightened to move. I felt that everything was a mortal sin, and in my scrupulosity considered my most innocent thoughts, words, or actions to be temptations to impure behavior.

I often tried to win my mother's approval by telling her things I thought were "great news." I also tried to be funny or witty to make her smile or acknowledge that I was talking to her. I can still see her standing in front of the stove without her ever looking at me or acknowledging my presence. These things hurt, but I kept trying. I used to do all kinds of work to surprise her; washing the dishes, cleaning the house, sweeping the entry-ways, weeding the flower beds, preparing meals, baking cookies, and taking care of my brothers and sisters. From the eighth grade and all through high school, I even mended my own clothes. My mother, however, acknowledged few of my efforts, and then only with a tight-lipped "thank you." I still wonder, when friends discuss their mothers or talk about motherhood, what it might have been like to have a mother. I never had one. That is how I feel!

When I graduated as valedictorian of my class and was photographed for a full-page insert into the high school annual, my mother refused to have my father even consider buying a copy. She did everything to discourage it, and pooh-poohed the significance of buying such a book even if it cost a mere two dollars. I tried so desperately hard all my life to please her—I never did. Now it does not matter.

Approximately three months after her first office visit, it was possible to start the patient on a course of insulin subcoma treatments[3] for relief of her severe fatigue, tension, compelling restlessness, and to release her long-repressed feelings. Her physical and neurological examinations were not remarkable except for enlarged pupils, moderately severe perspiration of the palms of her hands, slightly increased muscle-stretch reflexes with moderate extension of the reflexogenic areas, and their increase upon reinforcement. A five-hour glucose tolerance test gave the following blood sugar levels: 84—150—157—135—127—110—75mg%.

The results of psychological testing done elsewhere by a clinical psychologist unfamiliar with the syndrome of Emotional Deprivation Disorder were reported as follows:

---

3. Editors' Note: Insulin subcoma treatment is no longer in common use. This treatment is a type of shock therapy in which "insulin is given to produce sleepiness and to produce in the patient a sense of well-being." Although this treatment may still be found in certain parts of the world, psychopharmacological interventions have essentially replaced it. (Freedman, A.M., Kaplan, H.I., and Sadock, B.J., Modern Synopsis of Comprehensive Textbook of Psychiatry/II, Baltimore, MD: Williams & Wilkins, 1976, 1331.)

In summary, we appear to have here an exceedingly bright, talented young woman who has achieved considerable insight into her own immaturity, dependency, and unsatisfactory early mother-daughter relationship. However, despite these intellectual insights she apparently lives her life in a massive, compulsive, over-determined effort to test the love of mother-surrogates. She has tried the obvious neurotic conversion and psychosomatic routes for gaining nurturing with little apparent success. Her strong need for independence and autonomy come into direct conflict with these relatively direct means for satisfying dependency needs. At a more subtle level, she puts mother-figures to unrealistic "tests" and reacts with rage when they do not measure up. Her convent life has become a sibling battleground and she aptly describes her oversensitivity to the slightest sign of favoritism or inconsistency upon the part of her superiors.

I have mixed feelings about the prognosis here. I was initially very positively impressed by her fine intelligence, ability to express self-insights, engaging candor, desire for self-realization, and flashes of apparent spontaneity and warmth. Despite these genuinely positive assets, however, I was also impressed with the strong masochistic quality of her lifestyle and, in my experience, it is frustrating and difficult to find leverage for treatment with people who have this compulsive need to be losers. Add to this the related tendency to test, reduce, manipulate, and discredit the most significant potential need-satisfiers in her life, and the therapeutic challenge certainly becomes formidable.

The patient spent her first night in the hospital like many persons with Emotional Deprivation Disorder typically do—by cleaning her room from top to bottom, as she did not want to impose on the personnel. Both during the insulin treatments in the morning, and during the evening hours when we visited her, she relived many of her childhood experiences. Frequently these were accompanied by more or less violent abreactions with crying and screaming at the top of her voice. Halfway during these days at the hospital she bought herself a teddy bear which she named "Patrick," who never left her side, day or night. She derived much benefit from the kind treatment of the nursing staff, and at times she would remark, "They are real human beings." Mentally as well as physically she improved a great deal, and when she left the hospital, she was relaxed and possessed of great confidence that she would continue to grow and mature with further psychotherapy.

Here we offer the patient's own reflections on insulin therapy, as reported to us three years later.

If I had to do it all over again I would not hesitate for a moment. I had reached a point of no return when it came to being utilitarian. I simply could not stop working. Ever since my childhood, I had become accustomed during an emotional crisis to do some kind of work, usually hard physical work, to better repress my feelings. During my stay at the hospital, I finally talked about deeply traumatic experiences which I had never discussed with anyone. The most vivid episode was the tremendous relief I felt when I described a brutal encounter with my mother when I was sixteen. The incident was so charged with repressed feelings of my worthlessness and nothingness—to me it summed up a mother's rejection of me forever—that I was sure the whole hospital could hear me cry. And for once, I did not care. Since that day, this particular incident, like many others, has remained quiescent. I no longer feel that I am entirely stupid or worthless. During insulin therapy I took the first basic step toward building a positive self-concept, and the ever constant desire to commit suicide began to wane.

I feel that the treatments taught me my physical limitations, and I no longer force myself to continue working after reaching a point of physical exhaustion. The treatments taught me how good it is to rest. I also began to sleep again, at first generally during the day. For five years prior to therapy, I had slept only four or five hours a night, mostly fitful sleep, cut short by sickening spells of nausea and horrible nightmares. I always awoke from these nightmares screaming and so utterly exhausted that for a moment or so I could not get out of bed because of the pain in my joints, back, and muscles.

Following her hospital stay, psychotherapy was continued twice monthly in our office where she would sit on the floor with Patrick, the teddy bear, saying, "That is where little girls sit!" She expressed her feelings freely—anger, fear, despair, and sadness. She cried or screamed when she felt like it. She shared her life with us in these visits and also through long letters. In some ways life in the convent became more difficult for her as well as for her companions, for she began to express her opinions and feelings more freely. This caused reactions of concern and criticism that she was getting worse rather than better. Therefore, the feelings of fear and her wish to be dead returned, as well as more intense resentment toward many aspects of convent life. Fortunately, two people, her local superior and the principal of the school where she taught part-time, sustained her throughout with kindness and patience, although the situation was difficult at times. We prescribed a sharply reduced teaching schedule that would leave sufficient time for naps, rest, leisure activities, and a general relaxation of the rules so that she could sleep, eat, and pray when she felt like it. Once, when she had lost her appointment card and missed her visit, she wrote us the following:

> I need so terribly to grow up. To think I missed a single appointment! I am so afraid, so afraid that the time will run out. Mother Superior will get impatient, and I'll be pulled out, and I'm still so little. If you think that it would be better for me to come weekly, rather than bi-weekly, I'll give in. I have to grow up! But to me it seems better to make haste slowly, allow impressions so very contrary to all of my previous thinking, to sink in. If they will only give me the time, rather than to try to come weekly and "cram." I think I can see, that is, intellectually understand, what I have been doing all these twenty-nine years. The inability to eat, sleep, and all the hyperactivity were only the outward signs of my personal suppressed rage against people, real or apparent injustices, real and intolerable circumstances . . . therefore, I felt so guilty about my anger and rage that I turned it against myself. Even today I keep raging, picking at my stupid self because I made a human blunder by unwittingly depriving myself of an appointment . . .
>
> I can't rationalize the rage by trying to see the one hundred things I did well this summer . . . I am furious with myself! Child, Child, infant child! I want, will, must grow up soon, and fast!

By our constant affirmation of her, and by our encouraging her to dare and to trust her emotions more and more—she kept on growing. The feelings of fear and guilt gradually lessened. One day she wrote to us. "Last week you told me, 'That is the child in you, Sister, feeling so guilty'; that has made me feel so much better. Since then I have been able to dismiss this." Her desires to be dead disappeared after Sister X, for the first time, showed her some physical signs of affection. "I never had a mother, Doctor, now I want to live!"

Then suddenly, approximately fifteen months following the start of therapy, the sky fell down on her when she was informed by "headquarters" that she had to stop therapy immediately. No explanation was given either to her or to us. "You may change doctors," was the only directive given. The reaction which ensued was intensely disturbing: panic, bewilderment, anger, despair, horrible dreams of being deserted and then waking up to her own crying and sobbing. Also the fear of being given electroshock treatments by another doctor was a prime cause of alarm. Many of her previous physical symptoms returned with a vengeance: headaches, stomach pains, nausea, not being able to eat, and even some fainting spells. With it all, however, she was able to express her anger and resentment toward the provincial superior whose unfair and unprofessional conduct had with one word reversed her previous support and expressed approval of the therapist and therapy. She copied, in longhand, all her lengthy letters of protest and shared them with us until after several weeks, her protests, entreaties, and veiled threats paid off, and she was given permission, although begrudgingly, to resume therapy.

This shattering incident made the patient realize that she stood little chance of ever being allowed to be herself if she remained in her congregation. This was a hard step for her to take, for *intellectually* the religious life meant a great deal to her. This we learned from excerpts of her letters:

> I said absolutely "no" to God from age four until I was sixteen, when I decided that "yes" was the only answer I could make, being myself. I refused to join the "vocation club" with my brothers and sisters. Instead I prayed for a good husband every night. In my imagination I kept house for the boy I had a crush on, pretending that I was setting the table, etc., for him. The summer before I entered, I felt as if the day of doom was approaching. However, it seemed as if doing anything else would be ultimately to defeat my own happiness by defying God's will for me. I seemed to have the qualifications listed as the criteria for living the religious life: physical health and average intelligence—plus my talents seemed to lend themselves well to teaching. But I did not *feel* like teaching or entering at that time. I would have liked to go on to college first, and to taste life and drink deeply of all that existed outside the conventual walls. But once I had told my parents of my decision to be a religious, there was some pressure to enter soon.
>
> I felt as if I carried the weight of the whole world within me—I so dreaded and hated the thought of entering. My parents did not wish me to work away from home that summer, and it turned out that it was so hellishly hot that all crops were almost entirely lost. I was terribly depressed by the losses of so many farmers in our area. I worked feverishly that summer, on and on and on—never wasted a moment, getting ready, sewing endlessly. . .
>
> My concept of the convent was rather vague. I never wanted to settle for anything less than God. The desire was a greed—no matter what the cost, I wanted the religious life. I wanted it more and more as I grew older. As a teenager, the occasional enjoyment of teenage pleasure invariably left me in the middle of them; and

afterward I felt terribly empty and dissatisfied. And repeatedly I felt only one desire—one hunger to belong to God.

Since then, I have evaluated and thought through every facet concerning my vocation, and I think that it is because I am so rigid, so emotionally immature that I have not been living this life very successfully. When, where, and how has the religious life ever been a security, a sanctuary, a substitute mother for me? I transferred from mission to mission, and I cannot say that I ever hoped for anything but to please God. That is where the "mother-angle" may enter into the question, but I do not think I equate pleasing God or God's being pleased with me, with a mother's love.

I always felt that nothing less than God could ever really satisfy my hunger. Even when I had acquired some trinket, or some things I had really wanted, they soon meant no more to me than tinsel, a bauble. Only in convent living when I came to feel that people had failed me more and more, did material things become more important. Nevertheless, no matter how wide I now open my mind to another way of life, I am sure that I would still end up in a convent. But perhaps this is a compulsion?

If it was a compulsion, it gradually lessened during the few months of therapy. She then requested permission for exclaustration, and began to bargain-shop for a few of the bare necessities needed for living in the world. She showed us everything she bought, and modeled the few clothes she could afford to buy. Our affirmation of her, in leaving her free to plan for the future, built up her self-confidence and lessened her fears sufficiently so that when she left the convent she was able to stand on her own feet. She knew that various circumstances would of necessity reduce further therapy sessions to perhaps only once or twice a year.

Since she made this important step toward finding herself, twenty-three months after the beginning of therapy, she continued to grow and mature, as we learned from some of the letters she wrote during the first two years after leaving the convent:

> The gain I am most thrilled about is that you have truly left me standing, wobbly-kneed, yet able to go on and live without you, with no overdependent yearning... I have met an unusual number of real, genuinely good, and even great people, and thank God I feel that I am a good person myself. I can't deny, however, that I have problems. I think the worst of these is my fear of others. If I

can get over taking peoples' judgments and reactions to me as personal affronts and as final judgments, I know I'll make it. . . I have my ups and downs, but all in all, I know I am growing. At times I think about the convent, and consider returning, but I guess only because life seems purposeless now and then. Suddenly a week ago, I realized how guilty I feel because I had left the convent, a terrible conviction that God does not look at me, nor hear me, nor care about me anymore, because I had walked out on him. I can't say a prayer—God seems so far, and I wish to miss Mass on Sundays so that God will at least be aware of me because of my wickedness. I'm afraid, however, to miss Mass because I don't know if it would be justified. Sometimes I'm just too lazy or rather, too busy, busy, busy, to want to go. . . I believe the secret of my greatest contentment, and even joy in being alive, comes from the freedom to make my own decisions, choose my friends and leisure time activities as I wish—when I wish. I hated the convent because there was no room for spontaneity. Now, although I work long and hard, I still live like a butterfly. Outside of work hours, I keep no schedule or routine whatever. . . I realized again how much I have changed in just a few months on the basis of all the things you taught me. For instance, I found it hard to spend money for anything without feeling guilty, but when I began to buy a little better food for myself this summer, I found myself spontaneously wanting to do more good things for others. . .Whatever you gave me adds up to enough security to keep on risking, happily and eagerly, without wishing to be dead. I am still afraid. . . I did not go home to see my family because I simply did not want to. I wanted to stay here and enjoy my work and other people. Therefore, I did not go home but suffered the guilt instead. And now I have discovered I enjoy and do look forward to going home at the next opportunity. Somehow you gave me the freedom to keep violating the "ought to" feelings or compulsions that ruled my whole life. I feel guilt, but these feelings don't win anymore, and I have never enjoyed life and being alive as much as I do now!. . . It is so much more thrilling to feel accepted as lovable rather than as competent and useful. Most of the time I feel good and very happy, but I wonder if I am good in God's eyes. I don't go to church, don't pray, don't try to be anything, just live for the day. That is what I think you implied repeatedly—to trust my feelings and not force myself—to do this would be most pleasing to God—Whoever He is. I know I also have to find Him through my feelings! I often feel like the goat from the poem, "Prayer of the Goat." I want to share it with you.

LORD,
let me live as I will!
I need a little WILD freedom,
a little giddiness of heart,
the strange taste
        of unknown flowers.
For whom else are Your mountains?
Your snow wind? These springs?
The SHEEP do not understand.
They graze and graze,
all of them, and always
        in the same direction,
and then eternally
chew the cud of their insipid routine.
But I—I love to bound to
        the heart of all Your marvels,
leap Your chasms,
and, my mouth stuffed
        with intoxicating grasses,
quiver with an adventurer's delight
on the summit of the world!

AMEN!
(translated from the French by Rumer Godden)

Three years after the patient had left the convent, and shortly before this book went to press, we asked her to comment on her life so far. These are a few comments taken from her reply.

> It has not been a rose garden, but I have never been happier. Everything I achieved I did without financial help from family or congregation. I will soon obtain an M.S. degree in educational psychology, guidance, and counseling. I have never felt surer of myself. This past year teaching, I felt immensely appreciated by the children, their parents, and the school administration. It's really great! I am free at last to see children through my own eyes, and not as I am directed to view them in every parochial school I have ever taught in. . . Many people love me dearly, and they love me just the way I am. My biggest problem is not always being able to feel this emotionally, i.e., "at the gut level." The process of integrating emotions with the rest of me seems to be taking forever, and I suffer at times because of it. . . It sure is difficult to change a

lifestyle that has become almost, but not quite, comfortable. . . I love being able to make choices, even decisions, and to take the responsibility for both.

There is no doubt in my mind that I would have eventually ended up in one of the congregation's institutions for the mentally ill. I feel that I can never really describe to anyone the agony of my life up to the point of beginning therapy. I have gone to hell and back again. But since then I have experienced what heaven must be too, and this experience for me is simply the thrilling awareness of closeness to another human being, any one of my friends, whom I know in the innermost depths of personal emotion, who accepts and loves me exactly the way I am, and delights in the fact of my existence as much as he is aware of my delight in his.

Although my therapist was not the first person in my life whom I felt loved me, the relationship was the most meaningful and significant personal experience in my life. I felt I could say or be anything I wished, realizing more deeply each day, that for the first time in my whole life someone understood me, accepted me, and loved me very much *just the way I was*!

Years of pent-up feelings which I had never realized existed with such intensity came pouring out—and they had to be expressed. The beginning of getting to know and to accept myself began with recognizing and accepting these feelings. I had to have constant reassurance that it was proper for me to have feelings, and at first slowly, then in torrents, I emoted—tears of anger, rage, hate, hostility, resentment, and finally fear. It went on for months. I did not fully comprehend what was happening, I just trusted. For about six months I cried uncontrollably for two to four hours each night before I could fall asleep. As the emotional tension eased, my physical complaints subsided, and I was able to focus more realistically on life outside myself.

I feel like the ugly duckling who turned into a swan. But then he was always a swan! However, I do feel ordinary, but immensely happy. I am sure that the quality which attracts people to me as someone unique is simply the fact that they know exactly what I am feeling, and I can't help being honest. I am wired that way!

You asked me about Patrick. Yes, I loved him with such a passion from the day I received him in the hospital. I spent a great deal of psychic and emotional energy meeting his little bear needs. Until I left the convent, Patrick was immensely dear to me. But then I began to make real friends who were so lovable that poor Patrick was neglected. At one point I panicked. He looked so worn out I thought he was going to die. My father bought me another bear when I went home last year. And last summer after I had started to date, I bought still another one. This new bear is such a flirty, and independent-looking little scamp that I laugh aloud every time I walk into my room. He does not fit in with the other bears sitting on the sofa because he does not look sad and in need of loving like the other two bears. But he is cuddly! I think he represents the dramatic change that has taken place in my personality.

CHAPTER VI

PREVENTION OF REPRESSIVE DISORDERS

To know the laws of God in nature and revelation, and then to fashion the affections and will into harmony with these laws—this is education.

S. F. Scovell

IN EARLIER CHAPTERS, WE showed what the repressive disorders are, how they originate, and how they are caused by an incorrect and unnatural attitude toward an emotion. As a consequence, this emotion, having been buried alive as a result of the mechanism of repression, cannot come to rest, but remains active in the subconscious. In order to arrive at effective preventive measures, we must first investigate the factors influencing the origin and development of neurotic disorders, as well as the conditions under which repression becomes possible and has consequences so serious that repressive disorders begin to develop.

Three areas in the psychic life contribute to the genesis of repressive disorders: the pleasure appetite, the assertive drive, and the intellect and will. It is logical, therefore, to conclude that each of these three spheres contains elements which are significant for the origin and development of repression.

It may be safely stated that a basically sound disposition of the pleasure appetite is a favorable and even necessary condition for the development of a neurotic disorder. *People with cold and insensitive natures do not become neurotic.* They rarely repress, and when they do, it is a superficial process with slight effects that vanish rather quickly. It is a different matter in persons with a sensitive, rich emotional life who react promptly and intensely to all that life has to offer, good and bad, beautiful and ugly, up and down. Repressions in such people are deep and complete, and the repressed emotions do not let themselves be silenced. Buried alive as they are, in a manner of speaking, they continue to agitate incessantly for their emergence, and their rightful consideration and ordering by reason and will. In a sense, neurotic repression, and especially obsessive-compulsive repression, is proof of an emotional life that is richer than average. It constitutes a qualitative defect, and not, as many think, a sign of inferiority.

As the emotional life of the child has not yet attained the stability of adulthood and is not yet fully differentiated, it is to be expected that repressions will occur much sooner in children than in adults. At the same time, they will have more far-reaching consequences, for the emotional life of the child lacks any measurable degree of guidance by the intellect. The spiritual is still far from penetrating and ennobling the child's sensory life to the extent that this normally happens in the adult. Much more so than the adult, the child tends toward an object as a pure sense object and not as it is seen by reason. It follows that the attainment of a sense object is a much more fundamental requirement for the emotional life of the child than for that of the adult, since the former will not come to rest without sense gratification. Repression occurs much sooner in a child than in an adult for the simple reason that in the adult the intellect plays a much greater role in the evaluation of sense objects.

The normal development of the emotions of the pleasure appetite is an absolute requisite for the harmonious growth of the human person's entire psychological life. Whatever constitutes an objective good for human beings must also be experienced and felt by them subjectively as good. Humans beings are heir to an endless number of goods, due to the fact that their sensory cognitive life, ennobled as it is by the intellect, shares in the intellect's universality. These goods, however, must be made available to them to the full extent of their innate powers, if they are to mature fully and enjoy the richness of their human nature. Evidently, the richer and more sensitive the innate disposition of the emotional life, the greater will be its need to develop in its entirety.

This process of development is and must be a gradual one that proceeds from one emotion to the other. Every age level has its own task in this emotional growing process in response to the objects which vary from the most material to the most immaterial. All the varied emotions must grow in nuances and depth at their own specific and optimal times, and must assume their proper, and balanced places in the adult emotional life. It is, however, the task of developmental psychology to describe this process in detail. The only thing we want to say now, as related to the subject matter here at hand, is that in each developmental phase, all emotions specific to that phase must be given the opportunity to be experienced and satisfied and not held back and repressed. This holds true for all age levels—infancy, childhood, puberty, and adolescence—but the earlier these emotions become repressed, the graver the consequences will be.

In the early, formative years, the child more than anything else needs to feel and sense the mother's love through the stimulation of all its senses. Its many other needs must also be satisfied if it is to develop adequately in every respect. The child must have free access to everything associated with normal and healthy growth. It must be free to possess and enjoy these things, and by the same token to feel sad when reason dictates. This does not mean that the child must be given everything it desires or be free to do as it pleases. On the contrary, the child must be brought up in a reasonable manner, because it is after all a rational being even though its emotional life has not yet been subordinated to reason. Therefore, because the child is not yet capable of rational acts, it is necessary for the educator's reason—not caprice or whim—to assume the task of guiding and directing the child's emotional life properly. The child is directed by nature to this form of guidance and will find in it the natural harmony and peace—the *tranquility of order*—that it requires.

The child that grows up without intelligent guidance of its emotional life remains frustrated in its most fundamental need—to become fully integrated with and readily responsive to a properly informed reason in ordinary matters ("common sense") as well as in matters of morality (conscience)—and of necessity it remains undeveloped psychologically. Deprived as it is of rational guidance, it repeatedly performs irrational acts and becomes attached to improper and irrational objects. The ability of its own intellect and will to guide and temper its emotional life remains poorly developed, if at all, and the child grows up to be a person who is prey to the stirrings of his or her pleasure appetite. Such children become adults in whom one can recognize without difficulty the *spoiled child*. They become persons who, although not constitutionally unbalanced, develop psychopathic traits as a result of their upbringing, or lack of upbringing. They become persons who cannot deny themselves anything and must have their own way at all times.

On the other hand, it is also possible for the exact opposite to happen if parents and other educators fail to guide the child intelligently. Instead of becoming prey to the emotions of its pleasure appetite, the child may fail to develop them at all. This occurs when the parents unwittingly rob the child of its childhood by expecting the child to be so good, dutiful, and well-behaved that it does not make use of opportunities for play and fun. Although such parents do not forbid the child to find enjoyment in play and games, they do not encourage it either. This may happen when the parents themselves are excessively intent on work and utilitarian pastimes to the exclusion of vacations and leisurely weekends, while the child is serious and introspective by nature, eager to please and do good, and inclined to take a precocious satisfaction in such activities as helping with the household chores and supervising and taking care of younger siblings.

We have seen several severely neurotic patients whose parents had failed to encourage them to take part in the games and play of their friends, but instead had let them spend all their time baby-sitting for the younger children, helping the mother cleaning the house and preparing the food, or helping the father with chores on the farm. Some of these patients were married women who either refused to bear children or developed an intense resentment for their children once the neurotic disorder had become clinically manifest. Yet, these women could not be considered selfish, nor did they show any other psychopathic traits. None of them knew how to enjoy life or were able to relax without a sense of guilt. They either found their sole "enjoyment" in keeping a clean house by scrubbing floors, washing walls, and other routine chores, or they were gainfully employed full-time even though their husbands were able and willing to be the sole providers and preferred their wives to be at home with the children.

The second area of the psychological life bearing on the development of repressive disorders is the *assertive drive*. The greater the innate fear or energy of a person, the greater the ease with which he or she will repress pleasure emotions and their subsequent inclinations if for some reason or other such emotions are felt to be harmful. All people differ from one another as far as their natural dispositions or temperaments are concerned. Some are happy by nature and some are sad. Others have an innate tendency to be fearful or energetic and assertive. Racial and hereditary factors as well as differences in gender play an important role in this matter. We have already shown why women tend more toward the development of fear-based repressive disorders and men toward energy-based repressive disorders. Therefore, this matter needs no further discussion.

Experiences during childhood, however, also have considerable weight in the pathogenesis of neurotic disorders. The assertive drive is formed in large part during the first years of life. It may grow freely in a normal manner in an atmosphere of understanding where discerning parents recognize the importance of the emotions of this appetite and allow nature to take its course, eliminating defects without repression or distortion. On the other hand, in early years it may already become oriented to later neurotic disorders through hypertrophy of the natural emotion of fear or of emotional energy under the influence of misconceptions or incorrect attitudes on the part of the educators, or of the latter's own emotional immaturity or illness. The mother who treats her child coldly first of all readily creates, as we have explained elsewhere, an "existential" fear which frequently predisposes and sensitizes the child to unreasonable and exaggerated fear responses later on. Secondly, because such a mother is more often than not also excessively energetic and inclined to consider things from a strictly utilitarian viewpoint, she cannot fail to impress the child with the idea that an energetic and brave child cannot be allowed to be fearful. This naturally creates a conflict which forms the basis for a subsequent camouflaged fear-based repressive disorder.

The child is exceedingly receptive during its early youth and automatically makes the moods and feelings of others its own. In a manner of speaking, it *imitates the feelings of the people in its own environment*. When the mother laughs, the child laughs too; when the mother is downhearted, the child becomes sad. The same holds true for fear as well as hope and courage. If the persons in the child's immediate environment live continuously in a state of fear and worry, the child inevitably becomes disposed likewise. The child has even less chance to escape this fate if it is exposed to repeated admonitions to be careful, or to constant reminders to be brave whenever it is afraid and not to cry when it is sad because "big boys and girls don't cry." Of course, we are referring here only to exaggeration in these matters. Calm and capable direction which respects the child's emotional reactions cannot but have a beneficial effect. Teaching it to be careful and brave is not wrong unless it is an absolute which allows for no feelings of fear.

Another possible way in which the emotion of fear can become abnormally sensitized is mentioned here only for the sake of completeness. A child may experience something in its earliest years of existence by which it is terribly frightened. This isolated experience may sometimes leave such a deep impression that the child retains a permanent disposition to fearfulness.

As the emotions of the assertive drive are entirely normal, necessary emotions which manifest themselves early in childhood, they are tools that intelligent parents and educators use constructively in helping the child to attain what is good for it. Although it is true that these emotions may become the cause of a repressive disorder, there is no reason for parents to assume that they must be careful never to influence these emotions in any way whatever. One must not think for example, that parents should refrain from punishing a child because this might cause it to become fearful, or that they should never urge a child to be courageous, to work harder, or to do something unpleasant. One may be inclined to think that such actions could amount to repression because the child, who is yet incapable of determining its own actions in a rational manner, has no alternative but to control the emotions of its pleasure appetite by those of the assertive drive. Although this kind of control actually does take place in the child, it does not constitute an abnormal process.

Our discussions have always been based on the principle that as long as an emotion is guided by reason, it will always find a natural outlet and thus never lead to neurotic tension. Such rational guidance also takes place when the will informed by reason uses a utilitarian emotion to prevent the gratification of a pleasure emotion. In that case, the utility emotion has no independent action and acts entirely in the service of reason. Consequently, the pleasure emotion is not being guided by the utility emotion as such, but by reason; the natural order is preserved and abnormal conditions do not develop.

Essentially the same process takes place in the child, although here the guidance is provided not by its own intellect, but by that of the parents, to which the child's emotional life tends to be subject by nature of its love, respect, and need for increasing integration between emotions and intellect. As the child's assertive drive is subject to the reason of its educators, its pleasure emotions are thus, albeit indirectly, under rational control, and it would therefore be illogical to speak of repression in this context. Reasonable use of the emotion of fear, as happens when one punishes a child for sufficient cause, has nothing to do with repression. By the same token, a reasonable degree of prompting a child to greater effort and of encouraging it to bear disappointments or to suffer pain, is entirely different from repression. The only danger in this respect would lie in undue influence of these emotions to the extent that they become too strong and eventually do bring about repression.

Such abnormal development of the emotions of fear and energy in the child is often the result of a neurotic disposition of the parents themselves. *Parents with neurotic disorders raise children with neurotic disorders.* Nothing short of a cure of the parental disorder will benefit their children. However, there are many other factors which favor the later development of neurotic disorders in children irrespective of whether the parents have neurotic disorders or not. It is well to distinguish here between factors that act excessively on fear and those that do so on emotional energy.

Excessive stimulation of emotional energy may result if parents push their children too much and too often to attain certain goals. Ambition on the part of the parents is frequently the main cause of this. When a father has great expectations for his truly talented son, there is always the danger that the welfare of the boy will be sacrificed to the ambitious desires of the father. When the father is always after the son to work harder and forces him by threats or promises to apply himself to the limit of his capacities, there is no longer room for the various types of recreation and enjoyments that the boy needs just as much as he needs nourishment in the various stages of his physical growth. The inevitable result is that the assertive drive takes the upper hand. Because the boy begins to regard the things his father wants as the only good, he becomes more and more inclined to prefer the utilitarian good over the pleasurable good; the latter finally will be entirely repressed.

Another frequent cause for an excessively strong assertive drive is a desire for self-control that is not in keeping with the child's level. As neither the child nor the preadolescent is capable of complete rational control of the emotional life, it is out of the question to expect it to remain tranquil whenever a certain gratification is refused. Although this capacity of control increases with age, it never equals that of the mature adult. Children as well as adolescents have a much greater need to express emotion than do adults. In joy as well as in sorrow they must give free rein to their emotions so that they can grow up freely and develop their own personalities. Every intelligent educator recognizes this as true and applies this principle automatically.

Nevertheless, there are educators who are not so enlightened and insist on a more deliberate guidance of children. In their desire to bring boys and girls to a spiritually perfect life, these individuals recommend and impose various exercises of self-control, self-denial, and inner mortification which may serve these purposes well for adults but are far beyond the capabilities of children. What usually happens in such cases is that these children, presented with the ideal image of perfection, accept it with all the enthusiasm of which they are capable. They become exemplary boys and girls, the hope of their parents and teachers, who have the greatest expectations for their future. When, after several years, they suffer a "nervous collapse," they think that it is due to overwork and are ignorant of the real cause. Thus many a promising young life has taken this tragic turn simply as a result of overzealous and overambitious educators.

Even more important for the genesis of a neurotic disorder and thus also for its prevention are factors that act upon fear. Judging by our own psychiatric practices, the *excessive growth of fear* is one of the most frequent causes of childhood repression. It has also been our experience that of all fears, the fear of matters related to religion is the most important contributing factor to the development of a neurotic disorder. A deep-seated, deeply rooted fear of God and of acts against God is almost always present in persons with fear-based repressive disorders. The search for the cause of this fear always leads back to the earliest years of childhood and to the manner in which the child was made to be afraid of evil. Naturally, we do not dispute or doubt the teachings of the Christian faith and of theology in regard to the nature of sin, its seriousness, and its justly deserved punishments. We do, however, deny that the child who is taught these truths can understand them as they ought to be understood. God is an infinite spiritual good known only to an immaterial cognitive faculty. As a turning away from God, sin is an act of the will and is therefore understood only by those who understand the spiritual evil of sin. Similarly, a complete understanding of the essence of retribution for sin can be understood only by those who have grasped the true meaning of sin.

Children, however, are still a long way from possessing such immaterial knowledge. Thus, when told about such things they understand them in a childish, typically material fashion, and react to them with childish emotions which are not as yet controlled by reason. It is not surprising then that they begin to fear doing evil, and even fear the commandments of God. These fears have nothing to do with intellectual knowledge. They are strictly sensory fears. If such religious teachings are repeated often, fear will continue to grow, especially if those things are taught in a more or less dramatic fashion with the express purpose of frightening the child to prevent evil-doing. Undoubtedly, this is done with good intentions, but it cannot change the fact that sensitive, well meaning children can easily become obsessed with a fear of such pathological proportions that over the years they will become less and less capable of conceiving a rational idea of the meaning of sin. Moreover, fear will increasingly dominate all their psychological operations and repress every striving that they think might possibly be sinful.

This repression is particularly inclined to concern itself with the sexual feelings. Often, indeed, the concepts of evil and sin are associated almost exclusively in religious education with impurity. Although here again the good intention is obvious, it cannot be denied that in children, sexual matters are readily considered sinful when they are surrounded with secrecy, and because of the fear of educators themselves in matters pertaining to sex, and the repeated warnings against such things. This may enhance the fear so that in the end the emotional life may become distorted and these children may grow up with neurotic disorders.

Our own observations in psychiatric practice have taught us that in a considerable number of cases neurotic disorders originated in religious instruction and sexual education that were based on fear. A typical example of this was the early experience of one of our patients, an unmarried Lutheran minister, who for years had suffered from intolerable anxiety and panic states, sexual obsessions, and compulsions complicated by extreme fatigue, gastric ulcers, and severe depressions with suicidal tendencies. We diagnosed him as having a camouflaged fear-based repressive disorder superimposed on Emotional Deprivation Disorder. Here is his story in his own words.

> My very first memory pertaining to sex, at least as far as I know, goes back to the age of two or three, when my mother was giving me a bath. She was washing me while I played in the water. In the process I touched my penis but was told by my mother not to do that. As I had liked what I had done I repeated it, whereupon my mother scolded me harshly and slapped my hand. From this experience grew the idea that there was something very special and bad about my penis.
>
> When I was five some neighborhood kids and myself were playing in our garage. We all exposed ourselves and explored each

other's anatomy. It was then that I found out that girls were different from boys, although I did not understand why. Because I did not want my mother to catch us doing this kind of thing I told the kids to stop it and go home. I felt guilty about it all and never mentioned this to my parents.

Six or seven years later my penis started to hurt and I reluctantly told my parents about it. When my father told me to show him where it hurt I was very self-conscious as it had always been my mother who had given me baths. He told my mother to take me to the doctor who asked me for a urine sample. I did not understand what that meant as my mother always used German names for such things. Then the doctor began to do some cutting on my penis. I screamed and kicked as it hurt badly. He did not tell me why he did this and I concluded that I had done something very bad and that this was my punishment. I have had a fear of doctors ever since.

When I got to be a freshman in high school the boys had to take showers together. Each time I felt embarrassed and suffered untold agonies. I worried that I was different since the sex organs of the other boys looked different from mine. I finally told my mother about this ordeal at school, but she did not know what to say. That same year I accidentally discovered masturbation. Although I liked the feeling I had no idea what it was all about. Feeling guilty, I kept it a secret from everyone as I thought no one would understand. I thought I was different in some way. The following year I was sent to a private boarding school where the teachers told me repeatedly how wrong it was to masturbate. The harder I tried to stop doing it the more I did it. I felt as if I was caught in the jaws of a vise and did not know how to escape. As I feared the punishments of hell I tried desperately to be good and to please God, but I failed repeatedly. I became even ashamed of having spontaneous erections, and did everything possible to suppress them. It was very difficult at times but I succeeded even to the point of having no more nocturnal emissions. The latter, however, came about more gradually after I was sent to a hospital to have a complete circumcision. Before the lesion had healed I had an erection and the pain almost drove me out of my mind. As I had been told that all sexual pleasures outside of marriage were sinful I assumed that this terrible pain was the ultimate punishment for my erections, and I decided never to have them again. I was successful for more than ten years but then the accumulated tensions began to develop into the various physical and psychiatric complaints for which I finally sought help.

Stories like this one, and they can be multiplied many times, stress the need for a change in the methods of religious and sex education from the viewpoint of the prevention of neurotic disorders. Children should not be infected with the virus of fear in regard to God and moral evil; they ought to know God as the infinite good; they must be taught the truths of faith in such a manner that in later years, as adults, they will understand that the evil of sin is a spiritual evil, and will not consider such concepts as duty, law, and sin to be irrational simply because they are so frightening that they are incapable of forming a correct judgment. How this method of education should be carried out in practice must be left to competent psychologists and educators. We only want to stress that these things must be changed if we are to have more persons who are emotionally healthy.

Finally, we must consider intellect and will—the third dimension of the psychological life which affects the general conditions concerning the development of repressive disorders. Every striving presupposes knowledge, and thus the repressing emotion of the assertive drive is always preceded by a cognitive act which arouses that emotion. This cognitive act is in essence always an act of the utility judgment, as that is the power to which the inclinations of the assertive drive correspond directly. The utility judgment is the sensory power which forms concrete judgments as to what ought to be done here and now. It is the ennobled instinct of the animal. Animals have a natural, innate ability to recognize what is useful or harmful and to act accordingly, but in human beings this same power benefits, as do all the sensory powers, from the enlightening and ennobling influence of the intellect. As a result, this power loses its coercive quality and is able to make general judgments concerning the usefulness and harmfulness of concrete things. In this way, it becomes the guiding and tempering factor for the assertive drive.

Therefore, the inclinations of the assertive drive, and hence also the occurrence of repressions, depend on judgments formed by the utility judgment. If this arrives at an incorrect judgment—for instance, if it believes that a certain object should be avoided as harmful while in fact it is something good—the assertive drive will inevitably set the repressive process in motion. *Everything depends therefore on the correct formation of the utility judgment.*

There are several ways in which utility judgments can turn out to be incorrect. This may happen, first of all, when the intellect is given a dominant role too early in the life of the child. We have already explained in the first chapter that the penetration of the instinctive grasp of what is useful and harmful by the intellect is only a gradual process. Immediately after birth, the child's instinctive life predominates completely, although it is soon complemented, as in the animal, by the sensory power of experience. The child's potential intellect, however, is noticeable from the beginning, for a baby is never exactly the same as a young animal. Only gradually does the intellect penetrate the instinctive power and make it a fully developed human power. Before the onset of puberty, relatively little is accomplished in this respect, for no matter how logical a child's judgment concerning its own actions, it still remains an emotionally determined judgment in which instinct and sensory experience play a decisive role. It is not until puberty that the utility judgment begins to rise above the emotional level, to complete its growth in the adult human being.

This is nature's law of human psychological development. *It is never violated with impunity.* Yet this law is violated whenever the child's intellect is activated too early in the process, and the child stops acting spontaneously and instinctively and begins to act deliberately too soon. Such a child manifests an air of unnaturalness. Its emotional life has not yet developed sufficiently for it to deal with intellectual processes. Hence the child will act according to the dictates of the intellect although this constitutes merely voluntary motor activity. The emotions do not participate and are thus prevented from being expressed in a natural manner. Obviously, this amounts to a repressive process with all its consequences. Under these circumstances, the child typically becomes uncertain in all its feelings and actions. It loses the instinctive certainty proper to its age. It no longer acts according to its emotions, while at the same time it is not yet capable of possessing the intellectual certainty of the adult. If a child is allowed to grow up under these circumstances, the uncertainty will persist and become a characteristic neurotic symptom in later years.

There are different causes for this precocious intervention in the natural process of psychological development. It may result from an educational approach which aims at early spiritual and intellectual development because the role of the emotional life is distrusted: for instance, by letting the child start and finish school too early and by insisting on daily Mass attendance from the first day of grade school. It may also result from the early influence of modern communications media, particularly television, which all too often preempts time for play and games. Then again it may stem from an irreligious and anthropocentric mentality in which there is no place for faith and dependence on God and people are totally thrown back on their own accomplishments. Whatever the cause, it is always psychologically wrong and nature's penalty is a neurotic disposition.

This concludes our discussion of the most important factors predisposing to repressive disorders. Knowledge of them is of the greatest significance for the correct evaluation of the seriousness of the illness as well as for its prognosis. The difficulty of effecting a cure is proportionate to the seriousness of the combined predisposing psychological factors, which must be removed if a complete cure is to be achieved.

Only one more question remains. Where will the child be assured of the *optimum development of its emotional life*? To this only one answer can be given; namely, in *normal family life*. The family is the natural and ideal milieu in which the child can become an adult. It furnishes ideal relationships and conditions in which the child's emotions can be expressed and find their natural gratification. It provides, first of all, the natural bond with the parents, as well as the help, love, and protection the child needs. Moreover, it provides contact with brothers and sisters, and this enables the child to develop other aspects of its psychic life in a normal fashion.

A sound family life is the first requisite for the healthy personality development of children, and hence for the prevention of neurotic disorders. The family milieu, however, may be defective in two ways. There may be innate personality defects in the parents, such as emotional lability, mental retardation, extremes of temperaments, and so forth. These defects can hardly be avoided because they are the immediate results of the imperfection of human nature. They will reveal themselves to a greater or lesser extent depending on the compatibility of the parents, whose principal duty it becomes to try and prevent the consequences of these defects as far as their children are concerned. This they must do through mutual charitable tolerance and a sincere desire for self-improvement. Individuals who believe in the sacramental grace of marriage will find their greatest strength in the fact that this supernatural grace will do much for the married partners that their imperfect natures cannot do on their own.

In addition to these unavoidable defects, there are acquired defects which the partners should be able to control and correct with a certain measure of goodwill. Human nature and temperament form an inseparable part of them, yet neither the relationship between husband and wife nor that between parents and children necessarily has to be ruined because of innate defects. It would be even more inexcusable for parents not to try everything possible to create a wholesome family union, instead of allowing innate defects to be augmented by acquired ones. To the extent that parents succeed in correcting and minimizing disrupting influences in the natural order, will they eliminate many of the factors which contribute to the development of neurotic disorders in their children.

Whatever detracts from natural family relationships will tend to bring on psychological conflicts. Foremost among the factors that weaken the natural family bond stands the most radical dissolution of marriage: *divorce*. Apart from the emotional shock the child suffers when the father and mother, to whom it is tied by the strongest possible natural bond, go their separate ways, it also suffers in its further development through the lack of a most essential factor. Only through its relationship with both parents, not with either the father or the mother alone, is the child capable of optimal maturation. No matter what artificial means are employed to compensate for the absence of one parent, a multifaceted emotional life matures best and most fully if the emotions are experienced in regard to both natural parents. It is true that at times a divorce may appear to be better for the children too. If there is constant quarreling, fighting, and abuse between the parents, the child's personality will undoubtedly suffer severely. Yet a parental divorce causes still deeper wounds in the emotional life of the child, and is likely to result in even more serious consequences in later life. Parents whose relationship to one another leaves much to be desired should give this the most serious consideration, and should never forget that there is no more natural bond for the child than that with its parents as a unit. The child itself came forth from that union and its disintegration must of necessity produce the deepest hurt.

It is not enough, however, for the family to stay and live together. It should also *form a unit emotionally*. What nature has joined together, human beings must not dissolve. The father and mother must live for their family, for only then will the children find a natural milieu in which to mature. Although the father's work lies outside the house, the children must know and feel that he does this work to support the family, and that he engages in a labor of love aimed at the welfare of the union of which they form a part. The mother, on the other hand, exists, particularly during the pre-school years, for the family alone. Her task is in the home, not outside. Since her nature directs her to do the work required by her household, her husband, and children, she must dedicate herself to this task without reservations. Only in that way can the family become the indispensable union necessary for the normal personality development of children.

Children must be able to feel that this union is real and meaningful. It is absolutely wrong for the mother to leave the care of the children during the most important years of growth entirely to others. It is wrong for her to allow herself to become so occupied with social duties and entertaining that the children must live in a world of their own, so to speak, and see their parents only when called in to be "shown off to the guests." No other caregiver, no matter how dedicated and devoted, can replace the parents, and the parents owe it to their children to live with and for them, not only in theory but also in fact. The family ought to be a close union, with outside contacts, of course, but undisrupted by these contacts. In such a natural, healthy atmosphere, protected and cherished by an all-pervading love, the child's psychological life can grow until in due time it can accept with mature stability and confidence the full responsibility of its own existence.

As the *role of the father* in the prevention of a neurotic disorder is not always defined as clearly as that of the mother, we want to devote a few lines to the subject.

It is true, as it is said, that behind every successful man stands a woman; it is even more so that behind every authentically affirming mother whose tender love gives the infant its feelings of security and happiness, there is a father whose support and protection give her the strength and tranquility of mind to make her love truly creative. Any failure on the part of the husband in this important role will be reflected somehow in the child's growth to maturity through the anxiety and tension caused in its mother. The father's role begins during his wife's pregnancy and lasts through his presence on the way to the hospital and at the birth until the child, grown, leaves the parental home. The fact that many husbands fail at this is not surprising to anyone familiar with the effects on the husband-wife relationship of our occidental, matriarchal culture.

The father should be the first person to enlarge the child's world beyond its close and intimate relationship with the mother. Provided he is gentle, encouraging, and reassuring, the father can do much to lessen the child's dependency on the mother and to help it step beyond itself toward the rest of the world. The child, whether a boy or a girl, has the best chance to avoid neurotic adjustment if it grows up in an atmosphere of harmony between both parents, and in an atmosphere in which it can identify with a strong yet kind and loving father whose love makes it feel secure, and whose example offers it the opportunity for self-determination. Provided that the mother also looks up to the father as the rock on which she can lean and as the harbor in which she can always safely escape the storm, the child develops trust in itself and the outside world. For if nothing or no one, not even the outside world, can diminish the size of the father, the head of the house, or sap his strength, the world cannot be too bad a place to live and work in.

The *father's role in the family can be compared to the role of the orchestra conductor*, who brings order to the world of sounds produced by the members of the orchestra; the mother's role is that of the first violinist. The conductor encourages the sounds, yet also restrains them and guides them in their interaction without repressing or suppressing a single one. Similarly, the father of the family, provided he is truly mature, brings order to the emotions of the children as well as of his wife. But she too, even when not immature but simply because of her feminine nature, needs the guiding, directing help that flows from the intellect and sensitivity of the father, her husband. Homer showed his deep understanding of the nature of woman when, in his famous lines in the *Iliad*, he had Andromache bid farewell to her husband, Hector, with the following words, "Hector, you are to me all in one father, venerable mother and brother, you are my husband in the prime of your life."

It would be hard to describe in more beautiful and meaningful words what the husband means for the emotional life of the woman. All emotional support and help which the single woman finds at home are united later in the tie that binds her to her husband. He is the father who protects and defends her, in whose hands she knows herself to be safe, and to whom she can always flee when in danger. He is the brother whose companion and friend she is. All this is what the husband is to the woman; all this she expects from the one to whom she has entrusted her entire life.

Absent or weak fathers, especially those who are afraid of their wives, make it hard or impossible for boys or girls to become independent or self-sufficient and socially at ease with their peers and persons in authority. Such boys and girls readily become anxious, tense, and shy in school and social activities. They lack assertiveness, competitive spirit, social poise, and self-confidence. Depending on whether the earlier relationship with the mother was a positive or negative one, the resulting Emotional Deprivation Disorder, with or without a superimposed repressive disorder, becomes more or less severe in adolescence and adulthood.

It is the task of both parents, and of other educators as well, to create the most favorable conditions for a harmonious development of the child's emotional life. If they succeed in doing this, in due course the will can assume its rightful place in the guidance of the emotional life so that pathological deviations will not occur. Unfortunately, this does not mean that the prevention will always be complete, for not even the best educators can prevent personal conflicts from creating disturbances in the psychic life, or fully offset the effects on the child of its exposure to the modern mentality of the Western world, characterized as it is by an exaggerated utilitarian philosophy. There is little tranquility left in the world. There is too much pursuit of and wishing for greater achievements. One pursuit replaces the other so quickly that there is neither time nor capacity to enjoy what one has. As soon as one has obtained what one desires, there is only a momentary acknowledgement of it before one commences to pursue something else and a chance to enjoy the good obtained has passed by. The calm found in what is good is the natural goal of every desire, yet it recedes in the face of new desires. The *assertive drive has hypertrophied in our modern world*, and the irony of it is that the world praises this hypertrophy as perfection.

It is unavoidable that this psychological attitude, with its grave consequences for psychological health, should leave its mark on our youth. The unrest and agitation around them creates an unrest in their minds and disposes them to feverish pursuits, to an overstimulation of the emotions that brings on repression. For the youth of our times, solid instruction and education in a Christian family forms the best protective barrier against the onslaught from without. It is in this family milieu that children find the quiet satisfaction of their inclinations and begin to understand the relative values of all earthly goods. To construct such a wholesome family milieu is not a simple matter, yet by far a majority of people enter into a marriage contract without any qualifications beyond the blueprint of their own parents' example, and their own good intention of improving on it if it was obviously deficient. In our opinion, there is every reason for experienced educators to seriously consider the feasibility of establishing courses for the preparation of students who want to qualify for and succeed in marriage—the most important and challenging occupation life has to offer.

Finally, in view of certain popular but ill-conceived practices in modern education, we deem it necessary to state emphatically that prevention of repressive disorders is never accomplished by lowering moral norms. Just because certain persons with neurotic disorders are constantly living in fear of transgressing moral laws, and frequently do so anyway in spite of all their efforts not to, it is not logical to conclude that they can be helped by abolishing, or tampering with, these laws. Yet, this has been done, for example, by the authors of *Human Sexuality*, a study commissioned by the Catholic Theological Society of America.[1]

Others again are doing a disservice to the cause of the prevention of neurotic disorders in holding the opinion that authoritarian teaching of moral precepts to children induces psychological disturbances at a later age. They therefore advocate that children be allowed to develop their own moral standards according to their own feeling preferences. Although these persons are partially correct in their premise, as we have explained in this book, their remedy—e.g., courses in *Values Clarification*[2] and *Cognitive Moral Development*[3]—even if it would prevent the development of the neurotic disorders described in this book, does not safeguard the victims of these courses against developing other psychological disorders.

Another, equally mistaken view, is the one which holds that ignorance about sexual matters in early life is a frequent cause of emotional problems in later life. Yet, many years of sex education in the public schools, with its explicit discussion of sex, visual presentation of normal as well as deviant sexual behavior, encouragement of early sexual experimentation and the use of contraceptives by youngsters in both secondary and elementary grades, offer no hope that their future will be any more free of psychological disturbances than it was for the young people of past generations who were raised to repress their sexual feelings.[4]

1. Paulist Press, New York, 1977.

2. by Sidney Simon.

3. by Lawrence Kohlberg.

4. SIECUS' Sex Education in Schools. For more on this subject see Chapter IX, and also *Feeling and Healing Your Emotions* by Conrad W. Baars, M.D., Chapter 8, entitled "Erroneous Goings On."

CHAPTER VII

THE ASSERTIVE DRIVE

"... for it is peculiar to wrath to pounce upon evil. Thus fortitude and wrath work directly upon each other."

Summa Theologica II, II, 123, 10 and 3

IN THIS BOOK, WE have given many examples and case histories illustrating the pathological consequences of the repression of the emotions and feelings which serve the procreative drive. At the time of our first writings, the Victorian and Jansenistic attitudes toward things sexual and sensual seemed to be the dominant factor in the development of a repressive disorder. In the last two decades or so, however, we have become increasingly impressed by the prevalence of a similarly unwholesome attitude towards the emotions which serve the other fundamental, innate drive. We refer here to the assertive drive, commonly, though incorrectly, referred to as the aggressive drive.

In describing the human person's innate drives and emotions we prefer the term "assertive" to "aggressive." Webster defines "*assertive*" as: 1) characterized by, or disposed to affirm, to declare with assurance, to state positively; 2) to maintain or defend, e.g., one's rights or prerogatives." "*Aggressive*" is defined as: "tending to, or characterized by a first or unprovoked attack, or act of hostility; the first act of injury leading to a war or controversy." It would appear that an innate drive to defend oneself (assertion) is more properly expressive of human nature than an innate drive to attack without provocation (aggression). Similarly, the emotion of anger, like courage, serves the purpose of arousal toward overcoming obstacles and defensive action against danger (assertion), and not toward a first, unprovoked act of hostility or injury (aggression) in the absence of a danger. In therapy, too, it makes sense to help patients to become more assertive rather than more aggressive. Patients with neurotic disorders are more willing to cooperate in the former endeavor, but resist the latter.

The assertive drive is defined as the drive towards self-realization and self-preservation through assertiveness and competitiveness and by overcoming obstacles and threats against one's life and welfare. It is the human person's drive toward the realization in freedom of his or her potentialities and God-given talents. This fundamental drive utilizes the emotions of the assertive drive, particularly courage and anger, just as the procreative drive is served primarily by the emotion of love and the sexual feelings. Both drives, as well as the emotions which serve these drives, must function under the constant direction of reason.

At the risk of repeating ourselves, we want to restate our thoughts in a somewhat different manner in order to emphasize once again the *significance of the entire emotional life*—of each and every emotion without exception—for the total well-being of the individual. All emotions are psychophysiological reactions to the stimulation of the external and internal senses. They also occur in response to thoughts and ideas, the workings of the intellect, insofar as these bring to mind concrete associations; they serve but one purpose, namely, for the creature to be moved (as, e.g., "moved to tears"), and to act or to "move the person outward" as the Latin root of "emotion" indicates: *exmotus*, past participle of *exmovēre*. It is an immutable consequence of human nature that one is always stimulated to move toward the concrete good and away from what is not a good and pleasing concrete object.

The great importance of the emotions can be dramatized by considering for a moment a theoretical question: What would happen to an animal if it lacked nothing but its emotional apparatus? For instance, imagine a dog who sees and smells a fresh bone lying twenty feet away from it. Although the dog is physically and anatomically perfect, its visual and olfactory percepts will not move it to make the effort of walking to the bone. Lacking emotions, this imaginary dog, even when hungry, is not moved emotionally by what it sees and smells. Its sense knowledge is sterile as far as its being moved to desire the bone is concerned. Without this desire, its usefulness judgment will not arouse it to act to do what is useful, namely to walk toward the bone. The dog would be far better off if it were blind in both eyes, deaf and had a broken leg but still possessed the capability of emotional arousal as a result of smelling the bone. As long as its emotions are part of the dog, it will continue to desire what is good for itself and to act for the sake of survival. On the other hand, our imaginary dog without emotional apparatus is doomed to die. Apathetic people, i.e., persons with little or no emotions, would suffer a similar fate if it were not for the exercise of their will to do what is necessary to stay alive. All our emotions, or *psychological motors*, are necessary tools of our nature!

We mention this solely to demonstrate once more the *tremendous significance of emotions for the human being*. Of course, the emotions do not constitute the sole moving force of the human person. Human beings are endowed with an even more important moving force, the *will*. Since the will is free—at least in healthy, mature persons—it does not exert the same inexorable force as the emotions do in animals and similarly, although to a lesser degree, in very young children. In fact, the will diminishes this inexorable force more and more in the natural growing process unless constitutional or other forces prevent the natural integration of feelings and will. This happens, for instance, in a psychopathic personality, or in a person with a neurotic disorder when successful repression, or "mortification," of the feelings keeps the will at bay and so causes ceaseless struggle on a subconscious level without the benefit of the guiding and deciding action of the will.

Theoretically, human persons could act solely by virtue of the will. Persons with energy-based repressive disorders are an excellent example of this. Not choosing to trust their emotions, they must *think* and *deliberate* every move they make, and anticipate every possible consequence their move might have. Yet, even if their moves always turn out to be correct, their lives become more and more of a burden. The constant task of repressing all of their emotions takes increasing amounts of energy—energy that could have been spent on many more pleasant and worthwhile things. They lack the spontaneity and smoothness of action that their emotions would have provided if they had been taught to trust and accept them early in life. It is only when persons both *know* and *feel* that a certain act is proper that they act surely and confidently. Will and emotions must cooperate, not oppose each other, if life is to be reasonably smooth and comfortable. The emotions which serve the assertive drive are no exception to this rule, as we shall now discuss in more detail in connection with the emotions of *hate* and *anger*.[1]

Generally speaking, the understanding of the importance of these emotions has not kept up with the understanding of sexual feelings, with the result that these feelings are still repressed to the same extent that the sexual feelings once were—not that we are entirely out of the woods as far as the process of learning to accept and integrate sexual feelings is concerned. The pendulum is still swinging too much to the other side—sexual excess—and it may be expected to do so for some time to come. Yet the literature of the past decade or so presents evidence of progress toward a healthier attitude regarding this part of our nature and holds out the promise of a greater capacity to love others unselfishly and maturely, for contrary to popular belief, it is not one's capacity to hate or be enraged which interferes with love of others, but rather self-centeredness and preoccupation with one's own inner conflicts.

While the conflicts stemming from neurotic repression of sexual feelings are being gradually resolved in our day, those caused by the repression of assertive feelings continue to constrict man's horizon and reinforce his egocentricity. Daily we see patients in our practice whose mistaken attitudes and abnormal conditioning toward the emotions of hate and anger are at the root of their migraine headaches, backaches, hypertension, and other psychosomatic disorders; their unhappy marriages; their resentment[2] and addiction to alcohol; their apathy about social issues of grave import; their failures in the business and professional world; their dull though secure and uneventful lives; their attacks of anxiety and panic in the face of obsessive thoughts of an aggressive, even homicidal nature; and finally, of their loneliness and their often severe depressions and suicidal ruminations and attempts.

There are a number of causes of the development of such an abnormal attitude toward the emotions of hate and anger and for the resultant nonacceptance and repression of these feelings. These causes have the most

---

1. Since much of the following pertains equally to the emotion of hate, we include it in our discussion of the assertive drive.

2. The word "resentment" from the French *re-sentir* and *ressentiment*, "to feel over and over," beautifully illustrates the restless activity of the feeling of anger after its repression into the subconscious. The advice not to repress one's anger, but rather to experience it in a rational manner, is contained in Ephesians 4:26, "Be angry and do not sin; do not let the sun go down upon your anger" (meaning: go ahead and feel angry, but do not let your actions—determined by your reason or common sense—be sinful).

pronounced effect when they make themselves felt in the most impression-able period of one's life, the years of childhood; less so in adulthood when one begins to repress the same feelings which, until then, the individual had been able to handle without particular difficulty as psychophysiologi-cal tools through which one is aroused to oppose what is evil and harmful.

Perhaps foremost among these causative factors has been and is the *explicit teaching that hate and anger are bad and sinful*. For example, the *Baltimore Catechism*[3] teaches that anger is one of the seven capital sins. We find, of course, no fault with the teachings of this catechism, but we do want to state that, without qualifying remarks and further explanations, young children, especially when prematurely instructed, are easily misled into believing that it is a sin to *feel* angry when their father refused to take them fishing or to *feel* hate for their mother when she makes them clean their plate when they are not hungry, to give two very simple examples. Similarly, we find no fault at all with Holy Scripture and the beautiful teach-ings it contains, yet we must recognize that the language of the Evangelists, like our own, had no words to clearly differentiate between *the arousal of an emotion on the one hand, and its subsequent expression in word or behavior on the other*. The numerous references in Scripture to hate and anger are therefore vulnerable to serious misunderstanding, and hence may lead to potentially disturbing psychological reactions, for it is only the behavior and not the emotional arousal which is subject to moral evaluation. The emotions themselves are morally indifferent, neither good nor bad, but the behavior that follows—or for that matter, which was responsible for the arousal of the emotions—may be morally good or bad, depending on whether or not it fulfills the criteria set forth by moral theology.[4] The emotions themselves are not subject to either divine or human command-ments—only behavior is. In order to clarify this matter as much as possible in the brief space available, we want to discuss a few biblical quotations dealing with hate and anger, as well as their recommended counterparts, love and patience.

As a remedy against the "feared" emotions of hate and anger, the Bible recommends "*turning the other cheek*," gentleness, patience, and mildness, while in our Western culture the emphasis is on "not hurting the other

---

3. *Baltimore Catechism*, Paterson, NJ: St. Anthony Guild Press, 1949, A catechism of Christian doctrine, no. 3.

4. Whether a person is responsible for an objectively and morally evil act depends, of course, on the degree of freedom of the will at the time the act was performed.

person's feelings," being "nice," seeking "peace at any price" and "peaceful coexistence." We do not quarrel with the proper use of these terms but want to point out how and to what extent these expressions at times are no longer applied in a rational manner. For example, when we attempt to explain the goodness of anger as an emotion to individuals with a Manichaeistic religious background, they often retort, "But shouldn't we turn the other cheek if someone offends us or arouses our anger by some evil act?" These patients are referring to Christ's injunction in His Sermon on the Mount: "I say unto you, resist evil; if one strike you on the right cheek, offer him the other" (Mt 5:39). They do not seem to be aware, at least not in this context, that Christ Himself did not always act according to this injunction. For in John 18:23 it is clearly revealed that He did not turn the other cheek when He stood before the high priest and was struck in the face by a servant, but said, "If there was harm in what I said, tell us what was harmful in it, but if not, why dost thou strike me?" Thus it becomes immediately obvious that to interpret the injunction of the Sermon on the Mount literally and inflexibly is to misunderstand it.

Thomas Aquinas tells us that this injunction and all of Holy Scripture must be understood in the light of what Christ, His apostles, and the saints have actually practiced. The fact is that Christ and the apostles were not above being aroused by anger and from time to time also showed it in word and deed. This could be denied only by those of us who prefer to think of Jesus saying, without feeling or displaying any anger, "Scripture has it, 'My house shall be called a house of prayer,' but you are turning it into a den of thieves," (Mt 21:12, 13) after He had overturned the money-changers' tables and the stalls of the dove sellers. In that case, however, should we not have to assume that the seriousness of their offense would have escaped the money-changers if Jesus' behavior had been prompted solely by a movement of the will and had been devoid of any external sign of anger?

The same question can be raised when Jesus called the scribes and Pharisees, "you frauds, blind fools, blind guides, vipers' nest, brood of serpents," and similar epithets (Mt 23:13–33). If people believe that these words, if spoken without feeling tone, would hold the attention of the crowds and the disciples to whom they were addressed, they would soon change their mind by asking a person who is unable to feel and express his or her anger to read this long Scripture passage aloud to them. We often ask our patients to do so in our office to make them realize how seriously handicapped they really are by having repressed their emotion of anger.

Additionally, does it seem plausible to think that Paul spoke without being aroused with anger when he said to the attendant, who had been ordered by the high priest Ananias to strike Paul on the mouth, "You are the one God will strike, you whitewashed wall!" (Acts 23:3).

From these and many other Biblical examples we can arrive at but one conclusion, namely, that before we decide to forgive, we must first of all use our God-given natural tools—emotional arousal guided and directed by reason and will—to respond to all anger-provoking situations. This may be done for any and all of the following possible reasons: to take action for the purpose of correcting an injustice done us or those we love; to demand an apology, retribution or restitution for an offense; to protect ourselves against a continuance or repetition of a certain harmful act; to let the other know how we feel so he or she is given the opportunity to treat us more charitably in the future; and to defend ourselves, our loved ones and whatever we hold dear and valuable against any threat of harm.

Only when we have exhausted all reasonable means of action, or when we freely will to limit our response to an anger provoking situation for the sake of a greater good, only then and not before, should we turn the other cheek and bear the evil without bitterness toward our enemy. For Christ, that moment arrived when at last He was nailed to the Cross. It was then, and not before, that He asked His heavenly Father to forgive His enemies and executioners. That is what is meant by "turning the other cheek;" it is not a license, so to speak, for repressing the emotions which God made a part of human nature for each person's well-being and happiness.

Even superficial observation of persons whose conduct throughout their lives has been determined by a literal interpretation of the injunction of the Sermon on the Mount, makes it clear that the virtues of mildness and gentleness are not served by the repression of the assertive emotions. Such persons are better described as servile and fearfully submissive than as gentle, for true gentleness presupposes the capability of being aroused by anger and its ready mastery by the will, not its weakening by fearful or energetic repression. Just as chastity does not imply a weakening of sexual power but rather its ready mastery, so gentleness, of which it is said: "Possess thy soul through gentleness," does not imply a weakening or literal "mortification" (from L. *mortificare*—to kill, destroy) of the power of anger, but rather the easy response of anger to the guiding power of reason and will. True *meekness* presupposes a fully developed capacity to experience the emotion of anger and the freedom to act upon it in any one way one wills.

Before leaving this subject, we must remind the reader that what we have shown to be true for the proper understanding of the assertive emotions holds with equal force for the emotions of love and desire. Many individuals, those with neurotic disorders and those without, consider themselves poor Christians because they seem unable to live up to the commandments to love God, their parents, and their enemies. Many of them suffer unnecessary feelings of guilt when they do not feel this love and are rendered unable to progress by their self-blame in their emotional and spiritual growth. Since the *emotion of love* is not subject to legislations, it must be *love as an act* of a person's free will—volitional love—to which God's commandments refer, even though it is emotional love which by and large determines that subjective feeling of well-being and joy. One's feeling of love for God can only develop when one's spiritual relationship with God reverberates in a fully developed emotional life.

Persons with neurotic disorders often find little human joy in their religion even though their volitional love of God is perfect. The feeling of love that children have for their parents is determined mainly by the degree of love and goodness that parents constitute for their children. If parents were never good for their children because of selfish, cruel, harsh, and unloving treatment, the children cannot have a feeling of love for the parents. All they can do—if so disposed by virtue of higher motives—is to will their parents well, i.e., to love them, in spite of their shortcomings toward them. The same is true in regard to the Lord's commandment to love our enemies. He wants our will directed toward their good without necessarily relinquishing the feeling of hate for them, for it is by means of this emotion that we maintain our spontaneous *natural* protective alert against their hostile attitude or are spurred on to undo the harm our enemies want to do to us and others.

A second reason for repressing one's innate assertive emotions is found in rules for living based not upon God and His commandments and the moral laws but rather upon the conduct, feelings, and *expectations of other people*—usually neighbors, relatives, and friends. When children are *trained* to be docile and good in terms of what other people think is proper, trained to avoid certain behavior because of what the neighbors will say amongst themselves, trained never to talk back or disagree so as "not to hurt other people's feelings," and trained never to argue with relatives or neighbors in order to have peace in the family and the neighborhood, they cannot help but repress their assertive feelings and refrain from ever being themselves. Unless they dare to develop and adhere to more reasonable rules of conduct, they will become more and more fearful and ultimately will develop attacks of anxiety and panic when shopping in a store, being in a crowd, having a haircut at the barber's, or attending a church service, to mention only a few common examples. All these situations have one thing in common—the presence of other people who are regarded as judges of behavior.

Years of such conditioning leads to extreme fearfulness of offending others or of incurring their displeasure or disapproval even by a casual remark or an innocuous gesture or act. Such individuals are never sure what others think or expect from them. With persons they know well they usually can manage by simply avoiding any word or action they know to be offensive. With strangers, however, whose likes and dislikes, judgments and opinions are unknown, this becomes impossible, and, as a result, the situation soon leads to panic if it is impossible or very difficult to leave without drawing the attention of others. The only time such individuals feel at ease in a crowd is when darkness provides anonymity, as, for instance, in a movie theater.

A third reason for repressing one's assertive emotions develops in children *whose parents punish them indiscriminately* when they display a temper tantrum, become destructive in a fit of anger, or hurt others when angry. By indiscriminate, we have in mind here the failure to make it clear to the child that he or she is being punished for his or her behavior, and not for the underlying feeling of anger or irritation. Without such distinctions, children usually arrive at the conclusion that it is wrong to *feel* angry, especially when the parents are motivated in their attitude by their religious upbringing, as discussed earlier.

The proper approach for parent and educator in dealing with a small child's temper tantrum or with an older child's destructive or physically abusive behavior is essentially twofold. First, the affirmation of the child's feelings of anger by some appropriate remarks, and second, disapproval of the child's actions if they have hurt or could have injured others or their property. Since in the typical small child's temper tantrum nobody gets hurt and nothing gets destroyed, it is best to calmly wait for the tantrum to subside before letting the child know that one is sympathetic with his or her feelings of anger and frustration, and will be glad to learn the reason for the child's conduct. When a child learns at an early age that adults approve of his or her feelings of hate and anger but not of the expression if they are destructive, harmful, or disrespectful, the child will not be tempted to repress his or her emotions and instead will integrate them in freedom and reasonableness. There is no better way than this to prevent the development of the basic forms of the adult's intemperate anger—blind anger, resentment aimed at revenge, and bitterness of spirit. The pseudo-Christian attitudes which result in more or less successful repression of these emotions are, of course, the very causes of eventual outbreaks of uncontrolled anger and irritability and easily lead to ill-concealed resentments and bitterness.

As a fourth cause for the gradual elimination of the assertive emotions from the natural endowment for coping with every aspect of one's being-in-the-world, we must mention the impact on children of *repeated irrational and inconsiderate acts* committed in anger or rage by their parents or other adults. Chronic or repeated exposure to such conduct often results in fearful retreat and burial of the children's own assertive, emotional arousal, except in those whose strong innate drive for self-assertion leads them to resist and rebel in an often overly assertive, even aggressive manner. It is not always necessary that these harsh and angry acts or words be directed at the children themselves. For many, seeing loved ones hurt by someone's intemperate rage and angry vituperations, it suffices to create a conscious or subconscious resolve never to emulate their elders in this way. The determination to abstain from all angry behavior usually does not stop at this. These persons proceed to free themselves from even experiencing the very feelings and impulses which led to such painful and detrimental effects on others.

In our practice, we have seen many patients whose sole reason for their lack of self-assertion and consequent depressions was similar to that of a forty year old inventor and engineer who could not stand having anyone angry with him. As a child, he had never been in a fight with other children. He would refuse to win in any competitive game or sport due to fear that otherwise people would not care to play with him again. When he was older, he quit many a good-paying job rather than assert himself when treated unfairly. He was known for his quiet, impassive, and imperturbed ways. One day, he became acutely depressed, shot a mirror full of holes, and quit his job impulsively because he could not stand the irritating ways of a new co-worker. He had been raised by a loving, affectionate mother and an extremely irascible father who broke up practically every meal with his extreme temper and angry fights. The patient could not recall a single instance of his father speaking civilly to his mother or himself. His father had customarily criticized and fought with every member of the family, but at the same time he had the reputation of being the most friendly person in the neighborhood and at work. As a result of constant exposure to his father's angry and abusive behavior, the patient had decided at an early age never to be like him, no matter what the consequences to himself might be. He had succeeded in repressing his assertive emotions to such an extent that it was not until he entered therapy that he realized how unnatural and tense he had been under his mask of friendly tolerance.

Closely related to this cause for nonintegration of the emotions serving the assertive drive is the experience of individuals who as a result of an angry outburst *happen to have inflicted serious hurt or injury on another person*, usually in childhood or adolescence, and then made up their minds never to let such a terrible thing happen again. Patients with this kind of background have usually been seen in our practice because their relationship and communication with their spouses had deteriorated as a result of the fact that their successful repression of the assertive emotions had affected their other emotions as well.

We are reminded of a forty-five year old father of several teenagers who went to his family physician with complaints of anxiety and panic which he attributed to severe pains in the chest. When a complete physical examination was negative, he was referred to us. It struck us that his attacks never occurred at work, where he was most successful and respected, but only when it was time to leave or while he was on the way home from work. At first, he claimed that he was happily married and cited as proof that he could not recall having had a single difference of opinion with his wife in the eighteen years of their marriage. The patient had married her because she was "so unemotional," and he hated emotional people. For example, when his sister had "broken down" and cried at the death of their mother, he had felt disgusted with her display of emotion. Both the patient and his wife thought their marriage had been happy but during therapy began to realize that they had never been involved and had mistaken the absence of disagreements and arguments for happiness.

Actually, the acute onset of his illness had been preceded by years of increasing insomnia and fatigue, irritability, and lack of interest in his children. All of these complaints had been ignored and written off, however, as the inevitable result of a greater workload and more responsibility at his job. In subsequent interviews, he increasingly expressed feelings of hate and anger for his wife and her defensiveness when he tried to assert himself. He was increasingly irritated with her small talk, her overweight appearance, her passivity, narrow-mindedness, and many other things which he claimed he had not been aware of before. At first he laughed at suggestions that he might be uncomfortable with his assertive feelings, for, after all, there were times that he had "blown his stack," struck his fist through a plaster wall, and destroyed furniture in a fit of anger. However, these outbursts had all been followed by feelings of guilt and remorse, and he had "forgotten" them, preferring to think of himself as a calm and well-controlled man. It took some time to convince him that such occasional outbursts of violent anger are usually evidence of a long-standing repression of assertive feelings which accumulate to a point of such intense pressure that they can no longer be restrained. When persons interpret these outbreaks as temporary shortcomings of willpower, their feelings of guilt and determination drive them that much harder to renewed repression.

In this case, it was not until the patient recalled his own earlier history that he developed full insight and was able and willing to accept our help in learning new ways of dealing with his emotions. He recalled how in his childhood he had had a "bad temper," was inclined to rebel, and enjoyed aggressive sports, but angered easily when he lost. Once he had chased another boy for three blocks in order to beat him up with a baseball bat for winning a game. He'd had more than his share of fights, even with one of his sisters whom he had once given a black eye, for which his father beat him with a razor strap. We speculated that his aggressiveness might well have come under the control of reason and will in due time if it had not been for the fact that one day he beat one of his high school friends so badly that he had to be admitted to a hospital with a skull fracture, several broken ribs, and the loss of several teeth. For days he had lived in fear, guilt, and remorse until it was certain his friend would recover. Since that serious incident, the patient's behavior had changed abruptly. As his assertive drive had not yet been ready for reasonable control and guidance, he had no choice but to repress it through fear and determination. He feared that he might kill someone and determined that he would get rid of his anger once and for all, no matter what. Except for the aforementioned unavoidable outbreaks of pent-up anger, he had successfully repressed his anger for many years until finally the mounting tension affected his health.

Of course, there are many variations and combinations of the aforementioned causes for neurotic interference with sound development and integration of the emotions serving the assertive drive. Boys will find it

difficult if not impossible to become self-assertive if their fathers have always dominated them, ridiculed their efforts, and never expressed satisfaction with their accomplishments. Girls may become excessively shy and
fearful if their mothers stifle their attempts at self-expression and independence by making them feel guilty for "hurting mother's feelings" and by
taking away their initiative because "mother knows what is best for you."
To mention just one more instance of a family constellation which makes
healthy personality development practically impossible—perhaps the most
frequent one in the post-Industrial Revolution era—the family in which a
passive, submissive father relinquishes his natural position as head of the
family to a domineering, overbearing wife who despises him in particular
and all men in general.

A typical example of the consequences of this pathological matriarchal family constellation is the case of a fifty-two year old married man
who had become increasingly depressed, tense, and irritable. He ascribed
his symptoms to dissatisfaction with his work as a scientist since the arrival
of a gifted but arrogant and childishly irritating fellow worker, especially
because there proved to be not enough work for the two of them. He had
been sleeping poorly, and his dreams were filled with frustration and fearful expectation. He dreamed repeatedly of climbing a steep cliff yet never
reaching the top. Another dream was of being ambushed during the war.
He described himself as a shy and introverted individual, overly sensitive
to criticism, and without close friends, but successful in his work in the
laboratory. In the previous months, he had often felt like exploding, and
on one occasion he had told off one of his supervisors. He had quit going
to church, for on several occasions he had come close to shouting some
profane remarks during the service. He also had become quite concerned
and embarrassed about the fact that he felt very emotional while watching
movies or television shows and even during worship services at his church.

He had been the only son of a physically strong but otherwise weak
father who was submissive in every way to the patient's domineering, energetic and assertive mother. Ever since he could remember, he had pushed
himself through physical exercises, boxing, and judo to become as strong
as his father. He had never once cried, as far as he could remember, since
that was a sign of weakness. At the same time, he had also emulated his
father's submissiveness by going out of his way to please others and avoid
disagreements by giving in to all their demands. He had always detested
himself for this and, vaguely aware of the cumulative subconscious activity

of his repressed assertive emotions, had grown up with the firm conviction that he possessed a natural inclination to hate other people. During the war he had volunteered for commando training and was assigned to a special squad to kill noiselessly with knife or bayonet. He had killed many enemy soldiers and took it for granted that he did so in an unemotional and businesslike manner. Nevertheless, he had been puzzled by the fact that he always had to vomit each time he performed his duty as a commando.

In therapy, we came to know him as a sensitive, intelligent man who finally dared to cry over his war activities without feelings of shame or embarrassment. Before it became necessary for him to accept a transfer to another city, we were able to help him in becoming more comfortable with his long repressed emotions by reminding him of his expertise in judo. In that defensive sport he overcame the blow of his attacker not by rigidly and stubbornly resisting it, but by rolling with it, and, in the process, throwing the attacker off balance, thus rendering him harmless. As long as he considered emotions a threat and potentially harmful, he could learn, we advised him, to defend himself against them by using a similar approach of going along with them, by opening himself up to the emotions of others and by accepting his own. In that way he would neutralize them instead of keeping them with all his might. If he wanted so desperately to be a real man, he should learn to deal with some additional manly weapons, his emotions, not just willpower and physical strength. As this particular approach appealed to him, he began to show signs of emotional growth and his depression lessened. However, his transfer brought therapy to a premature end, and we lost contact with him.

Finally, we want to mention one more possible neurotic factor in irrationally expressed feelings of anger and hate. This factor is present in persons with Emotional Deprivation Disorder—persons who have not been affirmed in love by the important adults in their childhood, most often their natural parents. Since the affirmation process operates to reveal to the other that he or she is good, it follows that a lack of affirmation results in the other being left with an image of himself or herself as not-good, and what is more, the other will see the adult who has failed to affirm him or her as an evil, too. We are inclined to discern a relationship between this factor and the fact that the number of unaffirmed persons and persons with Emotional Deprivation Disorder is steadily increasing, as well as with the recently released figures of a study involving forty-eight countries showing the main cause of death among five to fourteen year olds to be accidents and suicide. We also ask whether the increasing incidence of crime could be related to the affective deprivation of the criminals and to their violent expression of anger against those who failed them or those who represent them and authority figures.

Be this as it may, we close this discussion of the emotions serving the assertive drive and of some of the main causes for their repression or suppression by briefly *summarizing* the consequences of this repression in later life: These include the inability to be oneself and to freely and spontaneously pursue one's goals by means of an easily controlled, readily guided assertiveness; a self-centeredness which cannot find happiness in the well-being of others; a lack of joy living with frequent deep depressions and psychosomatic disorders; and unavoidable outbursts of irritability, anger, or rage when the accumulated repressed feelings have built up so much pressure that the slightest stimulus can trigger an explosion, usually followed by feelings of guilt, fear, sorrow, or remorse.

Some of our thoughts on anger have been well expressed in "A Poison Tree" by William Blake.

> I was angry with my friend:
> I told my wrath, my wrath did end.
> I was angry with my foe:
> I told it not, my wrath did grow.
>
> And I water'd it in fears,
> Night and morning with my tears;
> And I sunned it with smiles,
> And with soft deceitful wiles.
>
> And it grew both day and night,
> Till it bore an apple bright:
> And my foe beheld it shine,
> And he knew that it was mine,
>
> And into my garden stole
> When the night had veil'd the pole:
> In the morning glad I see
> My foe outstretch'd beneath the tree.

CHAPTER VIII

FREEDOM OF THE WILL IN REPRESSIVE DISORDERS

Virtue exists not only in the intellect and will, the "moved mover," but also in the emotional life.

Summa Theologica, I-II,q.58,a.2.

MUCH HAS BEEN SAID and written about the freedom of the actions performed by persons with neurotic disorders. This question is undoubtedly an important one, and we think it proper to discuss it extensively.

We want to state at the outset that in our opinion such a discussion properly belongs to the province of psychology and not to that of moral theology. Moral theology is a science which teaches the norms by which human beings can attain their ultimate goal and the conditions that must be fulfilled for them to be able to strive toward God or turn away from Him. In other words, moral theology teaches that human beings must be free to be able to sin. It does not belong to the domain of moral theology, however, to judge whether freedom is present in any given case. Textbooks of moral theology must certainly contain some discussion of circumstances that influence the freedom of the will, if only for the simple reason that these textbooks are intended to prepare priests for practical pastoral duties. These discussions, however, are essentially of a psychological nature.

It is true that the priest in the confessional must form a judgment of the penitent's freedom of will, but this is essentially a judgment concerning a psychological matter which is then applied to a theological judgment concerning guilt. A priest's ordinary common sense and understanding suffice for the majority of patients. In special cases, however, particularly those involving psychological disturbances, the priest's knowledge will be insufficient except to provide a basis for reasonable doubt, for priests lack the specialized knowledge acquired in psychiatric and psychological studies. Consequently, the priest may require the advice of an expert in such matters; that is, of a psychiatrist or psychotherapist depending on the requirements of the penitent. It is the therapist's task to investigate and determine to what extent the emotional life of the individual involved responds to normal guidance by the intellect, and hence to what extent he or she can be said to be free. The therapist must avoid making decisions in questions pertaining strictly to moral theology, for in such matters he or she is a layperson. In this, it is the therapist's duty to follow the advice of a moral theologian. By the same token, the theologian must refrain from encroaching on the domain of psychotherapy; to do otherwise would entail great danger to the patient.

As it is up to the moral theologian to decide whether the psychotherapeutic opinion should be accepted; much will depend on the confidence the theologian has in the person of the psychotherapist. This, however, does not change the fact that it is the proper task of psychology to determine the extent of freedom in acts by psychologically impaired persons. This holds true for persons with psychotic disorders, personality disorders and psychopathic personalities as well as for persons with neurotic disorders. In all these different forms of psychological disorders the psychotherapist must decide to what extent the emotional manifestations are under the control of intellect and will. To do this, the exact nature of the disorder must be determined and a scientifically justified opinion based on facts must be given, founded on the therapist's equally justified insight into those facts. We intend to do this here for the repressive disorders, leaving the equally important matter of freedom of will in those with psychotic disorders, personality disorders and psychopathic personalities to be discussed at some other time.

Since in the repressive disorders we are dealing with repressed sensory emotions, the question is whether these repressed emotions still share in the free exercise of the will and whether the will is able to direct them. For a factual discussion of this question, we shall first consider the clinical data to determine whether the phenomenology of these disorders can teach us anything about freedom or lack of freedom in the activity of the repressed emotions.

As far as hysterical neurosis is concerned, we are immediately struck by the will's inability to control the repressed emotion. This clinical syndrome is characterized by the fact that the inadmissible and repressed emotion is made to vanish completely from consciousness while continuing to exert its influence in the unconscious in such a way that it manifests itself either in the person's conduct or in certain conversion symptoms of a somatic or psychological nature. The man who dislikes his work, but forces himself to ignore this aversion, develops a paralysis which incapacitates him from doing his work. The nun who wants to leave the convent, but stays on because she thinks it wrong to ask for a dispensation of her vows, suddenly is unable to walk. The repressed emotion can manifest itself in countless ways, as we have indicated elsewhere in this book; but no matter which symptom occurs, it is always the repressed emotion that brings it into existence.

The characteristic feature of this symptom is that it is *entirely out of reach of the will*. It is completely impossible for the will to exert influence on these psychogenic manifestations. No matter how much the patient wants the symptom to disappear, there is not the slightest chance that the conversion symptom can be influenced by mere willing. From the clinician's viewpoint there is no doubt that the conversion symptom is beyond control of the will. The only possibility for achieving something in the way of therapy is by attempting to influence the sensory life through methods such as suggestion, hypnosis and analysis with accompanied catharsis of the psychological trauma. Every appeal to the will-act is futile.

Evidently, we are dealing here with an activity of a repressed emotion which is absolutely beyond the control of reason and will, and entirely autonomous. Moreover, it should be realized that in these cases the repression does not need to have been particularly strong either in duration or intensity. Sometimes one single act of repression may be sufficient to produce a conversion symptom, while, as we have explained earlier in this book, the action of the repressing emotion is always less strong than that found in obsessive-compulsive repression. Whether the symptom becomes manifest depends entirely on the particular psychophysical disposition of the individual. If one is disposed to such a symptom, the repressed emotion, being obstructed in its normal manifestations, will seek to manifest itself by means of the symptom without any possible interference on the part of the will.

This same lack of freedom in the action of the repressed emotions *occurs in obsessive-compulsive repression*, even though the fact that the repressed emotion cannot be controlled by intellect and will is not so immediately evident, at least not to the layman. Here, in contrast to hysterical neurosis, the action of the repressive process is not terminated once the repression has taken place, for the repressing emotion continues to pursue the repressed emotion in such an intense way that it cannot become manifest again. In fact, the psychotherapist can frequently determine the nature of this repressed emotion only by studying the dream content. In the early stages of the illness, however, the repressed emotion will not betray itself outwardly in any way; it will begin to do so only when the tension becomes unbearable after prolonged and intensive repression.

The symptoms that appear then have a typical compulsive quality which obviously lacks control by the will. If the repressed emotion happens to involve the sexual drive, it may ultimately reveal itself in a compulsion to look at objects that stimulate the sexual drive, and although patients want to fight against this compulsion so that it will cease, and actually have the most resolute intentions to do so, it is to no avail. By forcing themselves, usually with great effort, not to look at such objects, patients are simply reinforcing the repression, and this, of course, does not diminish the compulsion. If this were really an urge that could be controlled by the will, one would expect that constant practice would lead to a habit. Yet, the opposite is true, for the more people try to control themselves, the stronger the compulsion becomes. There cannot be any question, therefore, of an act that is subject to control by reason and will. In these cases, the repressed emotion functions entirely autonomously.

One may object that these are extreme cases and that the foregoing observations do not prove that a single act of repression results in a loss of control by the will over the repressed emotion. It is true that the presence of obsessive-compulsive symptoms presupposes prolonged and intensive repression, but the controlling influence of the will could never have been eliminated so completely if each repressing act had not constituted a measure of withdrawal from the will's controlling action. The frequency with which the repression takes place does not alter its fundamental nature, but only the extent and depth of its consequences. Every repression to a certain extent affects the rational control of the emotional life, and what is obvious regarding hysterical neurosis likewise occurs in obsessive-compulsive repression. The only difference is that in the latter the autonomous action of the repressed emotion does not immediately become obvious, for the simple reason that every activity of the repressed emotion is encapsulated, so to speak, by the repressing emotion. In the earliest stages its manifestations are limited to the inner life; for example, to the imagination, as is seen in obsessive images which distract a person during prayer. Only later will it begin to reveal itself in compulsive motor behavior.

Because these facts are incontestable, in our opinion it cannot be denied that the repressed emotion is beyond rational control.[1] However, in making this statement, we do not claim that once a repression has taken place, all emotions of the faculty in question are beyond the control of the will. Strictly speaking, the *lack of freedom of will only concerns the actual emotion which was repressed and not the other ones.* Whether other emotions are devoid of rational control depends solely on whether they in turn have been repressed. Such a sequence is not an absolute necessity, for although every person represses to some extent during his or her life, the matter normally straightens itself out without difficulty. There is always the danger that the tendency to repress will become stronger once a repression has taken place, however, for once an object has been repressed, the person will be more inclined to repress anew when faced with the same or an analogous situation. In frequently repeated repression, especially if it began in childhood, the psychological pattern will be such that immediate repression will follow exposure to a certain object. If such an abnormal psychological condition has developed over the years, practically none of that person's acts, so far as they are related to the repressed emotions, will be free, because all related emotions are repressed as soon as they arise. Only when the repression and the abnormal and irrational activity of the assertive drive have been eliminated will it again be possible for that person to perform truly free and human acts. Only then can human nature take its normal course and enable the person to lead a rational life.

Now that we know that the will's lack of control over repressed emotions is a proven fact, we must attempt to learn the reason for it. This, of course, does not pose a problem for the deterministic psychoanalyst, but for those who accept the human person's innate freedom of will, the

1. This is also evident in those without neurotic disorders in the psychology of everyday life. We all know of people who shrug off an unpleasant remark, only to react the next time with abnormal vehemence to an unintentional slight. Likewise, who does not recall having suppressed a guffaw only to explode with laughter a little later against his or her will? The mechanism in such cases is always the same: after a person has repressed a certain emotion, it continues to function beyond the control of the will.

incontestable evidence of such non-free acts requires an explanation that does not do violence to the principles of general psychology and shows us why this lack of freedom exists and how far it extends.

Having explained the repressive process from the Thomistic psychological viewpoint, we shall determine whether it can explain the lack of freedom of repressed emotions and of the acts they bring about. Normally, when a certain emotion arises in a person in regard to a sensory object, it requires, by virtue of being a human emotion, direction by reason. The intellect must decide whether the sensory object also constitutes a rational good, and consequently, whether the gratification of the desire must be allowed or denied. Either decision provides a natural solution which does not disrupt the harmony of the person's psychological life.

There exists yet another possibility, however. As the emotion arises prior to the rational judgment,[2] it is possible that before the emotion receives its guidance from reason, another emotion intervenes and represses the first one. To understand this process we must realize that rational guidance means that the purely sensory object of the emotion becomes a rational-sensory object; and as the sensory appetite by nature tends to obey reason, it will make this rational-sensory object its goal. However, if repression takes place, this sensory object of the emotion cannot be subordinated to reason, for this object will also have become the object of the repressing emotion which, having won out, will represent it as such to the intellect. Thus reason will direct it, not as the object of the pleasure appetite, but as that of the assertive drive. It follows, therefore, that as an object of the pleasure appetite, it fails to be directed. If in some manner or other it persists in stimulating the pleasure appetite, it does so necessarily as a purely sensory object without the ennobling influence of reason. Obviously, intellect and will have no influence over this activity.

This explains why the repressed emotion is not subject to control by the will. We have used the metaphor of *the repressing emotion wedging itself between the will and the repressed emotion*; the foregoing explanation has made it clear that such a metaphor is justified and is as correct as saying that the intellect is above the senses.

If reason is to guide the repressed emotion, the repressing emotion has to be eliminated first. This represents the principle of our therapy: *to eradicate the repression and to eliminate the abnormal, irrational action of the repressing emotion*. Only in that way can the person with a neurotic

2. *passiones praeveniunt mentem*

disorder achieve an intelligent control over his or her emotional life, and this is the goal of all our therapeutic endeavors.

CHAPTER IX

EMOTIONAL MATURITY

The more necessary something is, the more the order of reason must be pre-served in it.

Summa Theologica, II,II, 153,3.

IN WRITING ABOUT THE various types of neurotic disorders, we have made occasional reference to psychopathic personality disorders which have clinical features resembling, to some extent, those of neurotic disorders. Although both are disorders of the emotional life, neurotic disorders are acquired, while, in our opinion, true psychopathic personalities are consti-tutionally determined.

Since the time when our main observations about the nature and dif-ferent types of neurotic disorders were made, researched in approximately 15,000 patients and put in writing for this book, we have observed in cer-tain individuals a kind of emotional immaturity and inner discontent not found in either neurotic disorders or constitutional psychopathic personal-ity disorders. The condition principally represents, we believe, an *acquired psychopathic state* resulting from mistaken psychoanalytic notions regard-ing the nature of the repressing faculty.

Since popular knowledge of the clinical discoveries and analytic theories of Sigmund Freud and others has become widespread, people in general have become increasingly concerned about the suffering and illness brought on by emotional repression and logically have reacted against this.

Never cognizant of the difference, however, between the neurotic mechanism of repression of the emotions and the natural process of guidance of the emotions by reason, people had no choice but to let the pendulum of emotional control swing to the other side and to give free rein to their emotions. This development was of course predictable, if one recalls that Freud believed the repressing factor to be the superego, encompassing conscience and thus also reason.[1] As a result, *conscience and reason, being the alleged perpetrators* of so much untold neurotic suffering in the world, became increasingly suspect. The more they fell into disrepute, the easier it became for unrestrained emotions to determine people's behavior. This is true for the emotions of love, fear, anxiety, worry, sadness, despair, and envy, and most of all, of course, for the sexual feelings. It is these sexual feelings, no longer neurotically repressed or rationally restrained, which, we believe, contribute significantly to the increase of sexual promiscuity and unwanted pregnancies, the legal enactment of liberalized abortion laws, the almost contagious spread of the contraceptive mentality, the growing revenues from pornographic trade, and the demands of "modern man" for a "new morality."

It may seem strange that we have not witnessed a similar reversal in attitude toward the feelings of anger and hate, also long repressed. Although unrest is admittedly more widespread and there are more outbreaks of violence in much of the world, the extent of this increase of aggressiveness is far less than the increase in sexual libertinism has been. Obviously, the violence and destruction which would follow if people were to give free reign to anger and hate has little to recommend itself when compared with the pleasures derived from unrestrained sexual emotions. On the other hand, in view of the generally low level of appreciation for the positive and necessary functions of hate and anger, it may be assumed that people, if at all concerned with their proper management, rationalized them away and instead focused their attention on love. Love, people thought, would be an ideal substitute for hate and anger. Stressing the significance of love would serve as an effective substitute for repressing the emotions of hate and anger. Moreover, for those who regard love and sex as virtually synonymous, this thinking affords an acceptable excuse for "unconventional" sexual behavior, deemed unavoidable if one were not to repress anymore.

---

1 ". . . the 'superego' or inhibiting and conscience-including component of the personality. . .. It acts as the supervisor of the ego . . . and, therefore, as the repressing part of the personality." Arthur P. Noyes and Lawrence C. Kolb, *Modern Clinical Psychiatry* (Philadelphia: W. B. Saunders Co., 1963), p. 21.

Partly for this reason, but also because the nature of human love and of its *component elements of emotional and volitional love* is so little understood, we have witnessed the emergence of *situation ethics* and its enthusiastic endorsement by many; a serious vocational crisis among priests and religious; a general upsurge in the divorce rate; a frantic search for a rapid, and therefore unnatural, build-up of the human person's emotions through sensitivity training and drugs; and a growing opposition to authority and obedience, on the basis that love, not law, should be the sole motive for one's actions.

We wonder whether it is coincidental that there has developed, in the wake of these changed attitudes from legalism to situation ethics and from prudishness to exhibitionism, a noticeable degree of *apathy*, not least among those who were affected most deeply by repression. Indeed, the rapid changes of the last few decades have led to a paradox: instead of having found happiness and bliss in an unrepressed attitude toward love and sex, men and women find themselves engulfed by countless social and moral problems and possessed with little more than apathy to cope with them. There are reasons outside of our particular field of competence for this growing apathy among so many people. As psychiatrists, however, we want to single out the unbalanced development of the emotional life, whether from repression or non-affirmation, as the most significant contributing factor. This unbalance consists of overemphasis on the feelings of love and sex, disapproval or fear of the emotions of anger and hate, and a general distrust of conscience and reason, associated as they are in the minds of many with the superego, the alleged source of neurotic sufferings.

If one is trained or, through deprivation, forced only to love and to suppress feelings of hate and anger, then the proper object of hate and anger, namely *the evil in this world*, both sense and moral evil, remains unopposed. One cannot love evil, nor can one hate it, and the result is apathy. One may oppose evil intellectually and volitionally, but without the moving force of the emotions of hate and anger, the effect is limited and the effort is feeble. The effectiveness of opposition to evil does not seem to increase noticeably when society attempts to promote an emotional response to what it considers the root evils—the triad of war, poverty, and racism. For many people in the Western world, these realities are too abstract to be capable of arousing an emotional response. At most, they lead to such predominantly willed reactions as pacifism, redistribution of wealth, or integrated housing and schools. A truly effective reaction against evil, complementing one's love of others requires—from early childhood—educational preparation based on a realistic appreciation and cultivation of *all* human emotions.

It is unfortunate that relatively little is being said publicly about the importance for the individual's psychological maturity of freely determined self-control, or, as we have called it elsewhere, self-restraining love.[2] We therefore describe and explain here the clinical characteristics of persons who have drifted beyond the point of nonrepression in the mistaken belief that rational restraint of feelings and drives would be tantamount to neurotic repression.

The emotional distress observed in the persons we referred to at the beginning of this chapter seems to stem from an excessive and premature pursuit of sexual gratification in the belief that such experiences are a necessary and desirable requirement for personality growth and personal fulfillment. In other words, these individuals, evidently influenced by popular existential philosophies, do not view sex primarily as something good and pleasurable possessed with an intrinsic, natural, other-directed purpose, but rather as something useful and therefore to be pursued in order to attain the desired goal of personal fulfillment. Disregarding the sex drive's natural aim of the creation of new human life, they gratify the sexual desire as such—but not so far as it is rational—by performing the sex act solitarily, promiscuously, unrestrainedly, perversely, or for its shock or "entertainment" value. In these individuals, we may say, the emotion achieves its sense object while reason is frustrated. This differs from the repressive disorders, in which one emotion represses another one in such a manner that the repressed emotion is gratified neither as such, nor insofar as it is rational. It is for this reason that we observe significantly more tension, anxiety, and restlessness in persons with neurotic disorders than in persons who pursue sexual gratification.

The mental characteristics of the persons under discussion resemble those of the constitutional or acquired psychopathic personality. The *constitutional psychopath* is emotionally unstable, impulsive, and prone to gratify every feeling immediately and selfishly because of an innate lack or diminished degree of integration between the emotional life and reason and will. The *acquired psychopathic state* develops in a normal child who becomes spoiled, sated, and bored with life as a result of being given

---

2. See *Healing the Unaffirmed: Recognizing Emotional Deprivation Disorder*, by Conrad W. Baars, M.D. and Anna A. Terruwe, M.D., Rev. ed. Suzanne M. Baars, M.A. and Bonnie N. Shayne, M.A. eds., Staten Island, NY: Alba House, 2002.

everything as soon as, if not before, he or she desires it. To understand the nature of the peculiar emotional immaturity of these individuals, a brief discussion of the development of the human person's capacity for happiness and joy is in order.

It may be stated that the extent of a *person's capacity for happiness*, i.e., the capacity for utilizing, appreciating, and enjoying all the things for which he or she was created, consists of the degree of adaptation of one's powers to their proper objects. Since all human powers possess and function by means of a material substrate, they cannot instantaneously acquire this disposition for optimal adaptation to their proper objects. This only occurs slowly and gradually. A few brief observations will show that this gradual process is required in the vegetative dimension as well as in the sensory and intellectual dimensions.

Physiological studies have shown that the maximum utilization of food requires the preparation of the gastrointestinal tract by means of secretion of enzymes and other substances which metabolize the ingested foods into their corresponding human elements. The full appreciation and enjoyment of many foods is not possible until we have developed a taste for them by gradually getting acquainted with them. Tactile perceptions in medical students and blind persons gradually become more refined through constant practice and experience. The fine points of a symphony are not understood and recognized until the ear has been exposed to many critical auditions. Maximum visual appreciation requires more than a casual glance at the endless variety of beautiful creations by nature and artists alike. In short, each sense must become fully adapted to its object if its owner is to be capable of maximal perception, and thus maximal enjoyment, of the more perfectly perceived objects.

The human person's higher cognitive faculties are equally subject to this principle. It takes many years of education and of exposure to and study of the works of the great minds of past generations—epic poets, philosophers, and others—before one can penetrate to the essence of created things and intellectually and spiritually appreciate their order and harmony.

There is no reason to exclude one's pleasure appetite and assertive drive from this principle of human nature. In fact, our clinical experiences have confirmed this. If we apply this principle, for example, to the *emotion of desire*, it is not difficult to understand that the more time and opportunity one has to know the many aspects of an object, to daydream and think about them, the greater the object's attraction will be and the stronger the desire for it. When at last one's desire finds its fulfillment in the possession of this object, one's joy will be greater and more intense than if the desire had been instantaneously fulfilled.

It is necessary that the child's emotions for all objects are allowed to grow consistently and intensify according to this principle. Objects must be made available in the proper order of significance for the growing child, from the most concrete and simple to the more complex and immaterial ones. The child's emotional appreciation of these objects must be increasingly exposed to a proper subordination to and integration with a correctly informed and disposed intellectual life. The child's emotional life will only develop to full capacity if these requirements are met. Only then, as an adult, will feelings of love and joy cultivated during childhood and adolescence enable him or her to experience the highest degree of human happiness.

In our discussion of the neurotic disorders in this book, we have shown that there are different ways in which a *desire may be blocked*. There is no need to repeat ourselves, but there is still another non-neurotic way in which a desire can be prevented from maturing which may lead to a grave psychological disharmony. This happens when the desired object is made available too soon, or even before the desire has had a chance to make itself felt. Anyone who has observed a typical *spoiled child*, whose every whim has been satisfied immediately, knows what we mean. Gradualness, imagination, wonder, expectation and awe, lack of fear and extravagance, and above all, order and reason are of the essence in the necessary cultivation of the emotions of love, desire and joy. The more complex, noble, and valuable the object is, the more time this approach will demand, and the greater the restraint must be in not making the object available too early.

This is especially true for the sexual desire as it grows under the ennobling influence of the intellectual life toward the person of the opposite sex—toward the happiness of that person and of the child which is the fruit of its fulfillment. No child can mature unless the growth of this desire is guaranteed in an atmosphere of rational norms and mature parental authority in which it is protected from the untimely gratification of its desires. This protection must always be based on rational motives. Fortunately, we have outgrown the era in which this was attempted by means of instilling fear of things sexual. There is no room here for fear, just as there is none for *false claims* that early acquaintance with sexual matters, random or forced sexual experimentation, and premarital, extramarital, or perverted sexual practices are guarantees of personal fulfillment and maturity. Sex education promoting these false claims is not worthy of the name education.

Modern-day practitioners of the theory of accelerated sexual growth— a backlash from neurotic repression—present a peculiar clinical picture of emotional immaturity. They are egotistic and preoccupied with themselves. Their sense of self-importance is exaggerated and unrealistic, often in spite of a defective sense of self-worth. They are blasé, sated, and bored with life. Their eyes and faces often reveal the absence of inner joy and contentment. Their erotic feelings are stunted, not refined. At times they have an aversion to the very sexuality they at first willed to possess so strenuously. Often, the remainder of their emotional life also shows a decided imbalance and disharmony. A cross-sectional view of these people marks them as typical psychopaths, even though their longitudinal histories reveal that they possess innately sound psychological constitutions. We must therefore classify them as acquired psychopathic personalities. We consider their prognosis *extremely unfavorable*, unless they possess superior intellectual capacities which they are willing to employ toward the proper ordering of their undisciplined emotional lives.

Although these individuals are in many ways emotionally overstimulated, they must nevertheless be considered emotionally immature, because the development of their reason and will has been relatively retarded. All graduates of Values Clarification classes (Sidney Simon), Cognitive Moral Development programs (Lawrence Kohlburg) and Sex Education programs (SIECUS) as well as Situation Ethics practitioners are the most likely victims of this particular type of immaturity. Emotional maturity, we repeat, is rooted in a full-grown, responsive emotional life—encompassing every emotion without exception—which is completely integrated with and penetrated by a well-informed intellect and "benevolent" free will. Or to say it differently, in the mature person reason listens respectfully to the emotions, while the will, acting upon the knowledge provided by reason, is itself spurred on and moved by the motor of the emotions.

Many of our patients consider it even more enlightening when we compare the relationship between the human person's intellectual dimension and emotional dimension with that between *a rider and his or her horse*. In this comparison, the horse represents the emotional dimension and the rider, the intellectual dimension.

The adult, emotionally mature human being is represented by a spirited, well-trained horse ridden to perfection by an experienced rider in full command of his mount. An excellent example would be a beautiful Lippizaner stallion ridden by the master of the Spanish Court Riding School of Vienna. Rider and horse trust and respect each other, each responds to the other, but the rider is always in command. The rider goes where he wants, in the manner he wants, readily and effortlessly, using his reins, weight, and legs to convey messages to the horse which are imperceptible to all but the most experienced onlookers. The strong, attentive, well-trained horse provides most of the energy necessary to carry the rider to his destination.

Of course, horse and rider did not achieve this smooth and easy interaction overnight. It started with the colt being allowed to run freely in the meadow, protected from harm by the surrounding fences. These early carefree years were followed by years of working together, of getting to know each other. The horse became familiar with the voice of the rider, learned to listen and respond to his directions, learned to rely on his judgment and will. The rider became familiar with the horse's temperament and idiosyncrasies, learned to put these to their best possible use, and helped the horse to overcome its weaknesses. Both rider and horse learned from their mistakes; both learned to improve their means of communication; each became more sensitive and responsive to the other.

In the end, the rider, having become an expert horseman, was free to go where he wanted because his horse had become a willing servant instead of a slave subdued by force.

The person with a neurotic disorder is represented by a big, strong, muscular rider mounted on a partially crippled, half-starved, nearly exhausted, pony-size horse. It requires much kicking, shouting, and pulling of the reins by the rider to make the horse go where he wants it to go. Every ride exhausts both the rider and the horse.

The person with a psychopathic personality is represented by a big, spirited, but untamed horse ridden by a seemingly experienced rider. On almost every ride the horse throws the rider and runs off aimlessly. The rider's efforts to train his horse are in vain—he never learns to control it properly. Only when the horse has grown old does the rider seem to attain a measure of control over it.

We have presented these comparisons for what they are—attempts at providing deeper insight into the nature of the relationship between the human person's emotional and intellectual dimensions, and the meaning of emotional maturity.

APPENDIX A

HUMAN DRIVES

FOLLOWING THE EXAMPLE OF Aristotle, Thomas Aquinas divides all acquired inclinations into two large groups. The first is made up of those which serve the innate drives of self-preservation and procreation.[1] The second group consists of the specifically human inclinations which serve the human person in sensitive, intellectual, and spiritual operations.

In the first group we find the desires for food, drink and sex, which correspond to the senses of taste, smell and touch. The senses of sight and hearing, as well as the internal senses of imagination, memory, and the usefulness judgment, serve more the specifically human inclinations; hence, greater penetration by the intellect. This distinction has been grasped quite well in the ordinary use of the word "sensual" to designate what some call the "lower" inclinations. One also uses different terminology to describe the gratification of the senses of touch, taste and smell, as distinct from the higher visual and auditory sensations.

The second group, the *specifically human inclinations*, contains two sub-groups. The first comprises the inclinations which have as their objective the inner growth and perfection of the human personality; the other includes those whose gratifications are not immediately required for the natural growth of the personality, but which contribute in a more or less accidental manner to the well-being of the personality.

The first sub-group is made up of those inclinations which are aimed at inner growth of the human person's being. It is the nature and purpose

---

1. Since the animal shares this group of elementary, subrational inclinations, Thomas Aquinas calls them animal desires (*concupiscentiae animales*).

of man and woman to *perfect their nature*, to use their natural talents for that purpose. As they are rational beings, this natural inclination must be developed in a rational manner; therefore their reason will spontaneously tell them that it is their first and greatest good to realize the fullness of their own being. For both man and woman there are natural inclinations toward independence, autonomy and maturity, sharing, etc. These natural inclinations include a difference of emphasis in the way each goes about growing in these goods. The man grows in shared autonomy with a natural emphasis on autonomy. The woman grows in shared autonomy with a natural emphasis on sharing. Because man and woman are different in the very depths of their existence—within their fundamental equality—their natural inclinations develop into different characteristics, or rather into common characteristics with a different emphasis. In men, the reasoning intellect and physical power are emphasized; in women, special sensitivity and the intuitive intellect are emphasized. These particular differences between man and woman, culminating so to speak in science and wisdom respectively, are complemented by many other ones to varying degrees. As space prevents us from describing the varied masculine and feminine natural inclinations, we want to refer the reader to *Human Sexual Ecology*,[2] and *Woman—A Contemporary View*.[3]

In addition to this first subgroup of inclinations that aims at one's inner growth and constitutes the first requirement of one's rational nature, there is an endless number of *other inclinations* whose gratification contributes *only incidentally* to human happiness. Their number is endless because one's sensory life may be attracted by an infinite number of goods. They may be arranged in several groups: goods which immediately satisfy one's personal meaning, not so much as an individual but as a social being, such as friendship, sympathy, devotion, gratefulness, and so on. The personal goods are again further subdivided into those that are mainly material, such as riches, and those that are mainly spiritual, such as honor. There are even goods that are in essence entirely intellectual-spiritual, such as knowledge and religion; but these, too, possess an emotional value because of the fact that the human being is not a pure spirit but a spiritual-sensory being, and all intellectual knowledge derives from and is linked to the sensory life.

2. by Robert E. Joyce, Ph.D., Washington, DC, Catholic University of America Press, 1979, pp. 65–82.

3. by F.J.J. Buytendijk, Ph.D., New York: NY, Newman Press, 1968.

APPENDIX B

THE AUTHORS PREFER THE use of the word "fear" in favor of "anxiety" throughout this book because of the confusion surrounding the word "anxiety" in American psychiatry. This confusion is so great that the psychoanalyst Sandor Rado once advocated that its use be abandoned altogether. This confusion has not noticeably lessened since the days of Rado. In fact, it has spread to the vernacular. Witness the almost paradoxical meaning of the word "anxious:" 1. full of anxiety, 2. eagerly wishing (Webster's New World Dictionary, 1979).

The psychiatric definitions of "anxiety" are many, yet all of them agree on one point, namely the assumption that anxiety is fear that has no object, at least no consciously known object. This is true in the type of neurotic disorder that was the subject of Freud's original and brilliant discoveries. However, his premature conclusion seems to have prevented Freud and his followers from uncovering a more basic characteristic of anxiety that also pertains to types of neurotic disorders other than hysterical neurosis, and even to normal persons.

Whenever certain circumstances prevent a person's fear from exercising this psychological motor's proper function, i.e. to move the person to protect himself or herself from the threatening evil through "fight or flight," this fear turns into anxiety. As a consequence, the person remains continuously exposed to the feared object, either on the subconscious level where it is "buried alive," or on the level of conscious awareness. In either case, the object keeps stimulating the person's fear, its psychological component as well as its physical. Since persons cannot be comfortable when any part of their being is constantly and uninterruptedly active, without ever having an opportunity to return to its resting state (awake—asleep; exercise—rest; noise—calm; pain—freedom of pain; etc.), it follows that a state of constant fear will have adverse effects.

On the psychological level, these effects are experienced as anxiety, panic or phobia; on the physical level as tension, restlessness, trembling, startle reaction, perspiration, palpitations, etc. As all anxiety is fear (but not all fear is anxiety) it follows that anxiety disorders, anxiety states, etc. are best understood by the consistent use of the word "fear" rather than "anxiety." Nevertheless, this is not a plea on our part for the abandonment of the word "anxiety." Properly understood it has its place both in psychiatry and the vernacular.

When is it impossible for fear to exercise its proper function?

1. When individuals are totally unaware of what they fear because the neurotic repression of the feared object is complete. It is hidden in the subconscious. This always takes place in persons with an hysterical neurosis, as Freud discovered (*see* Chapter III). Treatment: psychoanalysis.

2. When the repression is not so thorough and the person is partially aware of the feared object. This happens in persons with obsessive-compulsive repression, e.g. persons with fear-based repression. Their irrational fear is kept alive by a misinformed utility judgment (*see* Chapter III). Treatment: our mortification therapy.

3. When persons are fully aware of the feared object, but are psychologically too weak to come to grips with it in an effective manner. Their fear is a rational or existential fear.[4] Treatment: authentic Affirmation Therapy.

4. When healthy persons find themselves in a new and irritating living situation that cannot change, e.g. for fear of hurting someone's feelings. This happens in pseudo-neurotic reactions (see Chapter III). Treatment: helping these persons to do something about the source of their repressed irritation.

5. In normal healthy persons who are fully aware of what they fear, but are prevented from doing anything about it immediately, e.g. having to make an after dinner speech; stage fright; jungle fighting with invisible snipers, etc.

It is ironic that notwithstanding the greatly enhanced knowledge of neurotic disorders now available, the American Psychiatric Association

---

4. See *Healing the Unaffirmed: Recognizing Emotional Deprivation Disorder*, by Conrad W. Baars, M.D. and Anna A. Terruwe, M.D., Rev. ed. Suzanne M. Baars, M.A. and Bonnie N. Shayne, M.A., eds., Staten Island, NY: Alba House, 2002.

recently decided to eliminate the word "neurosis" from its 1980 *Diagnostic and Statistical Manual of Mental Disorders* (DSM III). This represents the American psychiatric profession's solution to the same dilemma faced by Dr. Terruwe in the 1950's: the growing number of patients appearing in psychiatrists' offices whose neurotic symptoms and complaints did not respond to established therapeutic procedures (in America chiefly the psychoanalytic approach; in the case of Dr. Terruwe her mortification therapy).

There can be little doubt that the development of two opposing ways of solving the same problem—in America the elimination of the term "neurosis"; in the Netherlands the discovery of a new clinical syndrome: deprivation neurosis *[De frustratie neurose; now called Emotional Deprivation Disorder]*—has its roots in American psychology's rejection of the language, concepts, and philosophic foundation of European psychology in the 1930's in its effort to establish an empiric science which preferred to view human behavior as a complex integration of basic biological needs and essential cultural adaptations.

The growing number of disillusioned psychiatrists in our time is an indication that once again American psychiatry stands at a crossroads. On one of the road signs worthy of consideration the following words can be read. They were spoken by the late P.J.A. Calon, Ph.D., professor of medical and developmental psychology at the University of Nymegen, Netherlands:

> In essence Dr. Terruwe's study centers on Aquinas's doctrine that man's emotions are directed by nature to be guided by his rational powers. She is fully justified in basing her ideas and their clinical applications on Aquinas's teaching about the emotional life of man. Until now it has remained unsurpassed in excellence by any modern hypothesis both in the splendor of its many facets, in the depth of its anthropological perspectives, and in the countless possibilities for its further development through modern scientific discoveries. . .. Dr. Terruwe's work is an important contribution to a synthesis in which the old is not rejected merely because it is old nor the new accorded *a priori* acceptance but a work in which major traditional thinking provided the light which guides us in the solution of problems in psychology and psychiatry.

Such a synthesis will make it possible to give more than lip service to the oft-heard claim by psychiatrists to the effect that they *treat the whole person*. As physicians specializing in the therapy of persons with a psychological illness, we can be healers only when we know what the human psyche is all about. More than anything else, this requires that the psychiatrist has the capacity to intelligently involve the spiritual dimension of the human person in therapy, without necessarily doing the same with the patient's religious beliefs. In conclusion, it must be said that psychiatrists and psychotherapists, as authentic healers of the whole person, cannot be satisfied with merely restoring their patients to their former level of useful functioning in society. They must go beyond solely utilitarian criteria of vocational performance or adjustment in business or profession.

For psychiatrists and psychotherapists treating the whole person, authentic healing means assisting their patients in attaining a level of happiness commensurate with their innate capacities and potentialities.

This generally involves a greater sensitivity for and keener intellectual appreciation of the true, the good, and the beautiful; a greater capacity to love and enjoy; a lesser emphasis on utilitarian pursuits and a decided tempering of the assertive emotions; and a greater harmony of interaction between sensory and intellectual life. It is by means of this more balanced and properly weighted inner life that our patients are led to attain the happiness for which they have been created—a happiness which requires an act of intellect, but also, and most emphatically, a ready responsiveness on the part of the emotional life in the stricter sense of the word, namely the emotions of the pleasure appetite.

APPENDIX C

'GUIDELINES' TO QUICKSAND
By Conrad W. Baars, M.D.

ACCORDING TO THE AUTHORS of the study *Human Sexuality*, commissioned by the Catholic Theological Society of America and censured by the Catholic bishops of America, their book was prompted by a desire to "provide some helpful and illuminating guidelines in the present confusion." Who or what brought on "the present confusion" the authors do not spell out, though they refer to "the inadequacy of traditional Catholic formulations and pastoral response to sexual matters."

Anxious then to help "beleaguered pastors, priests, counselors and teachers" the writers devote more than half of their text to their chapter on "Pastoral Guidelines," even though in the postscript they seem to doubt the validity of these guidelines: "We invite serious criticism and cooperation in the search for more satisfying answers to the mystery of human sexuality."

That the authors of *Human Sexuality* were seriously handicapped from the start in at least one area, the only area I consider myself qualified to comment on as a psychiatrist, is evident. In summarizing Chapter III on "The Empirical Sciences and Human Sexuality," the authors state:

Broad consultation from recognized experts in the social and behavioral sciences provided only inconclusive data on the issues of human sexuality, and failed to make clear what, if any, evil consequences to the individual or society follow upon practices thought of as somehow deviant, or that such practices are harmless.

It is not surprising that, for instance, homosexuality [same-sex attraction] is nothing more than a big question mark to these experts and authors, since there is nothing in this book to indicate familiarity with the fundamental, pre-behavioral aspects of the human person's psyche.

In the "Pastoral Guidelines," repeated reference is made to the need that sexuality and sexual behavior "be conducive to the creative growth and integration of the human person," implying, of course, that in the past this was impossible because of the "inadequacy in Catholic formulations on sexuality," which led to stunted growth and much psychological suffering.

As every Catholic psychotherapist knows, much emotional and spiritual suffering like scrupulosity, sexual disorders and obsessive-compulsive repression , has been and is related in some way to the manner in which the moral aspects of sexual behavior were presented in religion courses. However, to claim that the commandments and moral laws dealing with sexuality were and are responsible for this suffering is another matter entirely. Yet, this is precisely what the authors claim, when in the guidelines they advocate lowering and diluting such objective moral standards for the sake of "creative growth toward the integration of self-liberation, other-enrichment, honesty, fidelity, life-service, social responsibility and joyousness."

If this needs to be done through premarital sex, then all one needs to do is "judge what kind of intimacy is honest, self-liberating, life-serving and joyous." Or, if adultery and overt or commercial sexual relations must be considered a necessary ingredient toward growth, then we must give "special concern to the characteristics of being other-enriching, honest and faithful." Again, if contraceptives are necessary for growth—the authors seem to consider this almost a universal need—then "parents can be reassured by the availability of a great variety of methods" as long as they "consider honestly and carefully the medical, psychological, economic and religious implications of each method in regard to their (children's) total well-being." How the parents are to discover, for example, the psychological implications is left up in the air.

The authors' solution to society's confusion in sexual matters stems, no doubt, from the failure of their experts to advise them of the fact that the Freudian interpretation of neurotic repression has been successfully demythologized.

Freud held that the superego of the human person—that strange concoction of conscience, morality, social mores and religion—is responsible for the repression of unacceptable sexual and other feelings; thus he held it further responsible for the lack of integration of the personality, if not for sexual disorders and scrupulosity. Advisers competent in matters pertaining to the psychology of the "normal" human person, as well as of emotionally-spiritually afflicted persons, would have told the writers that sexual and other repressive disorders are *never* the result of repression by the superego, but rather of the *repressive action by another emotion or feeling.*

To give but one example: irrational fear of everything sexual can be engendered in early life not by the sixth and ninth commandments themselves, but by a fear-inspiring over-emphasis on these commandments, by an atmosphere of suspicion toward the human person's so-called lower nature, and by associated attitudes of fear of sex and of the sense of life on the part of religion teachers.

Because of this greatly improved understanding of the nature of neurotic disorders, it has been possible during the past thirty years to cure persons afflicted with scrupulosity and sexual disorders without ever tampering with objective moral standards.

This book, *Human Sexuality,* reminds me of Martin Luther's attempts to escape the unbearable tensions and sufferings of his severe Obsessive-Compulsive Disorder. His disorder began when as a young monk he shrank from no extremes of asceticism in order to realize a completely self-abnegating love of God. He tried to escape from his disorder by rebelling against the Church's teachings, some of which he considered responsible for his afflictions.

Whereas Luther cannot be faulted for this assumption, however, the same cannot be said for the authors of this book.

The book also reminds me of Chesterton's remark that Christianity has never been tried, or, to paraphrase, that Christians who once were recognizable by their love for one another, have over the centuries become masters at denying each other. Thus, Christians deny others when they say, even with the best intentions of helping them, "You may ignore the teachings of the Magisterium; God's laws are too hard for you." By that they say in effect, "You are not and never will be strong and good enough to adhere to these laws."

This, of course, is the very opposite of the mature, affirming Christian who says, "I see your unique goodness, your not-yet-fully developed potentialities, your weaknesses; but I believe in you and I am certain that you will learn to love and obey the laws that God gave us as guidelines for our growth toward living an other-affirming life; you can count on my help whenever you want it and I shall help you to discover all that is good and beautiful and true in yourself, in creation and in God."

Evidently the authors are not aware of the fundamental distinction between neurotic repression and mature self-restraining love, that unselfish love which restrains, when necessary for the well-being of the beloved, certain outward manifestations of love—without repressing love itself. Yet, it is precisely this crucial distinction between neurotic repression and self-restraining love which (together with an understanding of the mechanism of repression) provides the key to the prevention and cure of emotional-spiritual afflictions. This key is sound both morally and psychologically.

How tragic that the authors' desire to ease the sufferings of the rapidly growing number of neurotic and emotionally deprived Christians has resulted in "Pastoral Guidelines" which are little more than psycho-theological quicksand for the confused and "beleaguered" pastor, the disoriented counselee and unwary readers of this book.

GLOSSARY

abreaction — release of repressed emotion
afferent — transmitting impulses to the brain
analgesia — absence of pain sensation
anamnesis — the history of a particular case of disease
anergia — deficiency of energy
anesthesia — loss of sensation
anisocoria — an inequality in the diameter of the pupils
anthropocentrism — literally, man-centeredness
anthropology — study of the human being
aphonia — loss of speech
astasia — motor incoordination with inability to stand
astasia-abasia — Inability to stand or walk in a normal manner
asthenic — characterized by weakness
atrophy — wasting away
axiom — a recognized truth

catharsis — discharge of repressed ideas and emotions
clonus — series of muscle spasms (rapidly contracting and relaxing)
cognitive power — perceiving and knowing power
conative — striving
concupiscible — desiring
conditio sine qua non — indispensable condition
constitutionally — pertaining to the make-up or functional habit of the
                        body
corpus alienum — foreign body
cortical — pertaining to the outer layer of the brain

depersonalization — loss of sense of identity and personality

diurnal — occurring during the day

efferent — transmitting impulses away from the brain
electroencephalography — study of brain waves
empirical — depending on experience and observation
endocrine — secreting internally
enuresis — bedwetting
erudition — acquired knowledge, scholarship
exclaustration — temporary separation of a religious from his/her
                community

gastrectomy — the surgical removal of all or part of the stomach
glucose tolerance test — determination of the blood sugar level at regular
                intervals

hemisphere — one half of the brain
hippus — a rhythmic narrowing and widening of the pupil
hyperhidrosis — excessive sweating
hypertrophy — morbid enlargement or overgrowth
hypothalamus — center of the brain

immaterial — without matter; spiritual
irascible — easily provoked to anger

Lasègue's sign — neurological sign indicating disease of the sciatic nerve

mortification — practice of disciplining the emotions
mydriasis — dilation of the pupils of the eye

neuralgia — pain in a nerve
nuclei — centers

opthalmic — pertaining to the eye

pathogenesis — the production and development of disease
pathognomic — specifically distinctive of a disease
pathological — diseased
perceptual — by means of the senses

GLOSSARY

phenomenology — the study of phenomena
phenotype — the visible characteristics common to a group of individuals
phylogenetic — pertaining to the evolution of a race or group of animals
physiology — the branch of biology dealing with the functions and vital
        processes of living organisms
prognosis — a forecast as to the probable outcome of a disease
prophylactic — tending to ward off disease
psychasthenic — Janet's term for all non-hysterical neurotic disorders
psychogenic — originating in the mind
pyknic — having a short, stocky build

quadriceps femoris reflex — knee jerk

ratio — reason
repressed emotion — the emotion which is pushed into the subconscious
repressing emotion — the emotion which causes the repression
repression — conflict between two emotions, one of which is pushed into
        the subconscious by the other

sciatica — a painful inflammation of the sciatic nerve
scrupulosity — morbid sensitiveness in matters of conscience
Sensus communis — common sense
soma — body
soporifics – causing or tending to cause sleep
sthenic — strong
sub-sensory — vegetative

thalamus — anterior portion of the brainstem
transmutatio corporalis — bodily change

volitional — pertaining to man's will

BIBLIOGRAPHY

Aquinas, Thomas. *Commentary on Nichomachean Ethics*. Trans. C. I. Litzinger. Chicago: Regnery, 1964.

————. *Summa Theologica*. 3 vols. Trans. Fathers of the English Dominican Province. Westminster, MD: Christian Classics, 1981.

American Psychiatric Association: *Diagnostic and Statistical Manual of Mental Disorders*. Fifth Edition, Arlington, VA, 2013. Fourth Edition, Text Revision. Washington, DC, American Psychiatric Association, 2000. (2nd ed., 1968; 3rd ed., 1980; 4th ed., 1994)

Aristotle. *Nichomachean Ethics*. Mineola, NY: Dover Publications, 1998.

Arnold, Magda B. *Emotion and Personality*. 2 vols. New York: Columbia University Press, 1960.

Aumann, Jordan & Baars, Conrad. *The Unquiet Heart: Reflections on Love and Sexuality*. Staten Island, NY: Alba House, 1991.

Axline, Virginia M. *Dibs in Search of Self*. NY: Random House, 1964.

Baars, Conrad W. *Born Only Once: The Miracle of Affirmation*. Rev. ed., Suzanne M. Baars and Bonnie N. Shayne, eds., Eugene, OR: Wipf & Stock, 2016.

Doctor of the Heart. Staten Island, NY: Alba House, 1996.

————. *Feeling & Healing Your Emotions*. Rev. ed. Suzanne M. Baars and Bonnie N. Shayne, eds. Gainesville, FL: Bridge-Logos, 2003.

I Will Give Them A New Heart: Reflections on the Priesthood and the Renewal of the Church. Staten Island, NY: ST. PAUL'S/Alba House, 2007.

"Love, Sexuality and Celibacy" in Sex, Love and the Life of the Spirit. Chicago: Priory Press, 1966.

————, and Terruwe, Anna A., *Healing the Unaffirmed: Recognizing Emotional Deprivation Disorder*. Rev. ed. Suzanne M. Baars and Bonnie N. Shayne, eds. Staten Island, NY: ST. PAUL'S/Alba House, 2002.

Baars, Suzanne M. *The Abode of Love: Developing the Heart*. Canfield, OH: ST PAULS.

Boekel, C.W. Van. *Katharsis*. Utrecht: De Fontein, 1957.

Bowlby, John. *A Secure Base: Parent-Child Attachment and Healthy Human Development*. New York: Basic Books, 1988.

————. *Attachment and Loss (2nd ed.)*. NY: Basic Books, 1999.

————. *The Making and Breaking of Affectional Bonds*. New York: Routledge, 1979.

Boxtel, J.P. Van. "*Moraal en Affectiviteit*," in *De menselyke persoon in de christelyke moraal*, 1958.

————. "*Moraal en Gevoelsleven volgens Thomas van Aquino*," in *Tydschrift voor Philosophie*, June, 1959.

BIBLIOGRAPHY

Brennan, Robert E. *General Psychology*. New York: Macmillan, 1937.

———. *Thomistic Psychology*. New York: Macmillan, 1941.

Buytenduk, Ph.D., F.J.J., *Woman, A Contemporary View*. New York: Newman Press, 1968.

Calon, P.I.A. "*Ontwikkeling van de menselyke persoon. Consequenties voor de christelyke moraal." Voordracht gehouden op studiedagen voor de priestess van her aartsbisdom Utrecht en bisdom Groningen*. August, 1958.

and Prick, I.J.G. *Psychologische Grondbegrippen*. Salzburg: O. Müller, 1969.

Donceel, J. F. *Philosophical Psychology*. New York: Sheed and Ward, 1961.

Duynstee, W.J.A.J. *Verspreide Opstellen*. Roermond-Maaseik: J.J. Romen & Zonen, 1963.

Ford, John, C. *Religious, Superiors, Subjects, and Psychiatrists*, Westminster, MD: The Newman Press, 1963.

———, and Kelly, Gerald. *Contemporary Moral Theology*. 2 vols. Westminster, MD: The Newman Press, 1958.

Freud, Sigmund. *A General Introduction to Psychoanalysis*. Garden City: Garden City Publishing Co., 1943.

Guardini, Romano. *The End of the Modern World*. Wilmington, DE: ISI Books, 2001.

Harvey, John F. *The Homosexual Person: New Thinking in Pastoral Care*. San Francisco: Ignatius Press, 1987.

Harvey, Rudolf. *It Stands to Reason*. New York: Joseph F. Wagner, 1960.

John Paul, II. *The Gospel of Life*. NY: Random House, 1995.

Joyce, Mary Rosera. *Love Responds to Life — The Challenge of Humanae Vitae*. Kenosha, WI: Prow, 1971.

———, and Joyce, Robert E. *New Dynamics in Sexual Love*. Collegeville, MN: St. John's University Press, 1970.

Joyce, Ph.D., Robert E. *Human Sexual Ecology*. Washington, DC: University Press of America, Inc., 1980.

Kelsey, Morton T. *Healing and Christianity: A Classic Study*. Minneapolis: Augsburg, 1995.

———. *Caring: How Can We Love One Another?* New York: Paulist Press, 1981.

Kosnik, Anthony, Carroll, William, Cunningham, Agnes, Modras, Ronald & Schulte, James. *Human Sexuality: New Directions in American Catholic Thought*. New York, NY: Paulist Press, 1977.

Kreeft, Peter. *Summa of the Summa*. San Francisco: Ignatius Press, 1990.

Liedloff, Jean. *The Continuum Concept: Allowing Human Nature to Work Successfully*. Reading, MA: Addison-Wesley, 1985.

MacNutt, Francis. *Healing* (rev.). Notre Dame, IN: Ave Maria Press, 1999.

———. *The Power to Heal*. Notre Dame, IN: Ave Maria Press, 1977.

Mahler, Margaret S., *Separation-Individuation*. Northvale, NJ: J. Aronson, 1979.

Mahler, Margaret S., Fred Pine, & Anni Bergman. *The Psychological Birth of the Human Infant: Symbiosis and Individuation*. London: Hutchinson, 1975.

Montagu, Ashley. *Touching: The Human Significance of the Skin (3rd ed.)*. New York: Perennial Library, 1986.

Nicolosi, Joseph. *Reparative Therapy of Male Homosexuality: A New Clinical Approach*. Northvale, NJ: J. Aronson, 1997.

Noyes, Arthur P. and Kolb, Lawrence C. *Modern Clinical Psychiatry*. Philadelphia: W.B. Saunders Co., 1963.

Pfurtner, Stephanus. *Triebleben and Sittliche Vollendung*. Frieburg, Schweiz: Universitatsverlag, 1958.

BIBLIOGRAPHY

Pieper, Josef. *A Brief Reader on the Virtues of the Human Heart.* Trans. Paul C. Duggan. San Francisco: Ignatius, 1991.

———. *About Love.* Chicago: Franciscan Herald Press, 1974.

———. *Fortitude and Temperance.* New York: Pantheon Books, 1954.

———. *The Four Cardinal Virtues: Prudence, Justice, Fortitude, Temperance.* New York: Harcourt, Brace & World, 1965.

———. *Guide to Thomas Aquinas.* New York: Pantheon Books, 1962.

———. *Happiness and Contemplation.* Trans. Richard and Clara Winston. South Bend, IN: St. Augustine's Press, 1998.

———. *Leisure — The Basis of Culture.* Trans. Alexander Dru. Indianapolis: Liberty Fund, 1999.

———. *Scholasticism.* New York: Pantheon Books, 1960.

Pinckaers, S. *Morality: The Catholic View.* South Bend, IN: St. Augustine's Press, 2003.

———. *The Sources of Christian Ethics.* DC: Catholic University of America Press, 1995.

Rahner, Hugo. *Man at Play.* Trans. Brian Battershaw and Edward Quinn. New York: Herder and Herder, 1967.

Ratner, Herbert. *Nature, the Physician, and the Family.* Mary Tim Baggot, ed. Bloomington, IN: AuthorHouse, 1998, 2007.

Royo, Antonio, and Aumann, Jordan. *The Theology of Christian Perfection.* New York: Foundation for a Christian Civilization, 1987.

Ryan, Barbara Shlemon. *Healing Prayer: Spiritual Pathways to Health and Wellness.* Ann Arbor, MI: Charis, 2001.

Ryan, CSS, Gerard A. *The Rectitude of Mortification Therapy in the Pastoral Care of the Sexually Afflicted.* Unpublished manuscript, 2016.

Rzadkiewicz, Arnold L. *The Philosophical Bases of Human Liberty According to St. Thomas Aquinas.* Washington, DC: Catholic University of America Press, 1949.

Sanford, Agnes. *The Healing Gifts of the Spirit.* San Francisco: Harper & Row, 1984.

Smith, Vincent Edward. *The General Science of Nature.* Milwaukee: Bruce Books, 1958.

Terruwe, Anna A. *The Abode of Love.* St. Meinrad, IN: Abbey Press, 1970.

———. *Affectiviteit, effectiviteit: breekpunt van menselijk leven: over waarde-overdracht in het onderwijs.* Lochem: De Tijdstroom, 1988.

———. *De frustratie neurose.* Amsterdam· Anthos, 1998.

———. *De liefde bouwt een woning.* Bussum: Romen, 1978.

———. *De toename van agressie, suïcide en druggebruik binnen de consumptiemaatschappij.* Lochem—Gent: De Tijdstroom, 1986.

———. *Emotional Growth in Marriage.* Glen Rock, N.J.: Paulist Press, 1968.

———. *Geloven zonder angst en vrees.* Roermond: J.J. Romen, 1969.

———. *Give Me Your Hand.* Trans. Martin Van Buuren. Croydon, Victoria: Spectrum Publications, 1973.

———. *The Neurosis in the Light of Rational Psychology.* Trans. by Conrad W. Baars. New York: P.J. Kenedy & Sons, 1960.

———. *Opening van zaken.* In Usum privatum. Nymegen, 1964.

———. *Ouders en kinderen op weg naar de toekomst.* Lochem: De Tijdstroom, 1976.

———. *Psychopathic Personality and Neurosis.* Trans. Conrad W. Baars. New York: P.J. Kenedy & Sons, 1958.

———, and Baars, Conrad W. *Loving and Curing the Neurotic: A New Look at Emotional Illness.* New Rochelle, NY, Arlington House, 1972.

BIBLIOGRAPHY

————, and Baars, Conrad W. *Psychic Wholeness and Healing*. Staten Island, NY: Alba House, 1981.

————, and Kroft, A.L. *De stap over de drempel: moderne visies op hulpverlening bij menswording van mentaal gehandicapte mensen*. Baarn: Arbor, 1993.

————, and Van Cranenburgh, H.P. *Hooglied van de nieuwe liefde : antropologie van de weerhoudende liefde*. Baarn: Gooi en Sticht, 1996.

Tournier, Paul. *The Gift of Feeling*. Atlanta, GA: John Knox Press, 1981.

————. *The Person Reborn* in *The Best of Paul Tournier: Four Volumes in One*. New York: Iversen Norman, 1977.

Vanier, Jean. *Man and Woman He Made Them*. Mahwah, NY: Paulist Press, 1985.

Vann, Gerald. *The Aquinas Prescription*. Manchester, NH: Sophia Institute Press, 1999, 1939.

————. *The Heart of Man*. London: Longmans, Green & Co., 1945.

————. *Saint Thomas Aquinas*. New York: Benzinger Brothers, 1947.

————. *Morals and Man*. New York: Sheed and Ward, 1960.

Veldman, F. *Haptonomie: science de l'affectivité : redécouvrir l'humain*. Paris: Presses universitaires de France, 1998.

————. *Lichte Lasten*. Spruyt: Van Mantgem & De Does N. V., Leiden, 1970.

————. *Psysiotherapie*. Oosterbeek: Meyer & Siegers, 1964.

Virtue, William D. *Mother and Infant: The Moral Theology of Motherhood*. Pontificia Studiorum Universitas: Romae, 1995.

West, Christopher. *Theology of the Body for Beginners*. West Chester, PA: Ascension Press, 2004.

Wilhelmsen, Frederick D. *The Metaphysics of Love*. New York: Sheed and Ward, 1962.

INDEX

INDEX

INDEX

www.ingramcontent.com/pod-product-compliance
Lightning Source LLC
Chambersburg PA
CBHW050224270326
41914CB00003BA/556